THE NEW AMERICAN RADICALISM

Kennikat Press
National University Publications
Series in Political Science

The New
American Radicalism

*Alfred M. Bingham and Non-Marxian
Insurgency in the New Deal Era*

DONALD L. MILLER

National University Publications
KENNIKAT PRESS / 1979
Port Washington, N.Y. / London

Manufactured in the United States of America

Published by
Kennikat Press Corp.
Port Washington, N.Y. / London

Library of Congress Cataloging in Publication Data

Miller, Donald L., 1944–
    The new American radicalism.

    (National University publications)
    Bibliography: p.
    Includes index.
    1. Radicalism—United States. 2. Bingham,
Alfred Mitchell, 1905– 3. United States—
Economic policy—1933-1945. 4. United States—
Politics and government—1933-1945. I. Title.
HN90.R3M45   320.9'73'0917   79-570
ISBN 0-8046-9224-6

In loving memory of my sister
EILEEN MILLER
It was not what she did, but what she was, that matters.

ACKNOWLEDGMENTS

In writing this book I have been doubly blessed, drawing on the unfailing assistance of good family and good friends.

My most personal intellectual debts are to Charles Manoli, who introduced me to the world of ideas, the late Adrienne Koch, who inspired me to write history, and Donald Meyerson, who gave me an education in political economy.

Parts or all of the manuscript profited from being read by James B. Gilbert, Dan T. Carter, David Grimsted, Horace Samuel Merrill, Samuel Astorino, Michael Greenberg, Philip Donahue, Selden Rodman, Terry Summons, and Lewis Mumford. But it was Milton Cantor who literally shepherded it to publication, offering steady encouragement and searching criticism through its several revisions.

My thanks also to Larry Dowler of the Yale University Library for unearthing several boxes of "lost" Alfred Bingham manuscripts, and to Mr. Bingham for allowing me to examine his private papers at his home in Salem, Connecticut. Of one thing I am certain: this book could not have been written without the open-handed cooperation of Alfred Bingham.

Hilda Cooper of Lafayette College expertly typed the manuscript; Richard Farrell of the University of Maryland was there with help when I most needed it; and Jacob E. Cooke guided a rookie author through the final editorial preparations.

I owe a special debt to Peter Lowry, who offered his Scots' common sense and his cold editorial eye, saving me from countless errors. And he, Don Meyerson, Vincent Di Mattio, Terry Summons, Ted McConnell, Bob Leitman, Charles Hoxie, Jim Nestor, Fred Provencher and James

Dougherty were always there, with more than a little help for a friend. Writing, to be sure, is a deeply personal experience. Yet every page of this book is touched by these close and understanding friends. The book undoubtedly would have been completed much sooner had it not been for our countless nocturnal seminars; but it would have been a very different book.

Finally, this is Eileen's book. Her courage in the face of death gave me the courage to fight off a paralyzing despair and drive the writing to completion. Still, it would not have been possible without the comforting help of Leanne, Larry and Berni, and John and Sara. I owe a special loving debt to my parents, Donald and Frances Miller. In dedicating this book to Eileen, I dedicate it to them, as they know. This is, in an important sense, my children's book as well, for Greg and Nicole grew up with it. My deepest obligation, in every possible way, is to my wife Rose. She is my bright and morning star.

CONTENTS

THE NEW AMERICAN RADICALISM

ABOUT THE AUTHOR

Donald L. Miller is an Assistant Professor of History and Chairman of
the American Civilization Program at Lafayette College in Easton,
Pennsylvania. He has published articles in various journals and newspapers,
and has given numerous scholarly papers at universities and historical
conferences. His major areas of scholarly interest, both in teaching and
writing, are modern American social and intellectual history and American
urban history.

INTRODUCTION

This is a study of American radicalism during a decade of unprecedented crisis and opportunity. It describes the efforts of an important circle of non-Marxian insurgents to develop a socialist program and movement issuing from the unique conditions of American civilization and appealing to the middle classes as well as to labor and the most cruelly disadvantaged. Theirs was a spirited search for an expressly American radicalism, a native insurgency drawing on traditional American middle class values and ideals.

The Great Depression was America's gravest national crisis in the era between the Civil War and our own time. And the first years of that crisis were the most punishing of all. By the early winter of 1933, on the eve of Franklin Roosevelt's inauguration, unemployment had soared to over 13 million, the nation's banking system was in near ruin, its ramshackle relief system had proved incapable of meeting the needs of even the most desperately poor, while countless thousands of rural families struggled desperately to hold on to their lands and their homes in the face of a massive foreclosure movement.

Accompanying the economic decline and compounding its severity was a deep public unease about the nation's future. Three years of industrial paralysis and spreading misery had begun to erode the confidence of millions of Americans in the likelihood of a quick recovery. Yet while some angrily blamed capitalism itself for the crisis, the prevailing national mood was profoundly non-revolutionary, a curious compound of fear, bewilderment, and sullen discontent.

The depression, however, failed to affect all Americans in this way. There were some, in fact, who welcomed it as a supreme social opportunity. For America's radical intellectuals these were years of unbridled hope and feverish organizational engagement. The depression offered compelling substantiation of their long-standing indictment of capitalism, rekindling their hopes for revolutionary change. Here finally was the crisis that might offer them an opportunity to sweep to power. Everywhere on the Left there was ferment and fresh enthusiasm. And no radicals were more robustly confident about socialism's immediate destiny than the leaders of the Communist and Socialist parties, America's two largest Marxist organizations. After a decade of incessant sectarian in-fighting, government harassment, and lagging popular influence, the entire Marxist movement was charged with new vigor and fighting confidence. Yet it was the Communists who experienced the most stunning revival. More than any other radical organization, the party seemed intent on confronting the problems of the disprivileged with unflinching resolve; and this defiant activism drew scores of intellectuals to its standard. Even those who resisted official affiliation, finding it impossible to square their concern for intellectual autonomy with the party's insistence upon unquestioning ideological allegiance, found in Marxism an arresting analysis of political economy and a stirring program for human transformation.

Yet while Marxism was indisputably the dominant radicalism of the 1930s and the Communist Party the decade's largest radical organization, there were in these years a significant number of anti-capitalist insurgents who questioned Marxism's appropriateness to American society. America, they insisted, was a predominantly middle class nation, and only a radicalism appealing to the pressing material needs and aspirations of this majority could pretend to be adequate or hope to be successful.

Their intellectual meeting ground was the intrepid monthly *Common Sense,* which was launched in November, 1932, in the blackest hours of the crisis. Its contributors comprised a veritable "Who's Who" of the country's independent Leftists. John Dewey, Upton Sinclair, John Dos Passos, John Chamberlain, Harold Loeb, Lewis Mumford, Thomas R. Amlie, Paul H. Douglas, John T. Flynn, C. Hartley Grattan, Louis Adamic, Stuart Chase, James Rorty, Howard Y. Williams, George Soule, Henry Pratt Fairchild, and Selden Rodman all appeared at one time or another on its masthead. In one sense, these writers traversed the spectrum of ideas, plans, and aspirations of 1930s insurgency. They were not united by commitment to a single social program, nor did they all join *Common Sense*'s new party drive. Yet they shared certain important

social aims and ideals. All rejected the early New Deal as a pale substitute for the kind of sweeping human reconstruction they believed
the depression demanded. All urged the establishment of a collectively
planned economy. And all rejected Marxism and the existing Marxist
parties for a radicalism derived from the native tradition of dissent. The
insurgent idols of *Common Sense* were Thorstein Veblen, Edward
Bellamy, and Henry George, not Marx, Engels, and Lenin.

The editor of *Common Sense* and chief theoretician for the radical
movement it sought to inspire was a young recent convert to socialism,
Alfred Mitchell Bingham, son of the wealthy Old Guard Republican
senator and noted South American explorer Hiram Bingham. This book
is preeminently an analysis of Bingham's life in dissent, from his break
with the narrow conservatism of his father through his efforts to encourage a radical challenge to the New Deal, to his eventual disillusionment with radicalism and retirement from journalism and active political
life in 1945.

Bingham's insurgent career, however, cannot be considered apart from
those who joined him on *Common Sense* and in the new party cause.
This is then a history of an important segment of the decade's independent radicalism as well. It is also an examination of the origins of
a new kind of liberalism. For by the end of the decade the "New
American Radicalism" had given way to a cautious political reformism
that would emerge as the dominant liberal creed in the post–World War 2
years. Bingham was at the center of both these movements; he made a
crucial contribution to the new radicalism and to the new liberalism. An
examination of his career and intellectual achievement is thus indispensable for an understanding of the democratic Left in these turbulent years.

Any study of such a controversial subject as radicalism and reform demands a few preliminary words about terminology and methodology. While
some historians have called Bingham, Rodman, Dewey, and others closely
associated with *Common Sense* "independent liberals," citing their allegiance to certain unmistakably liberal ideals,[1] they are here designated
as independent radicals. Certainly they borrowed extensively from the
philosophic heritage of progressive reform, from the ideas of Simon
Patten, Lester Ward, Herbert Croly, and others; however, they broke
from this earlier liberalism in their clear intention to replace capitalism
rather than reform it. To call them liberals is to miss the decidedly
revolutionary aim of their political effort. Finally, the term "New
American Radicalism" is not my own. Bingham used it repeatedly to
describe *Common Sense*'s purpose and perspective. With the single exception of John Dewey, the regular contributing editors of *Common Sense*

refused to refer to themselves as liberals for fear of confusing their socialist position with the reformist New Deal perspective they so fiercely assailed. It is only later, after 1936, when they abandoned socialism and third party politics for an uneasy accommodation with the New Deal that they are here referred to as liberals.

While this is the first book exclusively on Bingham and his magazine, it is by no means the first to consider the ideas and political concerns of the decade's independent insurgents.[2] Yet it differs significantly from previous studies in its preponderant focus and controlling methodology. Most of the outstanding works on 1930s non-Marxian radicalism concentrate almost entirely on formal ideas, on the published writings of the decade's radicals. They fail to give comprehensive consideration to the critical interconnection between ideas and organizational action. This despite the fact that intellectuals like Bingham, Dewey, Douglas, and Amlie wrote expressly for, and actively participated in, a political movement that was to a considerable extent the organizational embodiment of their social ideas.

Nor has there yet been any comprehensive attempt to uncover the profoundly personal and subjective factors that influenced the formal thought and activist commitment of these important writers. Given the broad-reaching scope of most extant studies of independent radicalism, such scrupulous attention to the inner life or to a close examination of the two-way traffic between radical thought and mass action would have proved impossibly ambitious. But a book like the present one, with its narrower range of concern, can attempt what these sweeping surveys do not, exploring in the process areas of surpassing concern to the history of modern dissent.

A study of Bingham, in particular, affords a rich opportunity to examine the interplay between radical criticism and radical political action. Moved by the twin demands of thought and action, theory and practice, Bingham combined a spirited faith in the transforming power of ideas with a driving commitment to political activism. All ideas were for him merely a prelude to action. A self-styled revolutionary publicist, he sought to arouse through his writings a mass coalition for change and to supply that movement with a comprehensive political strategy and program. At the same time he placed himself in the organizational forefront of the movement, and this political work powerfully influenced his intellectual contribution, as every effort was made to adjust theory to the organizational problems he confronted daily. Radical theory and radical activism were then never separate affairs for him. To divorce his intellectual achievement from his work in the movement is to violate his own conception of the proper role and function of the insurgent intellectual.

Nor can Bingham's radical theory be properly considered apart from his character and inner life. "Political theories," as Peter Gay observes, "are never pure intellectual constructs. They emerge from a thinker's mind as the result of a fruitful combination of a number of things: the reading he has done, external events that tend to confirm his hunches, his sympathies, predilections and interests."[3] Admittedly, it would be impossible to sort out and detail all these tangled influences. But careful intellectual biography must attempt at least to describe the principal sources of a thinker's moral outlook and formal thought. Here an analysis of the inner life is essential; not necessarily a sustained psycho-biography but certainly a studious examination of the various personal, familial, and social factors that coalesced to form a thinker's social orientation. Mr. Bingham has generously allowed me access to the materials indispensable for such an inquiry; and I have attempted it here.

Aside from providing a more fully rounded understanding of Bingham, there is an additional reason for this kind of analysis. I share with Kenneth Keniston the conviction that the radical commitment arises from and is sustained by a set of inner moral principles and instincts.[4] This moral center is the crux of the radical experience. Formal thought emerges later, an intellectual elaboration of beliefs deeply held. In our case, a search for the moral center of Bingham's radicalism provides answers to three of the most absorbing questions the historian can ask about the insurgent intellectual: What initially impelled him toward radicalism? What determined the kind of radicalism he advanced? What sustained his commitment to radicalism in the face of the enormous difficulties that assail all who challenge the dominant orthodoxy? Finally, it should explain why Bingham eventually spurned radicalism for a milder liberal reformism. We will have then not simply a description of Bingham's thought and activity, but an explanation of it as well.

Beyond this, an analysis of Bingham's inner life can give additional explanation to the deep ambivalence that characterizes so much of the decade's radical thought. Richard Pells finds, quite correctly I believe, an underlying layer of conservatism in 1930s radical criticism. The decade's radicals were, he argues, "at once critical and supportive of traditional American ideals."[5] This insight bears particular relevancy to Alfred Bingham, so much of whose social thought was either decidedly bourgeois or downright conservative. And the roots of these tempering influences are to be found in his conservative New England education and upbringing.

Bingham's radicalism does not fit the pattern and character of so much of the century's insurgency. Christopher Lasch has shown that the revolt of the twentieth-century intellectuals "often took the form of a rebellion against the conventional family," since this patriarchal family was the transmitter of a bourgeois culture the new radicals found stale and oppressive. Estranged from the conventional family and the reigning values of bourgeois life, these radicals often identified with other "outcasts"—with the poor and the disadvantaged—and "tried to look at the world from their point of view." This deliberate effort to see society from "the bottom up," Lasch tells us, is one of the distinguishing features of modern cultural radicalism.[6]

Bingham, like so many of the radicals Lasch describes, was raised in an environment of order, affluence, and Protestant righteousness. Yet his turn to radicalism never involved an estrangement from the core values of his upbringing. Instead, he embraced socialism as a means of preserving and extending to all Americans the material advantages and outstanding values of this comfortable bourgeois world. Like an earlier New Englander, Edward Bellamy, Bingham linked the triumph of socialism with the universal extension of the culture of the educated upper middle class. For both men, socialism came to mean the replacement of a brutishly exploitive capitalism by a chastened commonwealth of culture, charm, and enhanced spirituality. The cooperative community Bingham would later render in the pages of *Common Sense,* with its lush green landscape, its clean and spacious garden cities, its material plentitude, its polite manners, and vigorous cultivation of the arts was scarcely more than the ordered world of his youth writ large.

This sheltered middle class environment not only influenced Bingham's vision of the socialist future; it determined his choice of the historic agency for its realization. Unlike most modern radicals, Bingham never strongly identified with the proletariat, never sought to view society "from the bottom up." Isolated from and always guardedly suspicious of the industrial poor, he preferred a revolution spearheaded by men of his own class and temperament, middle class intellectuals of considered judgment, committed to the material and moral regeneration of both the plutocracy and the poor. Far from being a rebellion against his bourgeois culture, Bingham's radicalism was an effort to realize it in a purer and more universal form. The middle class strategy he urged for the achievement of socialism did not simply emerge from a disinterested analysis of American socio-political development, as some historians imply. It stemmed initially from the particular cast of his background and upbringing. Here is compelling evidence of the inseparability of personality and political theory.

Chapters 1 and 2 examine in fuller detail these and other pe·
factors essential to an understanding of Bingham's radical contribu..
Since I have proceeded on the assumption that political theory and
behavior emerge from a core belief or faith, these chapters set the
basis for all that follows.

Throughout the remainder of the book I have used Bingham's career
in dissent to point up some of the principal ideological, organizational,
and profoundly personal difficulties that arise from attempts to encourage radical change through the American democratic process. Bingham, like most non-Marxian radicals, chose the ballot rather than the
bullet for the achievement of socialism. This commitment to con-
stitutionalism forced him to confront what Peter Gay has aptly called
"the dilemma of democratic socialism"–how to cling to principle while
pursuing power?; or put more directly, how in a democracy to fashion a
movement that remains both indisputably radical and politically consequential?[7]

Every determined radical seeks power, seeks in some way to transform the society of his time. Yet radicals in this country have never
attained considerable national power or influence, and this has had a
devastating impact on the movement, driving countless dissidents to
compromise their ideals and temper their policies in the hope of gaining
greater public effectiveness. And for so many of these radicals this
odyssey of disillusionment has been powered by the conviction that the
full achievement of socialism is impossible in a nation so resolutely
middle class.

Bingham, for a time, thought otherwise. He confronted the "dilemma
of democratic socialism" supremely confident that he could encourage
the creation of a democratic movement that was both radical and
politically successful. Ultimately, however, this effort to pursue both
power and principle ended in failure, impelling Bingham, too, to moderate his radical ideas in the search for wider public influence. In fact,
his very concern for political power caused him to cast his radicalism
in a form that was dangerously close to the liberalism he assailed,
smoothing the way, unwittingly, for his eventual turn to reformism.
This book, then, is not so much an examination of the reasons for the
failure of American radicalism, a hugely complex question that such a
modest inquiry cannot hope to answer in full, as it is a study of the
concerted effort of a group of democratic insurgents to reverse that
record of political frustration and defeat. It is a book about what it
means to be a democratic radical in modern, middle class America.

Finally, it is not an indictment of Bingham's retreat to liberalism. While I have found much that is morally compelling and socially astute in Bingham's radicalism, I have also found much that is narrow, naive, and even downright dangerous. My overriding purpose, however, has been to understand and explain, not to judge. For there is an element of the tragic in the effort of Alfred Bingham; and that resides in his inability to resolve a dilemma no American radical has yet successfully resolved. We have yet in this country to connect socialist vision to a powerful political movement, to fashion a radicalism broadly attractive to the mass of Americans. Here is the real importance of Bingham's dissident career and contribution. He was one of the decade's only radical intellectuals to examine searchingly the middle class character of American industrial society and to develop a strategy congruent with these ascendant class and cultural tendencies, a radicalism that avoided the worst features of the Marxian Left—its crude dogmatism, its cult of revolutionary violence, its obsession with theoretical purity, its slavish duplication of Marxism-Leninism, and its excessive reliance upon the Soviet Union. In seeking to free American radicalism from its reliance on foreign revolutionary models, he addressed a problem of continuing concern to the democratic Left. If his career in dissent evokes the frustration and failure that have been the hallmarks of the radical experience in this country, it also poignantly reveals the exceedingly difficult, some would say impossible, task of squaring radical ideals with American realities.

1

A BINGHAM STRAIN OF REBELLION

In early November, 1932, at the approach of the hardest winter of the Great Depression, the New York newspapers announced the publication of *Common Sense,* a new radical journal inspired by Thomas Paine's stirring revolutionary broadside. Recalling the insurgent spirit of '76, its editors declared for a "Second American Revolution" to recapture liberties lost through a selfish concentration of economic wealth. Only a sweeping national reconstruction—political, economic, social, and cultural—could, *Common Sense* proclaimed, regain the freedoms for which an earlier generation of revolutionaries had fought and died.

Common Sense's two chief editors, Alfred Bingham and Selden Rodman—young, impatient, and passionately idealistic—hoped to awaken a dispirited public to the failure of capitalism and to encourage a movement aimed at its replacement. Yet both rejected Marxism for a distinctly American radicalism capable of appealing to the middle classes as well as the proletariat. "What is needed in the United States," Bingham proclaimed, "is a native American radicalism, a radicalism free from affiliation with any of the existing organized groups."[1]

When reporters rushed to interview Bingham at his *Common Sense* offices, they were, however, not so much interested in his insurgent ideas as they were in his father's reaction to the magazine. For *Common Sense*'s ringing call to revolution collided with the bedrock conservatism of Hiram Bingham, the Republican senator from Connecticut. Here was the age-old generational conflict boldly reenacted, the father ardently championing the capitalist status quo in speech after impassioned speech on the Senate floor while his rebellious son plotted the revolution. Not

11

surprisingly, when Senator Bingham picked up the first issue of *Common Sense*, with a caricature of his old friend Andrew Mellon spread across the cover, he angrily ripped it to pieces, never to read it again. "In politics," young Bingham told inquiring newsmen, "my father and I no longer talk the same language."[2]

A towering man, with deep-set eyes, high cheekbones, and an impressive shock of silver hair, Hiram Bingham epitomized New England respectability. His family traced its lineage back to the founding fathers of Connecticut, and its history was replete with colonial governors, revolutionary war heroes, and renowned Congregational ministers. Hiram, whose parents and grandparents had been pioneer Calvinist missionaries to the South Pacific, entered politics early in the Harding years, following a brilliant career at Yale as an historian and world-celebrated South American explorer. With a boost from the Connecticut political boss J. Henry Roraback, he was elected lieutenant governor in 1922. Two years later he captured the governorship but never served his term, being chosen the following month in a special election to fill the United States Senate seat vacated by the death of Frank Brandegee. In Washington for the next nine years, Bingham championed the interests of the eastern financial wing of the Republican Party, fiercely assailing all efforts at government regulation of capitalist enterprise.[3]

Away from the Senate, in his spacious home outside New Haven, Bingham ruled over his family like a stern patriarch, urging his seven sons to follow him into public service as advocates of an austere Yankee conservatism. As a youth, Alfred rarely questioned his father's political views; even his later radicalism bore the impress of Hiram's unvarying commitment to individualism and decentralization of public responsibility. At Yale Law School, at his father's urging, he had served as chairman of the Hoover for President Club and aimed toward a career in Republican politics. But immediately after graduation, troubled by a nagging social conscience, he took off on a two-year world tour that inspired his turn to radicalism. Armed with some newspaper credentials and a letter of introduction from his father, Bingham swept through Europe and Asia, interviewing Mussolini, Gandhi, Chiang Kai-shek, and other world leaders. But it was a three-month stay in Soviet Russia that dramatically changed his life.

The month Bingham entered Russia, the Bank of England went off the gold standard and Soviet newspapers were headlining hunger riots in America. All the while Russia was making startling economic advances. Her people seemed filled with a surging pride in the revolution, and Bingham caught their enthusiasm. What most impressed him, however, was the perspective he got from Russia on his own capitalist world, which seemed to be "crumbling into ruin." Revolution, he became convinced, would soon sweep the globe, transforming the world for which he had shaped his career. "I realized," he later recalled, that if I "was to have a hand in politics and government in this world it would not be by going into a New London law office and taking the traditional political road through the state legislature and into Congress."[4]

Russia shook Bingham with the force of a religious conversion, igniting in him a passion to commit America to a revolution equally thoroughgoing. Yet he hoped that his own country could make the transition to socialism peacefully and bloodlessly through the agency of a democratically elected party. With Russia as an inspiration, not a guide, he returned home in mid-summer of 1932 intent on a career as a publicist and theoretician for a new American radicalism. The launching of *Common Sense* signaled the beginning of that ambition.

While Russia triggered Bingham's turn to socialism, the roots of that rebellion lay deep in his family background and personal history. Bingham's radicalism seems, at first glance, a rude departure from a stolid family heritage of political standpatism and Calvinist orthodoxy. This, at least, is how the press saw it. Yet a closer examination of the Binghams of Connecticut yields a fascinating strain of nonconformity and moral insurgency. The same righteous reformism that inspired Bingham to the cause of social revolution moved his nineteenth-century ancestors to give their lives to missionary service. And while Hiram Bingham later spurned the faith of his missionary parents, he possessed in a full-bodied but more secular form the same questing, adventuresome spirit and urge for personal commitment that drove them to establish a Calvinist beachhead in the primitive Pacific islands.

This missionary Protestantism powerfully influenced Alfred Bingham. Although he, like his father, would reject traditional Christianity, the religious habit of thought persisted long after the dogma ceased to have meaning for him. The messianic impulse, the grim intensity, the resolve to lead a life of moral conviction, the lofty idealism, the imperishable faith in the righteousness of the cause, the shining confidence in the possibilities of conversion, and the forbidding fear of the apocalypse remained strong in Bingham; they were embodiments of his matured radicalism. His ancestors, sure in their faith, had found in missionary service an outlet for these profoundly religious energies; Bingham turned instead to radical politics. Radicalism became for him a means of spreading moral enlightenment and expressing the implacable Protestant urge for service upon which he had been reared.

Hiram Bingham, who had been touched in his own way by the same impulse, saw it reemerge in a different form in his son. "Am I wrong in thinking," he wrote to Alfred a decade after the latter's conversion to radicalism, "that Missionary zeal led you—as it did my father and grandfather—to be prejudiced in favor of the heathen, the outcast, and the unfortunate?"[5] For Bingham, then, the Russian adventure was merely a powerful catalytic factor in a personal transformation that began early in adolescence. In this anxious quest for a secular calling capable of giving release to energies essentially religious, we find the source and animating inspiration of Bingham's radical faith. And the haunting influence of the family missionary heritage loomed large in this process of personal discovery.

Bingham's great-grandfather, Hiram Bingham I, was born in 1789 in Bennington, Vermont, the son of a moderately prosperous Yankee farmer. The Binghams were resolute Calvinists, and when Hiram graduated from Middlebury College in 1816 he went directly to Andover Seminary, where he caught the crusading reformism of his tutors and vowed to dedicate his life to the foreign missionary service. Following his ordination, he and his new bride Sybil Moseley sailed from Boston on the brig *Thaddeus* with the first American missionary group bound for the Sandwich Islands.

On arriving in the islands, Bingham and his company were visibly shaken by the crude primitivism of the natives. "Can these be human beings?" Hiram asked of his converts-to-be. "How dark and comfortless their state of mind and heart! How imminent the danger to the immortal soul, shrouded in this deep pagan gloom! Can such beings be civilized? Can they be Christianized?" Yet Bingham, it appears, never seriously doubted the contagious power of the gospels. With a curious blend of soft persuasion and pious authoritarianism, he and his fellow missionaries eagerly set about spreading Christianity and Yankee habits among the local tribes. First they mastered the island language, reduced it to a simple alphabet, and began teaching the natives to read. Then followed simple gospel lessons. Here Bingham led the way. In 1922 he published his *Elementary Lessons in Hawaiian,* a primer communicating the fundamentals of Protestantism. The natives were next educated to civil habits. They were instructed to hide their nakedness in cotton clothing, to sanction their sexual concubinage in Christian marriage, and to refrain from drinking the rum they purchased from English sailors. Hulas were strictly prohibited; nor were the islanders permitted to decorate their bodies with flowers. Some missionaries even established temperance societies patterned after those in the States. It was not long before all the natives were ordered to take the pledge.

Less than a decade after his arrival in the islands, Bingham was preaching in a pole-and-thatch tabernacle in Honolulu to a congregation of 2,000 fully clothed converts. Around the Honolulu mission he became known as "King Bingham," and for twenty-one years he ran the settlement there with a hard-fisted discipline.[6]

Bingham and his wife labored in the islands until 1840, when Sybil's illness forced their return to New England. Their work for the gospel, however, was carried on by their son Hiram II, who after training for the ministry at Yale and Andover left with his young wife for missionary duty in the equatorial Gilbert Islands. For seven years the young couple preached and taught in horrid conditions on the tiny coral island of Apaiang until Hiram's failing health drove them back to the mission headquarters at Honolulu, where Bingham devoted most of the remainder of his life to providing a Christian literature for the Gilbert Islanders. When he died in 1908, he had completed a Gilbertese translation of the Bible, edited a Gilbertese dictionary, and written a host of religious tracts and hymnals in Gilbertese.[7]

It was here in the more settled surroundings of Honolulu that the Binghams raised their youngest son, Hiram III, who was marked from birth to carry forward the family's Christianizing effort in the Pacific. After early training at the mission school in Honolulu and later at Yale, however, Bingham abruptly abandoned plans to enter the ministry and went on to pursue graduate work in history and politics, first at the University of California, then at Harvard, where he gained the Ph.D. in 1905. His decision to change careers was prompted by a love affair with Alfreda Mitchell of New London, Connecticut, an heiress to the fortune of the art jeweler Charles Tiffany. Their marriage in 1900 gave Hiram the financial security to launch a wide-ranging career in teaching, exploring, aviation, and politics. His son Alfred would later draw on the same Tiffany fortune, through the generosity of his mother and grandmother, to support his radical magazine.[8]

Hiram Bingham was an irrepressible adventurer, a man of extraordinary versatility and robust enthusiasm. As a young lecturer in Latin American history at Yale he organized and led a series of pathbreaking geographical expeditions to South America. On one of these he discovered the famed "Lost City" of Machu Picchu, the magnificent citadel city the Incas had built high in the Andes to escape the encroaching Conquistadors. While on subsequent expeditions, he located

Uitcos, the last Inca capital, led the first ascent of Mt. Coropuna, one of the highest peaks in the Andes, and made the first survey of the Pampaconas River. His published accounts of these discoveries helped to incite interest in the United States for the serious study of Latin American history and led to his promotion to full professor at Yale in 1915.[9]

The Binghams' stately home on Prospect Hill, just outside New Haven, with its sunporches and broad terraces, flanked by woods and rolling meadows, provided an idyllic setting for Hiram and his wife to raise their children. Alfred, the third of their seven sons, was born on February 20, 1905, at Cambridge, Massachusetts; but his first childhood memories go back to the day his family moved into the spacious home near Yale. Bingham recalls his youth being spent in "an environment of sunshine and green fields, of nurtured health, of space to run in and grow in." Blessed with inherited wealth, pleasant surroundings, and affectionate parents, he felt as a child that he had been "born into a perfect world, where no change was desirable or possible." "The world in which I grew up," he wrote years later, "was an 'economy of abundance.' I cannot remember ever doing without anything I wanted because it cost more than my family was able to spend."[10]

Bingham spent his youth in an unusually sheltered environment. Barriers of wealth and education combined to segregate him and his brothers from the world beneath their social class. Trained at exclusive private schools and shipped off to the family's sprawling country estate in northern Connecticut in the summers, they rarely met children with backgrounds different from theirs. This encouraged an attitude of privileged superiority which was remorselessly reinforced at home. Hiram strictly forbade his sons to associate with the tough working class boys, or "muckers" as he called them, who lived in the squalid tenements that scarred the valley below their Prospect Hill home. Poverty, he told his sons, was the curse of those not capable of advancing their own welfare.[11]

Education at Groton and then Yale only fortified Bingham's class and cultural insularity. Groton was a special world, a prim and arrogantly elitist retreat from the turbulent industrial world that had grown up around it. The headmaster, Rector Endicott Peabody, who had an enormous influence on Bingham, once announced that Groton stood for "everything that is true, beautiful, and of good report."[12] In an important way, Groton was an extension of Bingham's family upbringing. Peabody himself personified the lusty Christianity and civilizing zealotry of the Bingham missionaries. Students crowded into chapel regularly for his stern lectures on Christian character, duty to country, and right manners. Peabody encouraged Grotonians to enter public service to work for a Christian world; yet Groton did little to equip them for the discordant realities of political life. Emphasis in the classroom was on the humanities, European history, and classical languages, with the masters usually teaching by rote; and, of course, students remained securely sheltered from any but their own kind. Peabody's conception of reform, moreover, was hopelessly anachronistic. It encompassed little more than sound political morality and a solicitous concern for the needy. "Politics to Peabody," one writer has observed, "was a kind of crusade in which Grotonian knight-errants, presumably dressed in Eton collars, would charge eagerly into the political arena and clash noisily with the forces of evil."[13]

Bingham's parents did not belong to an organized religion, yet he had received a moral training at home congruent with the dominant mood at Groton. There he experienced a spiritual revolution which culminated in his baptism in the Congregational Church. A relentlessly intense student, he burned with the urge to live a life of Christian conviction. He even seriously considered entering the ministry. His religiosity and precocious aestheticism (he was an excellent pianist and a voracious reader) set him apart from his classmates, who tagged him with the nickname "old Mother Hubbard."

Yale did little to challenge his view of the world. There Bingham also found little connection between what he learned in the classroom and the industrial world beyond the gates of the college. "New Haven," he wrote later, "was a manufacturing town, a railroad center, a favorite resort of sweatshops only seventy-five miles from the nerve center of American finance. But . . . I learned no more of the reasons for wealth and poverty than if I had still been living" on Prospect Hill.[14]

In his senior year at Yale Bingham finally decided on a career: he would follow his father into politics, a decision not unrelated to his vaulting moralism. Since early in his Groton years he had been afflicted by a strong Protestant urge for service, his aim was to achieve self-fulfillment—"moral greatness," as he called it—in the struggle for a "higher" human cause. A life in public service would allow him to exercise fully his creative energies while working for the public good. Immediately after graduation, at his father's urging, he entered Yale Law School to prepare for his life's work.[15]

Yet always there were doubts. While politics would perhaps allow him to work for his motivating ideals, he began to question whether he was living close to those ideals. He was particularly troubled by his privileged circumstances. He had never been entirely comfortable knowing his wealth was inherited; nor had he fully accepted his father's preachings about the poor. Could he continue to blind himself to the fact that millions of Americans struggled to stay alive on an income less than his vacation allowance? Writing to his grandmother from Yale to thank her for a generous check, Bingham questioned "whether it is entirely good for us to have an easy time financially."[16]

These guilt pangs conjoined with his soaring idealism to nurture a still vaguely expressed social ethic. More curious than ever about the world beyond his class and social station, he decided to spend the summers between law school traveling through the land, living and working among the poor and the disprivileged, seeing for himself "how the other half lived."

Bingham spent his first summer as a farm laborer in Massachusetts, working at back-breaking chores for a dollar a day. The following year he took a job in a Waterbury, Connecticut, brass factory. The grind and monotony of both jobs, one agricultural, the other industrial, powerfully disturbed him. Waterbury was an especially distressing experience. There listless men and women toiled ceaselessly at a robot-like pace amid the clamor and soot of industrial machinery. The pay was abysmal, the work hard and intensely boring. This was Bingham's first concentrated encounter with the frightful human toll of industrialization, and the impact of the encounter would continue to haunt him. "I decided then and there," he confessed, "that unskilled factory labor made a travesty of human life." Somehow this kind of work would have to be eliminated. Perhaps technology, at Waterbury an instrument of oppression, held the key to the workers' liberation?

As a farm worker, Bingham had been awed by the amount of human labor that could be eliminated by the use of power-driven machinery. His work at Waterbury verified his perception of the liberating possibilities of the machine. There his job was to inspect the products of several machines, some operated by women, the others fully automated. It occurred to him that with a slight increase in plant investment the entire operation could be automated, freeing the women from the poisonous environment of the factory. But it was not, he quickly realized, that simple; for "freedom" for these unskilled workers meant "unemployment and empty pocketbooks." Bingham left Waterbury confused and troubled about the coming reign of the machine. "I saw the automatic machine as a bringer of freedom—and fear."

The following summer Bingham went west in search of the disappearing frontier. After a brief stint as a traveling salesman in Oklahoma City, he bought a run-down Chevrolet, hooked up with a band of itinerant farm laborers, and followed the wheat harvest north through Oklahoma, Kansas, and Nebraska, picking up work where he could find it.

But work was hard to come by, for "the combine had conquered the grain belt, and the men it had displaced were tramping the roads in forlorn thousands." Unemployment and poverty were everywhere, as gaunt, sun-scorched harvest hands moved in lockstep pattern from farm to farm in a desperate search for work and the next meal. Once again the machine seemed a mixed blessing. It had saved the wealthier Plains farmer untold labor time, while releasing countless thousands to a life of cruel uncertainty.

These labor experiences quickened Bingham's critical sense. He was particularly struck by the vivid contrast between the "industrial waste-lands" he encountered in his summer odysseys and the "sunny green pastures" of his family's estate at Salem, Connecticut. "I had a dim Utopian yearning," he recalled years later, "to see the rank wilderness I had glimpsed in my summer wanderings reclaimed to the same care-fully tended trimness and beauty and comfort of the garden world in which I had been brought up." Yet his revolt, as he admitted, was "more aesthetic than ethical. The disorder and planless anarchy of the worka-day world horrified me; the sordidness of poverty filled me with dis-gust rather than pity."[17] While alive to the inequities of industrial capitalism, he was not yet prepared to condemn the system outright. But now there were doubts where earlier there had been inflexible certainty.

Bingham approached his law school graduation in an intensely troubled state of mind. Already he had spurned or massively modified many of the ideas he had carried with him to Yale. Yet he had still not found a wholly satisfying alternative philosophy of self and society. He had begun to question capitalism; but his grudging faith in indi-vidualism and broad personal freedom prevented him from embracing socialism. Collectivism of any sort would, he still believed, dangerously encroach on that wide area of freedom essential for creative self-fulfillment. And creative self-fulfillment he still judged his principal life aim.[18]

By this time Bingham's robust individualism had become a militant life faith, causing him to throw off traditional Christianity for a libera-ting atheism. In "ASA: A Young Man's Creed," a personal manifesto he wrote just after finishing law school, we have a revealing affirmation of the exuberant individualism and resolute commitment to personal fulfillment through human service that would underpin his radical faith.

"ASA" is written in the form of a dialogue among college friends, with ASA, or Bingham, as the central character. Its dominant note is an Emersonian celebration of the dignity and full-bodied potential of man. "Man," ASA rejoices, ". . . [is] the only true God;" his searchings, his quests, his achievements, and his consummations the only true reality. Nothing was sacred, then, but the integrity of one's life. This faith, Bingham realized, placed huge responsibilities on man, enlarging the significance of all his activities. He could look to no ulterior sanction, neither secular nor spiritual, for solace or support; he set his own standards and bore full responsibility for his actions. In an affirmation almost radically anarchistic, ASA declares that "no one should venture to direct another's life or make rules for it. That is the highest prerogative of the individual himself." In this faith, a life well-lived became the supreme achievement. But living well, to Bingham, meant more than personal "happiness." This in itself was a counterfeit ideal. To live well was to live fully, to advance always in the direction of one's ideals and transcendent expectations. Each individual, in Puritan fashion, had a sacred responsibility to set his aim high, to seek to fulfill all his creative and moral possibilities. "To have an ideal of greatness," ASA proclaims, "is essential to the highest kind of active life."

Yet Bingham was not advocating here an extreme individualism, free of social aim or responsibility. Rather, he seemed to be earnestly searching for a social faith commensurate with his vaulting idealism. "A man with a motivating faith," ASA declares, "is a bigger man than one without." And while still unsure of the specifics of this faith, he was certain of one thing: that it must be immediately connected with the here and now. The richness of any philosophy, ASA states, is intensified by its immediateness, by its intimate relation to everyday social living. "Take philosophy in its highest sense as directed living—intelligent purposeful life—. . . and it cannot be . . . relegated to the white-haired recluses. We ought to direct our whole minds to intelligent living individually and socially." It is remarkable that Bingham had not yet read John Dewey, for here he approached him so closely.

But "ASA" is more than a personal testimony; it is the beginning of a social analysis as well. All institutions, ASA argues, ought to be "in the service of man," their dominating purpose the encouragement of his creative possibilities. This was the crime of the factory system: it cramped the spirit and cut off the possibilities for creative self-fulfillment. Somehow each worker would have to be given full opportunity to exercise his skills and imagination; and again Bingham turned to the machine as the solution. Technology, properly directed, could eliminate the life-destructive jobs in industry, releasing workers for more richly creative pursuits. Those who remained in the factory—the engineers, technicians, and production managers—would truly run it; and for them this would be "real life, power, significance." Bingham had still not resolved the dilemma of technological unemployment. But he had moved beyond the crippling confusion he had felt on the Waterbury job toward a fresh confidence in man's ability to solve the problem of work and wealth in the coming power age. Now he proposed as the chief business of man the erection of a social system guaranteeing universal material security and purposeful creativity. He had left behind the comforting dogmas of his upbringing. His was still a faith in search of a program. But that faith was informed by the "very positive notion . . . that a proper ethical system and a proper social system must be directed toward the enlargement of the scope of every individual life." This belief would form the core of his matured radical ethic.[19]

"ASA" is a work of soaring enthusiasm. The writing throughout is passionately, almost embarrassingly, extravagant. Bingham's rebellious idealism and lofty confidence animate every page. There is little doubt that he felt himself marked for greatness and that he was certain that this greatness would come early; for youth he proclaimed as the floodtide of life.

> When it comes to the materials out of which life is built, real life, of blood and tears and joy, [ASA cries] it is not the aged philosopher who counts as often as the young one. It is the young Shelley, the young Joan of Arc, the young Christ, who lights the new torches by which men may live. . . . Old men dream dreams. . . . It is the young men who see visions.[20]

Or again, in a poem he wrote while at Yale:

> I am horse, rider, lecher, saint and emperor
> My kingdom is youth
> And you, grim future, are my jester
> God be damned to hell
> I am I[21]

On finishing law school Bingham found it impossible to square these outsized ambitions with a career in law and state politics. His faith in conventional politics, moreover, had been rudely shaken by an experience as a delegate to the Connecticut Republican convention. He found the state party ripe with corruption and bossism; while the Democrats struck him as no better. This mounting political disillusionment was compounded by the knowledge of his father's own moral failing. In 1929 Hiram was censured by the Senate for a breach of legislative ethics. As a member of the Senate finance committee charged with setting rates for the Smoot-Hawley tariff he had smuggled into a closed hearing as his "secretary" a top official of the Connecticut Manufacturers' Association.[22]

Bingham was also laboring under the strain of family problems. His parents' marriage was failing; and he blamed his father for this. Hiram was also insistent that his son go immediately into law and politics. Yet Bingham hungered for something larger. "Life," he wrote in "ASA," "is an adventure . . . a sacred flame . . . the ideal always being individual fulfillment through the pursuit of greatness."[23] Another of Bingham's law school poems captures this intense yearning for a cause to which he could give himself completely:

> Oh God, give me a sword
> My hands were not fashioned with power revealed
> In sinews and strength for a battle gage
> That I a dullard pen should wield
> To scratch a dullard page
> God, give me a sword, and a cause for the fighting[24]

Years later Bingham would describe his attitude at this time as one of total alienation from the world for which he had prepared. One thing was certain; he would postpone his entrance into the practice of law. Just after passing his bar exams, he was encouraged by his grandmother to take a world tour as a way of rounding out his education. She would pay his way. Bingham eagerly seized the opportunity. This would give him the needed time to work out his personal and career problems, to press on with the search for a secular calling. In September, 1930, he sailed from New York for Europe and the Far East.[25]

2

A BOURGEOIS MEETS BOLSHEVISM

Bingham's world tour took him by way of Europe and the Near East, then on to China, across the vast reaches of Russia, and finally back through Turkey, Greece, Italy, and England. It was an exhilarating and turbulently exciting experience. Everywhere he went the atmosphere was alive with great restlessness and change as new ideas and leaders seized the imagination of millions. In India Gandhi's nationalist movement was challenging a rotting British hegemony, while in China Mao Tse-tung's Communist armies, then locked in combat with Chiang Kai-shek's Kuomintang, were widening their control over the countryside. All the while, at the headwaters of insurgency, the Soviet Communists were fashioning a radically new human order. Nor was Western Europe immune to the spreading contagion of change. There Fascism was the great transforming force. In Italy a triumphant Mussolini had already staked out his corporate order. And in Germany economic crisis, parliamentary ineptitude, and anguished memories of Versailles had fostered a swelling Nazi movement that would soon menace all of civilization. It was a time of shattering transformations, the furious beginnings of a new international order. From the moment Bingham arrived in Europe to begin his travels, he felt himself in a world "tense with change," as the "economic foundations" of the postwar era "gave way little by little."[1]

Bingham's credentials as a free-lance correspondent for several Connecticut newspapers, along with a letter of introduction from his father, gave him access to the seats of power. He could also have traveled in high luxury. Yet wherever he went he tried to reach the common people, to seek to understand their aims and outlook, to gauge for himself the dynamic power of the new ideologies that were sweeping the globe.

Bingham had been educated to Kipling's conception of the white man's civilizing mission in the underdeveloped world. But on the first wing of his trip, through Egypt, the Arab Near East, and on into India, his childhood illusions were blasted to pieces. In India he met "picture-book Englishmen—beautiful, charming, arrogant—living in 'oriental luxury,'" coldly indifferent to the harrowing poverty all around them. As he talked with the leaders of these people, including Gandhi and Jawaharlal Nehru, he realized that a new form of nationalism, a combination of ideas from the Indian past and Western socialism, was preparing India for independence, by revolution if necessary. Here, too, were ideas that threatened his smug "world of Anglo-Saxon snobbery."

China redoubled his growing uneasiness about the future of the capitalist West. There a boiling revolt against Western imperialism was in full swing. "I had the chilling experience," Bingham recalled years later, "of being spat at as I drove through the noisome slums of Shanghai." Revolution, it seemed, had decisively established itself as a world-transforming force. Perhaps his own country would soon feel its destructive fury?

After a brief layover in Japan Bingham returned to Manchuria to prepare for his Russian journey. What he observed in China and India, the revolution yet unfulfilled, made Russia immensely important to him. Here was the source of upheaval and the model for the modernization that was sweeping the underdeveloped world.

When Bingham loaded his baggage on the trans-Siberian express, he was in a confused and unsettled state of mind. Years later, in a semi-autobiographical work, he wrote of entering Russia in August, 1931, with a sense of grave foreboding, fearing he was about to approach "the center of the disintegrating forces that were wrecking civilization" and half-expecting "to be spotted as a capitalist, taken out at some Siberian way station and shot."[2] Yet the diary he kept of his Russian journey reveals a different mood. His fears, it appears, were overlaid by a ready enthusiasm. "I feel I may be starting on a complete internal revolution as well as seeing the beginnings of a complete world revolution," he scribbled in his journal just after crossing the Soviet-Chinese border. "I already have a dim sense that equality and fraternity are realized here as nowhere ever before."[3]

Bingham spent three fascinating months in the Soviet Union. His journey took him through Siberia as far as Novo-Sibirsk, then southward over the new Turkestan-Siberian railroad to exotic Tashkent, across Turkmenistan and the Caspian Sea to Baku, thence north to Moscow and Leningrad, and finally to the Ukraine and the magnificent ancient city of Kiev.

Speeding through the heartland of Russia on the trans-Siberian express, he gathered his first impressions of the revolution from the hundreds of Soviet citizens he met on the crowded train; and it was this, the "human side" of the revolution, that most impressed him. Reared in a family keenly sensitive to class distinctions and plagued himself by childhood-bred fears of the "crude" proletariat, he was shocked by the warm kindness and generosity of the Russian workers. Some of his fellow passengers viewed him with detached curiosity, a few with guarded suspicion, but most were openly friendly. These were the exalted proletariat and, truly, the revolution had ignited in them a refreshing spirit of equality and camaraderie. "Here I am," Bingham wrote somewhat incredulously from his railroad car, "among what at home would be distinctly 'lower class' people; but there is simply no feeling of class; or at least everyone seems to feel they belong to the ruling class." Even the secret police did not appear to frighten these vigorously confident people. The revolution, they were convinced, was theirs. When Bingham asked several young Russians about the "dreaded GPU," they laughed, insisting that only the bourgeoisie need fear them.[4]

Everywhere Bingham traveled in the Soviet Union he found the same social confidence he had first noticed among the peasants and laborers on the trans-Siberian express. Certainly not all Russians shared this enthusiasm for the revolution. Bingham met enemies of the regime who informed him of the overbearing hardships of Soviet life: the pitifully low living standards, the absence of luxuries, the burdensome taxes, the forced labor, and the savage terror in the countryside against the kulaks. But despite it all, the majority of Russians he encountered pridefully supported the developing Communist state. Certainly life is difficult in the Soviet Union, Bingham conceded in his diary. Yet those with "the vision to see the magnificent adventure on which Russia is embarked and those who have some controlling part in carrying it out, find themselves in an exciting realm where the petty dullness and hardships of life can be ignored."[5]

A young Communist journalist Bingham met in Novo-Sibirsk powerfully summarized what Bingham took to be the prevailing mood. We are building a "new world," she told him. "Yours is worn out. Think of the joy of building now, from the beginning."[6]

It was this—the revolution's surging faith—that underlay Bingham's early enthusiasm for Russia. And of all the Russians, the Communists seemed most passionately committed to this visionary ideal. As a Communist engineer Bingham met on the trans-Siberian express eagerly insisted, it is not a question of "our believing" in the inevitability of a classless future: "We don't believe, we know."[7] The stern intensity of these Communists, their utopian enthusiasm, their "burning missionary spirit," proved irresistibly attractive to Bingham, who was in search of much the same kind of secular calling. "How thrilling it must be," he marveled, "to believe, and work for the belief."[8] The Bolsheviks were extreme men, men of no compromises, and Bingham, like countless other Western intellectuals who made the pilgrimage to Russia in these years, often experienced a sense of reverential awe in their presence.

On one occasion, while teaching an English class in Moscow, Bingham was invited to the home of the revolutionary Michael Borodin, who several years earlier had virtually masterminded the Chinese revolution. For an entire evening the two men talked excitedly about China, Russia, and Marxism. Toward the end of the evening, Borodin told Bingham that his criticism of capitalism ran deep enough for him to become a Communist. Bingham immediately disagreed. But later, rethinking Borodin's remark, he became "disquieted." The inspirational pull of Communism was for him not unlike the impulse to piety he had experienced at Groton.[9]

In the end, however, Bingham could not accept Marxism. He felt himself "too sophisticated, too well educated in skepticism, to come to the fold, and believe with all the fervor of the faith." Nor could he reconcile his extreme individualism with a creed that treated doubt and criticism as heresy. "I am afraid," he wrote after only one month in Russia, "that I can never be a communist, at least as they are understood here; for to reach the proper stage of faith one must cease to think intelligently. One must accept the rigmarole of a creed. Communism . . . demands the revolutionary dogmatism which I could attain only with my tongue consistently in my cheek."[10]

Bingham's rejection of Marxism, however, did not entail a complete rejection of the Soviet experiment; nor did he dismiss the full Marxian theory and program. Instead, the appeal of Soviet Russia threw him into an emotional and intellectual quandary that he would finally resolve by embracing a highly personalized radicalism congruent with his underlying middle class sympathies.

Bingham was impressed by the material as well as by the spiritual ideals and accomplishments of the revolution. Everywhere he traveled in Russia he encountered signs of astonishing physical growth, whether in the form of huge modernized factories, towering government office buildings, or sprawling collective farms worked by thousands of former peasants. This was the third year of Stalin's Five Year Plan, and all the nation's productive resources were being harnessed to the aims of the revolution. But it was the economic plan itself that most impressed Bingham and transformed forever his economic thinking. In place of a chaotic, loosely regulated capitalism, the Russians had substituted a comprehensively planned economy. This idea of using government planning to achieve a balance between production and distribution intrigued Bingham; even more appealing was the Communists' concern "with production, rather than finance, with making goods, rather than making money." In Russia the monetary system and the profit motive were "subordinated" to the production schedules of the overall economic plan; whereas under capitalism profit reigned supreme, controlling the pace and direction of the entire economy. "This Russian economy," Bingham recalled later, "was devastatingly logical. I did not know how to refute it." While Russia still lagged behind America in industrial productivity, the superiority of comprehensive production-for-use planning seemed "unquestionable" to Bingham.[11]

Bingham was equally impressed with the collectivization movement, the agricultural aspect of the plan. While he was not permitted to go out into the rural districts to observe collectivization first-hand, he talked extensively with foreign technical experts recently returned from the countryside. They reported to him of empty houses, "of begging children, of arrests, of seizures of all food and movable property from suspect peasants, of a suspicious and fearful atmosphere where every man distrusts his neighbor as a spy." Still, Bingham refused to denounce the entire program. "To convert backward villages into modernized collectives and ignorant individualistic peasants into communistic proletarians," he wrote to his father, "is a task requiring the most extreme measures."[12]

Even the absence of political liberties in Russia failed to dampen Bingham's enthusiasm for the regime. "Democracy," he wrote from Moscow in early 1932, echoing what had already become a standard apologia of Soviet sympathizers, "is an ideal and a fact under Russian Communism, but it is to be understood in a different sense from what is common in other countries. . . . Liberty in Russia is the liberty that economic security gives to the worker, rather than civil or political liberty as it is understood in America." Bingham was convinced, moreover, that the dictatorship was a "temporary, stopgap measure," that full political democracy would be established with the achievement of the primary aim of full economic democracy. In the meantime he was prepared to tolerate the dictatorship. "In the present era of building socialism, unity of spirit and unity of control are essential. The Communist party secures it."[13]

The reports Bingham read in the Moscow newspapers of the deepening economic depression in his own country redoubled his enthusiasm for Russia, clearing the way for his turn to radicalism. "To read the papers here," he wrote from Moscow, "is to see capitalism all going down in a lump in the greatest fiasco of all history." From Russia, America, indeed the entire capitalist West, looked to him "like imperial Rome, with its wealth, luxury, beauty, idealism, side by side with vice, poverty, and crime." Just as Christianity had brought down Rome, so communism, he now suspected, would bring down capitalism. "How strange it is," he wrote, "to feel oneself on the verge of the apocalypse, to see doom hovering over one."[14]

Bingham had been troubled by these same premonitions of social catastrophe in India and China. But where before he had associated revolution with senseless bloodshed and wholesale destruction, in Russia he glimpsed the possibilities of a "brilliant dawn" after the black days of terror. "I had long supposed," he admitted in his diary, "that revolution with its atmosphere of hate and fear would have killed all the humanity in the Russian people; instead it seems to have brought it to flower." Perhaps revolution could produce a "higher type of humanity" in his own country?[15]

But could *he* be a revolutionary? He was still unsure. Here again his diary proves revealing. At one point late in his journey he writes that he is "almost converted" to the cause of revolution. Yet in the very next sentence he admits to doubts and misgivings. "Perhaps I never shall be [a revolutionary]. I have too much to lose myself; how can I see my mother and my home, and my career all in the ordeal of revolution?"[16]

This was the rub. Revolution involved the destruction of so much he cherished. The Bolsheviks had ruthlessly demonstrated this with their disparagement of all that Bingham considered genuinely admirable in Czarist culture—its architecture, its music, its literature, its tradition of civility. In its place they had substituted a "stunting" materialism, a worship of the factory and the machine. In Soviet Russia, Bingham derisively noted, "the tractor had become the symbol of the communist future. Even flower beds were laid out in its likeness."[17]

Bingham was thus pulled by two instincts, one social, the other deeply personal. The revolution had brought enormous social gains, promising in the end a more secure life for all. Yet its brutalitarian methods and its thoroughgoing materialism powerfully offended him. Bingham caught the gist of his own ambivalence in a diary entry he made just after arriving in Moscow: "As my enthusiasm for the new regime rises, my despair at its lack of charm grows deeper. Comfort and security for all may come . . . but must the world see an end to comeliness? No, we must have culture and we must have gentility, and we must have beauty."[18]

A sensitive and sheltered New Englander, Bingham obviously lacked the moral outrage and ruthless singlemindedness of the convinced revolutionary. Nor could he unequivocably endorse the proletarian ideal. While he admired the revolutionary enthusiasm and rough-hewn character of the Russian proletariat, he confessed that he could never live comfortably among them. "I am soft, so horribly soft . . . [and] this Russian Revolution is utterly hard. I am afraid of it from the depths." Even the difficulties of travel in Russia appalled him. Just before retiring for the evening in a run-down Russian hotel, he wrote of his yearning for "tiled bathrooms, good food served beautifully, and hot, by trim servants, glowing lights—or again of . . . rustling woods where there is no fear of wild animal or proletarian 'tough.'" After a performance of Chekhov's *The Cherry Orchard* in Moscow, he noted that the play portrayed "along with the fatuity of the old system. . .so much of its touching charm, a beautiful spacious home, with sun and quiet, idyllic fields and hills, and a family knit by the most delicate affection and sympathy."[19] Fond memories of Prospect Hill rushed to the surface. And while certain now that a revolution against capitalism was both necessary and inevitable, he hoped that somehow in America the best of this old world would be protected and preserved.

Bingham left Russia by way of Odessa and the Black Sea in November, 1931. As he boarded the ferry bound for Constantinople, he was overcome with a surge of relief. "I am leaving tractors and shock workers," he rejoiced in his diary, "and taking the road of gentle romance . . . to the magic land of the East." Out of Russia he no longer felt "a criminal for not being a proletarian." On approaching the Bosporus at dawn he had a sudden awareness of all he had missed while in Russia. "There were white villas set among cypresses, the

bronzing oaks, and the clustering harbor with sailboats and fisherman. . . .
Here was grace and beauty and gentleness. . . . Here was the old world
breathing more easily." After anchoring on the Golden Horn and rowing
ashore in a tiny boat, Bingham walked the streets of Istanbul where he
encountered well-dressed businessmen and beautiful women, shops
crowded with exotic food and gay articles, and fine restaurants alive
with conversation. Finally he settled into a luxurious hotel "with car-
pets and courtesy and real cleanliness." For a glorious moment Russia
with all its coarseness and crudity seemed "preposterous."[20]

Still, he realized that he would never be the same after experiencing
the revolution. The Soviets had demonstrated to his satisfaction the
superiority of socialism; and more than this—that "devotion to the
community can take the place of religion."[21] Yet though he left Russia
with the conviction to work for the classless brotherhood the Communists had set as their aim, he could not accept revolutionary Marxism
completely. The dilemma he confessed to in Moscow continued to
trouble him. Finally, while spending the winter in Greece and Italy,
the resolution to this predicament came to him in the idea of a middle
class revolution. Revolution, he was sure, would soon cut across the
entire capitalist West; but if the concerned middle class could spearhead
this revolt it need not duplicate the bloody Soviet example. America,
he wrote just after leaving Russia, can find "vast hope and inspiration
in the example of the Soviet Union," but it would be senseless to follow
the Bolshevik example. Revolutions, after all, had to be adapted to the
"spirit and temperament of each nation." Class warfare and proletarian
dictatorship might have been necessary in backward Russia where the
"aristocracy and monied classes were comparatively small, and the dictatorship of the working class found much to favor it." In America,
however, "a frontal attack by the working class on the privileged would
have less chance of success and would be vastly more costly."[22] Bingham
combined this apprehension about the success of a class revolution with
a deep fear of the consequences of an "uprising of the propertyless"
for a man of his class. "I see myself," he wrote from Moscow, "back in
a revolution torn country without means of livelihood and trebly [sic]
suspect. Oh they would be bitter times." Deeply distrustful of the
American "proletariat," so many of whom he found "wholly without
taste, loud and flashy, vulgar in the worst sense of the word," he looked
to a revolution directed by the middle class, a revolution that would
respect the finest features of bourgeois culture. In this way he was able
to resolve the inner struggle that had delayed his acceptance of radicalism. He would become a "communist," he told his brother Mitchell

when they met in Greece in the spring of 1932, but it would be his "own variant" of communism.[23]

But what would be his role in the coming revolutionary transformation? Just after returning for a second and briefer visit to Russia in the spring of 1932, Bingham decided on a career as a radical publicist. "A weekly journal," he noted in his diary, "seems the best way to combine my propaganda and my livelihood."[24] As a theoretician and publicist for a uniquely American radicalism, he hoped to be the directing force of a new kind of social revolution. And in "Common Sense and the Community," a personally revealing essay he wrote just before returning to the United States, he described in rough form the kind of revolution he envisioned.

The main body of "Common Sense and the Community" is a plea for a new cooperative social ethic and a new cooperative social order. However, as much as he abhorred violence, Bingham rejected a revolutionary strategy calling for a gradual and entirely peaceful change through the existing organs of democracy. "No matter how decent and reasonable Socialism may seem," he declared, "its enemies will not be overcome by gentleness or Utopian dreams."[25] The overthrow of capitalism would, he feared, be impossible without some bloodshed. Writing to his grandmother in the spring of 1933, Bingham advocated the use of violence if it were the only available way to destroy the "stupid tyranny of capitalism. . . . I believe that violent methods are justifiable," he added, "when they prevent prolonged disintegration of civilization and great wars. . . . So I say that a revolution probably cannot be accomplished without considerable cost, much as I should prefer to see it come easily."[26]

Yet Bingham, never the uncompromising revolutionary he sometimes claimed to be, pulled short of urging a bloody class reprisal. Rather, in "Common Sense and the Community" he suggested a revolutionary strategy designed to speed America smoothly toward socialism.

The propagandist figured prominently in Bingham's agenda for change. There could be no revolution until large numbers of Americans were educated to the need for a new economic society. This would be the purpose of his new magazine: "to awaken an intelligent revolutionary public opinion" by exposing the inadequacies of capitalism and "depicting the possibilities of a rational and decent social order." In the meantime, even before sentiment for revolution had crystallized, there would have to be established a "disciplined" revolutionary organization. Once this party secured massive popular support, it would (Bingham did not specify how) call into existence a "constitutional convention" of economic and political experts elected by the major "functional interests" in society. The convention's mandate would be the framing of a new federal constitution, the old Constitution, especially the Fourteenth Amendment, being an implacable barrier to radical economic changes involving property rights. Then the convention, acting in the interests of the community, would move to "dispossess the owners of productive industry . . . and set up institutions for planned control of the national economy."

If the revolution commanded the allegiance of the broad body of Americans, and if it was intelligently directed by a disciplined central party, it would, Bingham claimed, overcome the opposition "easily" with little bloodshed. If, however, the capitalist interests coalesced to forcefully prevent the new constitutional convention from meeting, "more violent means" would be necessary, and perhaps even "something more or less like a dictatorship won by force" might be required. Bingham seemed to be alluding here to a provisional dictatorship of the revolutionary party that would abdicate once the transition to socialism was secured.[27]

While proclaiming himself a supporter of "full and complete" democracy, there was an unmistakable strain of class elitism in Bingham's analysis, a profoundly undemocratic inclination only partially connected with his advocacy of a temporary dictatorship. This emerges full-blown in a letter he wrote to his grandmother in the spring of 1933 complaining of the apathy and inertia of the mass of Americans. The people, he charged, "are content to live in slums provided only they have a little security." Perhaps "men would have to be 'forced' to be free. Certainly the people . . . who are able to change society to any extent, are always a small minority. They must be superior to the masses whatever class of society they come from."[28] Bingham never supported a meritocratic government of disinterested experts, free from popular control. But in the first years of his radical commitment he strongly suggested that a listless public would have to be aroused and then carefully shepherded to socialism by a morally and intellectually superior revolutionary vanguard. Unlike most radicals he had scant confidence in the insurgent potential of the American "proletariat." He preferred that the revolution be led by men close to his own class and temperament, intellectuals of considered judgment, resolutely committed to the material and spiritual uplift of those less fortunate. The Christian missionary imperative strongly undergirded his radical faith.

Nor was his vision of socialist America as revolutionary as his rhetoric implied. If we ignore his occasional references to a "temporary dictatorship," an idea he would soon abandon, Bingham's conception of revolution was marked by an abiding attachment to traditional American democratic principles and institutions. In his radical blueprint he urged, for example, that both the political and economic institutions of the new revolutionary republic be based on the time-honored traditions of democracy, decentralization, and federalism. The tentative economic model he suggested in "Common Sense and the Community" rested on "decentralization of the broadest and most popular kind"; it was a federalized system with maximum decision-making power invested in the hands of local industrial units controlled by the workers and production engineers.

Considered together, Bingham's writings throughout the early 1930s reveal a man who never sought to erect through revolution an altogether new human setting. Even in his most radical phase, from 1932 to early 1934, he urged a "Second American Revolution" principally in order "to regain the liberties which our economic development has submerged."[29]

In the spring of 1932, just after completing "Common Sense and the Community," Bingham returned to America to work for the cooperative society Communism promised but had not yet achieved. He had begun his world travels in search of a purposeful career, a personal cause appropriate to his vaulting idealism. In "ASA" he had given vent to his restless hopes and ambitions, but they had no clear body or aim. Life, he had made it clear, had little meaning for him except as he was able to achieve fulfillment through work for the social good. Yet he had found no satisfying social philosophy or social aim. This was the importance of Soviet Russia. There he found a revolutionary faith and a social ideal that transformed his vaguely felt humanitarianism into a sharply articulated radicalism. Now he called himself a "communist." Revolution would be his life's work. His anxious quest for a cause, a "sword for the fighting," had come to an end. He had his commitment; he had his creed. Writing late into the night on the eve of his departure for America, he exuded a serene confidence in his ability to succeed. "With my eyes open to my weakness, and to the dangers I run, I choose to try to lead. . . . I think it possible I can be great. Others have thought so too. I will try."[30]

3

"COMMON SENSE" AND REVOLUTION

Bingham returned to America in mid-summer of 1932 bursting with
revolutionary confidence, expecting to find the mass of Americans
prepared as he was for open revolt against capitalism. This was the
most difficult summer of the long depression. Nearly one-quarter of
the work force was unemployed, and all across the land there were
appalling signs of economic want and spreading despair. In the coal
fields of Appalachia evicted families slept in battered tents, cooked
over open fires, and sent their children to school gaunt and hungry,
while in countless towns and cities growing numbers of the dispossessed
crowded together in squalid "Hoovervilles," their dominating daily
concern survival rather than employment. In Detroit, Philadelphia, New
York, and Chicago, all over urban America, long queues of dispirited
men huddled daily outside the doors of soup kitchens and rescue
missions waiting shamefully for a meager handout. Others, more
desperate, scavenged for scraps of food in the city dump. And everywhere that summer ragged armies of the unemployed tramped the roads
in an aimless search for opportunity. "Fifty years ago," complained one
Pennsylvania miner, "we used to work six months a year and live
good. . . . Even in Cleveland's administration, when Coxey made his
march, I ain't seen times like these."[1]

As the depression reached this, its third terrible year, the *Saturday
Evening Post* asked the British economist John Maynard Keynes whether
there had ever been anything like it before. "Yes," he shot back, "it
was called the Dark Ages and it lasted 400 years."[2]

Yet however grim their plight, surprisingly few Americans had given
up on capitalism. Anxious to find a public embittered by poverty and

poised for radical action, Bingham found instead most Americans suffering patiently and quietly, still unwilling to blame capitalism itself for the crisis. The hollow-looking unemployed he encountered on the streets of New York begging for nickels and listening to soapbox orators seemed "hardly sufficient," he later remarked, "to terrorize the 'bourgeoisie.'"[3]

Others in 1932 sensed this same absence of revolutionary ardor, this pervasive mood of blank despondency and aimless confusion. The young writer William Saroyan, touring depression America, found among the poor and the unemployed a strange resistance to radicalism, coupled with a paralyzing apathy. "Hardly anybody is interested in anything much," he reported. "Hardly anybody is at all." The millions of unemployed continued "law-abiding. No riots, no trouble, no multimillionaires cooked and served with cranberry sauce." Instead of blaming capitalism for their failure, Americans blamed themselves, experiencing a private kind of shame and humiliation at being unemployed. In the words of Studs Terkel: "No matter that others suffered the same fate, the inner voice whispered, 'I'm a failure.'"[4]

To impatient young radicals like Bingham, this desperate attachment to "the system" was both disheartening and unreasonable. "The American people still believe the Ballyhoo that has been thrown at them for decades by politicians, publicists and advertising," Bingham observed bitterly just after returning from Russia. They plod along with the cruelly mistaken impression "that this is 'only another depression,' that our institutions are God-given and immutable, that prosperity is around the corner."[5] Still, he remained confident in the possibilities of revolutionary change. The prevailing public inertia made the radical's mission doubly difficult, yet hardly impossible. Clearly, however, before there could be a revolution there would have to occur a thoroughgoing change in the dominant orientation and strategy of the American radical movement, for the movement itself was largely to blame for the reigning mood of confusion and political despair.

Bingham interpreted the public's stubborn attachment to capitalism as a failure of American radicalism. Millions of distressed Americans, he was convinced, were powerfully disenchanted with capitalism but clung to it nevertheless because existing radical parties had not addressed themselves to their immediate social needs, had refused to appeal to them in language they readily understood. The Socialist Party, as Bingham saw it, was a party dominated by churchmen and intellectuals, hopelessly out of touch with those it proposed to organize for revolution. The Communist Party, on the other hand, while defiantly committed to working class revolution, was too closely associated with Soviet Russia to incite a mass following, even among the most grievously oppressed. But the principal problem of both these parties, in Bingham's estimation, was their Marxist program and orientation, a program and orientation ill-suited to the prevailing American middle class mentality.

Bingham was certainly no reflex anti-Marxist. In Russia he had taken the Marxist classless ideal as his own, being careful to distinguish between Marx's richly suggestive theoretical contribution and the vulgarized "Marxism" of Soviet Communist officials. He understood, as well, that the American Communist Party's slavish reliance on the Soviet Union and its scriptural duplication of Soviet Marxism-Leninism were in direct violation of the advice of Marx and Engels, who had urged socialists to pay "special regard . . . to the institutions, customs, and traditions of various lands" when organizing for revolution. Yet his was not an attempt to reshape Marxism to American socio-political realities. Rather, he set out to free American radicalism completely from its reliance on Marx and the Soviet Union and to develop a distinctly Americanized socialism. Naively perhaps, he assumed that if Americans were presented with a radicalism growing out of their native traditions and directed toward their pressing material concerns, they could be enlisted for revolution. This would be the purpose of his new magazine.[6]

By the early fall of 1932 Bingham had assembled a skeletal staff for *Common Sense* and was ready to go to press. Selden Rodman, a recent Yale graduate, was made co-editor, with C. C. Nicolet of the *World-Telegram* as managing editor. Walter W. Liggett, an experienced investigative reporter, and C. Hartley Grattan, an Australian born radical correspondent, also helped to put out the first issue. But by the spring of 1933 Nicolet, Liggett, and Grattan had all left *Common Sense*, leaving only Bingham, Rodman, and a shifting staff of amateurs to run the journal. Up until the outbreak of World War 2, *Common Sense* was the joint effort of these two men, Bingham being almost solely responsible for its editorial policy, with Rodman handling the daily responsibilities of managing editor.

Bingham had been introduced to Rodman in New York in the fall of 1932 by the journalist William Harlan Hale, a roommate of Selden's at Yale. Only twenty-three years old at the time, Rodman was a brash cultural radical with a passionate commitment to art, poetry, and revolutionary politics. As an aspiring experimental poet at Yale, he had teamed with Hale to found and edit the *Harkness Hoot,* an irreverent literary journal specializing in satiric accounts of the Yale scene. But his driving aim was to edit a national radical magazine.[7]

Bingham and Rodman launched *Common Sense* in a mood of intense optimism, confident that it would incite the first stirrings of a revolt against capitalism. In choosing the name *Common Sense* for his magazine, Bingham was undoubtedly aware of another of Paine's works, the *Appeal to Reason,* for like Paine he had a vigorous faith in the liberating potential of science and informed intelligence. "I believed [then]," Bingham later recalled, "that the economy could be managed to avoid unemployment and depression, that fiscal deficits and a national debt were bookkeeping, not moral problems . . . that by the application of intelligence and good will to the management of human affairs war and poverty would be abolished and something like the millenium brought to pass."[8] In the first issues of *Common Sense* he and Rodman described the problems of depression America with engaging simplicity, insisting that if only capitalism were replaced by a socially managed economy every American could enjoy undreamed of material plenty with only four hours work a day. Visionary and hugely simplistic, the animating ideas of the early *Common Sense* grew out of Bingham's confidence in man's capacity to solve even his most complex social problems.

From the first, *Common Sense* sought to distinguish itself from other progressive journals like the *Nation* and the *New Republic.* These journals, Bingham believed, were too "highbrow" to attract a wide popular readership. And while critical of capitalism, they failed to offer their readers a constructive program for its replacement. Unlike them *Common Sense* would deliberately seek to reach the "ordinary American" with a clear and decisive program of revolutionary change.[9]

In their initial efforts to reach a mass readership, Bingham and Rodman employed many of the publishing techniques of the larger commercial magazines. With an eye to building up newsstand sales, they went to a tabloid format, with an arresting, colorful cover design. *Common Sense* was also inexpensively priced; and its articles and editorials were written with the general reader in mind (although in later months they became increasingly sophisticated). Inventive art work and cartoons ridiculing fat plutocrats and grasping politicians gave it a breezy satirical flavor that balanced well with the seriousness of its editorials and feature pieces. And on the back cover of the early issues were photographs juxtaposing the ostentatious living habits of America's leisure class with the bitter plight of the unemployed.

For the elaboration of its political and economic message, *Common Sense* called on the country's most prominent non-Marxian insurgents, including in the early years John Dewey, Upton Sinclair, Lewis Mumford, John Dos Passos, Harold Loeb, Stuart Chase, John Chamberlain,

George Soule, Paul H. Douglas, John T. Flynn, Congressman Thomas
Amlie of Wisconsin, Governor Floyd Olson of Minnesota, Charles
Beard, and James Rorty. Despite their numerous political and philosophic differences, all these contributors were united with Bingham
in the belief that American radicalism had to turn away from Europe
and "attempt to solve its own problems in its own way." More than
any other magazine of the depression era, *Common Sense* consciously
identified itself with the historic tradition of American dissent. Hardly
an issue failed to contain some reference to a noted American insurgent. Henry George and Thorstein Veblen were special favorites of the
editors; but it was Edward Bellamy whom they singled out as America's
greatest social philosopher, citing his efforts to fashion an Americanized
socialism attractive to the middle class, his opposition to violent class
conflict, and his earnest concern for preserving and extending the finest
features of middle class culture. Bellamy also had a passionate faith in
machine technology, sharing with Bingham the belief that an orderly
organic culture would emerge with the intelligent social direction of
technology. And for both men economic change was merely the prerequisite and basis for a life-forwarding spiritual regeneration; middle
class New Englanders, their rebellion against capitalism was animated
by the moral intensity of the Puritan. If revitalized and refitted to
modern conditions, Bellamy's ideas, Bingham insisted, could form the
philosophic underpinnings for a new kind of American radicalism.[10]

While Bingham kept an iron control over *Common Sense*'s editorial
policy, his feature writers backed up his editorials with some of the
most unrelenting anti-business writing of the decade.[11] The common
theme of these exposés was the alignment of the forces of wealth
and privilege against the mass of Americans, criticism designed to draw
the readership to the economic program Bingham was developing in the
lead editorials. Bingham called his alternative economy a "production-
for-use" system; and for the next four years this term came to define
the radical message of *Common Sense* and the political movement its
editors worked to encourage.

Bingham, as we have seen, first became impressed with a "production-
for-use" arrangement in the Soviet Union. The Soviet economy, as he
saw it, differed from the American in its preponderant concern with
production, as opposed to profits. Under capitalism production depended upon the businessman's reasonable expectation of a profit. When
ample opportunities for profit existed, businessmen produced. However,
when various unregulated economic forces conspired to reduce opportunities for profit, they cut back production and the entire public

suffered. Modern technology, Bingham was convinced, had already solved the problem of production, moving America from an "age of scarcity" to an "age of potential abundance." Yet this enormously efficient technology was tied to an antiquated distribution system that subordinated the pressing needs of the citizenry to the pecuniary interests of the capitalist. The need clearly was for an economic system like Russia's, where the entire monetary and financial mechanism was programmed to meet the production schedule of the national economic plan.[12]

When Bingham began *Common Sense,* his economic education was scanty, the product of a few college courses and a cursory study of the Soviet planning effort. The economic manifesto he enunciated in its first issues was technically unsophisticated and hopelessly vague. Yet however elementary his knowledge of technical economics, he began his analysis of capitalism with a simple but profoundly important question: What is the leading purpose and function of an economic system? His answer: serviceability—the production of ample goods and services for the entire community. And it was precisely here that he found the Soviet system superior to capitalism. Yet while the Russian planning effort would influence all his subsequent economic writings, it was the quixotic ideas of a group of American economists and engineers that most directly shaped the economic program of *Common Sense.* In the published findings of the Technocrats, as this group came to be called, Bingham found ample statistical and theoretical support for the rudimentary production-for-use ideas he presented in the early issues of his magazine.

A few days before the first issue of *Common Sense* hit the newsstands, an article appeared in the *New Outlook* reporting the existence of a research team of engineers, social scientists, and technicians who were using offices at Columbia University to conduct an "efficiency study" of the North American economy. The survey's director, Howard Scott, an eccentric Greenwich Village engineer, claimed to have overwhelming statistical evidence of capitalism's "unworkability." The nation's marvelously efficient productive machine, Scott claimed, was being sabotaged by an antiquated capitalist distribution system. Only by moving to a rationally planned system, run by expert engineers, could the nation reap the full harvest of its technological advance.[13] Reporters rushed to Scott's offices to question him about his findings, and within a matter of weeks the ideas of Technocracy swept the country, inciting an instant popular craze.

The Technocrats derived most of their basic assumptions about the workings of the industrial system and the centrality of the engineer in the production process from Thorstein Veblen. Veblen saw the nation's industrial plant as capable of introducing virtually limitless prosperity. Yet the dream of universal plentitude was being subverted by the capitalist businessman, who regularly curtailed production in the interest of profit. In *The Engineers and the Price System* (1921), regarded by some as the "manifesto of technocracy," he laid down a plan for a bloodless revolution by the engineers and technicians, those who actually performed the essential work in industry. Since these groups were indispensable to the productive process, they could, through the threat of a general strike, bring down capitalism with little violence or disruption of the going technology. Once in control, they would move to replace "absentee ownership" with a "soviet" of economic experts whose supreme concern would be the full release of industrial production.[14]

Yet Veblen, always the pessimist, doubted the immediate likelihood of such an engineer's takeover. A successful engineer's revolt would, he admitted, demand the "tolerant consent of the population at large, backed by the aggressive support of the trained working force." The workers, however, were "out of touch and out of sympathy with the technical men," while the general population was still in thrall to the "Vested Interests," soundly convinced of the superiority of capitalism. Even the engineers themselves, Veblen argued, were a placid lot, "consistently loyal . . . to the established order of commercial profit and absentee ownership." Thus, like so many other American social thinkers, Veblen searched vainly for a group capable of spearheading a radical reconstruction. For in the end his hoped-for revolutionary agency, the production-conscious engineer, was a symbolic construct; and Veblen freely conceded this. Sardonically appraising the possibilities for radical change, he concluded that there was "nothing in the situation that should reasonably flutter the sensibilities of the . . . absentee owners, just yet."[15]

"Just yet." Here Veblen seemed to leave open the possibility of a future engineers' revolt. In preparation for such a change in historic circumstances, he organized shortly after World War 1 a small study and research group to explore the possibilities of a peaceful industrial coup. If capitalism failed, this group could become the nucleus for his proposed "soviet of technicians." But Veblen's group, which met regularly at the New School for Social Research, soon disbanded when its members found themselves hopelessly divided on a number of questions. As an outgrowth of these discussions, however, Howard Scott and several of Veblen's other admirers, including Stuart Chase, Frederick L. Ackerman, Charles Steinmetz, and L. K. Comstock, established in 1919 the Technical Alliance for the purpose of drafting a blueprint for a production-for-use system. Occasionally Veblen himself joined their discussions. But financial difficulties, Veblen's failing health, and dissension between the enigmatic Scott and other members of the group soon killed the organization. Scott nonetheless remained committed to the original research objectives of the alliance; and when the economic crash he predicted came in 1929, several of his old associates and a few new converts joined him in New York to reestablish a research project along the lines of the old Technical Alliance. In the late spring of 1932, they began an energy survey of North America in space made available to them by Columbia University; the following winter they published their fantastic economic findings.[16]

The Technocratic analysis was strikingly congruent with Bingham's first crude explorations in economic theory. Like Bingham they found the cause of the depression in capitalism's antiquated market system. An ever accelerating technology had already solved the problem of production, making it theoretically possible for every American to enjoy an income adequate to his needs. The problem, however, was that capitalism's distribution system was attuned to an "age of scarcity." That is, a businessman would not produce unless he was assured a profit, and this profit depended upon a supply "more or less scarce." So long as scarcity conditions prevailed, capitalism worked reasonably well. But this scarcity was being rapidly eradicated by an expanding productive system. Modern technology, "the offspring of capitalism," was thus killing the parent: the symptoms of this paradoxical dilemma were idle factories, rising unemployment, and an escalating debt burden that would soon, if left unchecked, bring on total economic ruin.

The Technocrats urged capitalism's replacement by a system that disregarded purchasing power (which dropped when goods were plentiful) and distributed goods according to social need. Yet how were the real economic needs of an entire citizenry to be calculated? Present economic measurements, Scott claimed, were too imprecise and unstable to fix accurately the value of commodities; he therefore urged a system of distribution and valuation based on energy rather than specie, the value of commodities to be precisely determined by tabulating the amount of energy, or ergs, necessary to produce them. With prices no longer left to the caprice of the market, consumption and production could be properly and permanently balanced.[17]

Technocracy burst upon the public consciousness at a time when millions of Americans were searching desperately for a magic cure for economic recovery. Here was an economic message replete with convincing data, couched in the authoritative language of science and engineering, offering both an explanation and an easy answer for the economic crisis. Unlike communism it contained no mention of class conflict, outright confiscation, or proletarian violence. Technocracy's simple and single message was the promise of a future of unsurpassed prosperity. When asked how he planned to implement his engineer's utopia, Scott, an unusually long-winded speaker, was strangely taciturn, saying only that he was indifferent to political action.[18]

Scott's public evasiveness on the question of political tactics, his overblown estimates of the nation's productive capacity, and his failure to announce a specific economic program to restore prosperity eventually exploded the Technocracy fad. But in the dark months before Roosevelt's inauguration his ideas enjoyed extravagant popular acclaim. Scott's economic analysis held a special appeal for independent radicals like Bingham, Upton Sinclair, and John Dewey, who while repelled by Technocracy's vision of an engineer's future, saw in his findings a uniquely American challenge to capitalism.[19] "The basic conclusions of Technocracy are true," Bingham insisted, "whatever doubt may be cast upon individual statements." Yet while he and Rodman would found the economic program of *Common Sense* upon certain Technocratic principles, they remained suspicious of the movement's political and cultural assumptions. The Technocrats never arrived at a political strategy for carrying out their ideas, but Bingham and Rodman were disturbed nonetheless by the undemocratic implications of many of their proposals, fearing that the sudden flare-up of interest in Technocracy might lead to a demand for a dictatorship of engineers. To prevent this, they urged *Common Sense* readers in sympathy with Technocracy's critique of capitalism to join them in creating a political movement expressly dedicated to a more democratic future. Rodman noted that Veblen himself had recognized the unlikelihood of the engineers alone taking over the productive system. "Only as the people are persuaded to adopt political methods," Rodman warned, "can the engineer's goal [of a rationally directed economy] be made practicable."[20]

Bingham was also disturbed by Technocracy's shallow materialism, its spiritless emphasis on economic abundance and technological advance as the highest social achievements. The Technocrats' unbounded faith in science and machine technique, their dreams of a smoothly mechanized future, struck him as a more perverse form of the deadening materialism he found at the heart of Soviet culture. For Bingham, material abundance was merely a preliminary step toward a new democratic culture and life standard. The reorientation of cultural and social values he saw emerging from man's emancipation from want would, he hoped, lay the foundations for a cooperative community in which life-forwarding values transcended the pecuniary craving for material gain, a society that allowed its freely cooperating members full opportunity to exercise their creative powers of feeling and thinking to reach that kind of Emersonian self-fulfillment he had earlier idealized in "ASA."[21]

Bingham rendered his ideas of "The New Society" in a series of utopian essays that appeared in *Common Sense* in early 1933. These essays, actually an update and revision of Edward Bellamy's classic vision of industrial democracy, convey the decidedly middle class character of his radicalism. They are easily the most personally revealing of his political writings. Like William Dean Howells's *Altruria* and Bellamy's Boston of the year 2000, Bingham's is a community shaped by an older set of values, a clean and prosperous middle class republic unscarred by class conflict or rancorous dissent. As in the seventeenth-century Puritan village, consensus is the crucial condition of community; only this consensus has been secured, not by fealty to a transcendent spiritual ideal, but by technologically produced abundance, which has eradicated economic competition, curbed men's selfish appetites, and provided each citizen a comfortable standard of living. Yet although economic plentitude and full equality have produced a harmonious consensual community, each individual stands out as a "distinct personality," and society as a whole is marked by the broadest cultural diversity. Bingham would have community; but he would also have full individuality. He never considered the two irreconcilable.

Bingham took his *Common Sense* readers to an America transformed into "a garden of verdure and beauty, a vast park landscaped with trees, woods, [and] meadows." In the meticulously planned garden cities that grace the terrain, crowded, noisome tenements have been replaced by attractive community buildings and spacious residential parks. The air is clean and clear, for the central power stations that provide energy are located at mine heads and water power sites, far from the population centers. But the cleansing process went beyond this. Salesmanship, advertising, commercial law, brokerage, and banking, all the sleazy enterprises of a moribund capitalism, have been eradicated. Here was an entire social world cleansed of the "misery and falsity of commercialism."[22]

Bingham's model republic embodied all that he cherished in his New England upbringing. Utilizing the techniques of modern social engineering, he constructed a kind of idealized New England village on a grand scale. In an important way his was an effort to recapture the organic community life of his Puritan forebears. Order, civic placidity, and moral rectitude are the ideals his community enshrines.

Yet Bingham's utopia was not simply an effort to revivify an earlier organic community consensus. At the heart of the utopian plan was an unequivocal acceptance of industrialization and an awareness that new institutional and administrative reforms would be necessary to insure that all citizens participated openly and freely in the public decisions that touched their lives. Collective effort was to be balanced by the fullest participatory democracy.

In these "Good Society" essays Bingham wrestled with what remains one of the crucial public questions of our time—how to balance individual freedom and public control. This effort to strike a creative reconciliation between democracy and collective planning would mark his writings throughout the decade. In these articles, his first sustained confrontation with the problem, he suggested the institutional outlines of an industrial republic guaranteeing broad individual freedom within the framework of socialist planning, a society that sanctioned and encouraged two apparently contradictory public ideals—collectivism and individualism.

Like his intellectual mentor Edward Bellamy, Bingham was both a socialist and confirmed individualist. Both men saw unregulated capitalism ravaging the individualism they cherished; and both looked to a democratized collectivism to recapture this disappearing ideal. But while Bingham borrowed many of Bellamy's ideas in constructing his idealized future, he jettisoned what he took to be the more authoritarian features of Bellamy's utopia.

In Bellamy's *Looking Backward* ultimate power rested with a governing bureaucracy of social experts possessing encompassing public powers. While intensely committed to the national welfare, these officials did not draw their authority from the community of working citizens. Only those over forty-five and not connected with the industrial army had meaningful power. To permit members of the industrial corps to vote, Bellamy argued, would "be perilous to its discipline."[23]

On this issue Bingham split with Bellamy. Bellamy's meritocratic socialism would, Bingham believed, merely substitute the veiled authority of expertise for the bared tyranny of the robber baron. Yet how to balance government planning and democracy? Bellamy had not resolved this question satisfactorily, nor had anyone else Bingham had read. Bingham was thus thrown back on his own incomplete knowledge of political economy; and what emerged was a curious amalgam of Italian fascism and American political federalism, a democratized version of the corporativist state.

Bingham first encountered corporativism during his brief stay in Italy in 1932. Initially he was impressed by the similarities between Fascist economics and Soviet planning. "Fascism like Communism," he wrote at the time, "means putting the welfare of the community ahead of selfish gain. . . . It has honestly declared that the social welfare must come before the individual welfare." Under Mussolini the state had broadened its control over the economy and had instituted a complete system of social insurance, as well as a thriving network of community organizations for work and leisure. These were sure harbingers, Bingham was convinced, of a more humane economic order. In a long private interview with Bingham, Mussolini underscored those areas of similarity between Fascism and Communism. When Bingham commented that the outstanding difference between the two systems was that fascism seemed intent on working out a compromise with capitalism, whereas communism aimed at its destruction, the Duce paused, spread his arms wide apart and boomed gustily, "But this is communism. This is socialism."[24]

Bingham could not agree. Socialism remained for him a more compelling social ideology and a surer and saner road to a cooperative future. In Mussolini's hands, moreover, corporativism seemed in immediate danger of becoming a reckless ideology of national expansion; while at home Bingham saw corporativism fast evolving into a "centralized paternalistic bureaucracy." As a practicing model of industrial democracy, Italian corporativism, he was forced to conclude, was a failure. But in the corporative conception of government, he found an institutional construct that influenced his political and economic thinking throughout the 1930s.

Actually, of course, the "corporative" idea was not a fascist invention. It was instead, Bingham recognized, a synthesis of nineteenth-century Catholic social doctrine, guild socialism, and syndicalism. Its overriding ideal "grew out of the Syndical theory that all powers should be in the hands of self-governing industries." Ideally, or as Mussolini had originally presented the plan, corporativism was to rest on a foundation of thousands of associations of workers, employers, and professions. These associations, or syndicals, were in turn to be organized into federations and local bodies for mutual cooperation in which workers and employers were equally represented. The corporations were to have powers over industry in matters like wages, hours, and conditions of work, while a central council of corporations was to be charged with ultimate direction of national economic life. Thus under corporativism, as Bingham understood it, all industries were to be subject to state control, yet each was to be largely "self-governing within its own sphere."

In practice, the institutional shell of Italian Fascism might have resembled this theoretical model, but in fact Mussolini had centralized all real power in his office. Yet Bingham remained convinced that the theory itself, if properly implemented with every group interest represented in associations that managed local economic and political affairs, could combine the benefits of industrial democracy with the efficiency of central planning.[25]

The community of Bingham's "Good Society" articles is essentially a corporative state, with certain Technocratic features. It is, however, a democratized corporativism. All industrial units are nationalized and combined into huge trusts, or corporations, run by workers and production engineers. Each industry has its own democratically elected planning board composed of representatives from labor, the production engineers, and the consuming public, while overseeing the entire national economy is an elected central planning board, charged with drafting a national economic plan. However, in matters of general social policy it is subject to the legislative control of Congress. Thus, the people through their political representatives determine the social ends the economy seeks; and only in matters affecting the economy as a whole does the central planning board issue decrees, leaving "all other matters to each industry to determine itself." Such a democratized and decentralized collectivism would, Bingham believed, combine the overall planning and direction essential in any advanced economy with the maximum amount of economic democracy for the individual worker and citizen.[26]

Bingham's industrial republic was not a perfect society, an ordered world free of pressing human problems and the noisy clash of men and ideas. There would always be, he acknowledged, dissension, struggle, and conflict in any human setting. These could be minimized, not eradicated. Yet while Bingham's was an orderly world, it was not a repressive one. The spirit of Bakunin, in fact, flickered faintly in his vision of the future. The citizens of the new industrial republic, Bingham wrote in one of the final "New Society" articles, had not yet reached the "ultimate goal toward which man had struggled for ages—complete freedom and absolute lack of outside restraint on the individual." Yet with the functions of government radically curtailed, they had already begun to anticipate the day when the state would "wither away" to be replaced by the anarchist dream of a "free association of men in the fellowship of common life."[27] Thus, unlike most collectivists Bingham's writings pointed ultimately toward a decentralized community of enlarged freedom and broad cultural diversity. Much like Marx he believed that, having solved the problems of production and distribution through collective controls, the community would begin to be self-regulating, with the powers of the state trimmed to a bare minimum.

Nor did Bingham nurse the illusion that the fellowship of man could be had through social engineering. There would always be deeply human problems that no amount of social planning could eradicate. Socialism, Bingham warned, promised not an end to all human ills—only to those growing out of the economic, social, or political conditions of life. Having mastered these inequities, men could at least begin to live decently, with dignity if not perfect bliss. On this point, Bingham endorsed the wise realism of the Marxist philosopher Sidney Hook. Under communism, Hook once wrote, men would cease to suffer as animals but would continue to suffer as human beings. They would move "from the plane of the pitiful to the plane of the tragic."[28]

Bingham's willingness to concede the impossibility of social perfection, his perception of the need for ongoing and dynamic change in any society, and his rooted distrust of centralized power distinguished him from most modern utopians. Since the advent of the industrial revolution, the literature of utopian thought, both American and European, has been characterized by a driving "rage for order," a yearning for an ordered and predictable world free of tumultuous social change.[29] Alarmed by violence and class action, utopian writers have generally so ordered life in their fictional futures as to remove all possibilities for genuine individuality or meaningful change. "The pervasive character of all utopias," in the words of Lewis Mumford, "is their totalitarian absolutism, the reduction of variety and choice, and the effort to escape from such natural conditions or historical traditions as would support variety and make choice possible."[30] "Utopia," George Kateb writes, "is a dream of order, of quiet, of calm. Its background is the nightmare of history."[31] Most modern utopias, as a result, are grimly regimented societies peopled by contented but lifeless automatons with no personal distinction whatsoever, people as lifeless as the machines that service their every whim. Utopian writers have also been reluctant to admit the need for a recurring change in the community's institutions and values. Once erected, they blithely assume that their institutional designs will richly serve all subsequent generations. Utopia, after all, is perfection; and is it not impossible to improve upon perfection?

Bingham, there is no doubt, was as alarmed as any previous utopian writer by the mounting class violence and unruly change of industrial society. His also was a dream of order and consensual communalism. Yet this "rage for order" was balanced by a resolute Yankee individualism, by a deep and continuing regard for the principles of democracy and decentralization he had learned at home. A pragmatic relativist, he also understood that a society's values and institutions, its most sacred customs and mores, must be continually challenged and reshaped in response to dynamic changes in the material world. Of all the material forces at work in the world, easily the most consequential, to his mind, was industrialization; and only a democratic culture, a culture that grew in free and often unpredictable ways from a cooperative pattern of life could master the machine for truly human purposes. Thus in the fourth year of the depression Bingham held out to his readers the engaging possibility of a prosperous democratic community compatible with organic development and fully responsive to the social and spiritual needs of its citizenry.

By the spring of 1933 Bingham had fashioned the beginnings of a radical program that included a sweeping indictment of capitalism and an intensely personal vision of the socialist future. He had also begun to address the most crucial public issues of his day: the relevance of Marxism to American society, the problem of establishing a revolutionary movement in a prevailingly middle class nation, the relationship between collectivist planning and individual freedom, the place and function of technology in America's future, and the question of violent versus democratic change. Yet while committed to revolution and certain of the kind of future he wanted, he had still not given his readers a clear indication as to how America was to make the historic leap from capitalism to socialism. By the spring of 1933, when he published his utopian essays, his political thinking had advanced little beyond the naive speculations of "Common Sense and the Community." He could not give his readers a political program because he had none himself. It is not surprising, then, that in the first year of *Common Sense* the economic issue predominated.

Bingham, of course, was not alone in this concern. Economic planning was the commanding intellectual issue of the early 1930s. Anticipating a new public receptivity to change, intellectuals rushed into print an amazing array of economic schemes, some democratic, others decidedly undemocratic. The general character and specifics of these economic proposals are of more than cursory interest to the student of the decade; for these economic strategies provide a revealing insight into the political orientation of their authors. This was especially true of Bingham, whose program for expanding abundance through the orderly introduction of democratic planning had a decisive influence on the political strategy he would eventually urge for his new party movement. Before considering that political strategy and movement in detail, therefore, it is important to analyze more searchingly his and other *Common Sense* intellectuals' plans for a new industrial order. If there was such a thing as an ideology of American independent radicalism in these years, it received its classic economic expression in these various proposals.

4

TOWARD A NEW INDUSTRIAL DEMOCRACY

Bingham's "New Society" essays convey the fervid social optimism of early depression radicalism. Fired by the possibilities of wholesale change, intellectuals filled dissident journals with their plans and programs for a new America. Some, like the Southern Agrarians recoiling from the excesses of unbridled industrialism, called America back to an earlier and simpler era, before the hegemony of the machine, when men were knit together in intimate communities, close to the land and united by a common heritage and a rich organic culture. But the southern romantics did not speak for their age. Most of the visionary programs that appeared in the literature of these years were founded upon a realistic acceptance of the machine and upon the need for more collective controls and more collective order. Even Lewis Mumford, a persistent critic of machine culture and industrial regimentation, called for a sensible integration of the machine into the fabric of society and for greater collective social discipline.[1]

At the heart of the new economic literature was, above all, a commitment to public planning, a compelling urge to subject the machine to human direction. Planning, to be sure, had long been central to American reform thought; but the depression dramatically accentuated this emphasis. Then there was the Soviet Union, whose spectacular industrial growth offered unqualified evidence of the possibilities of economic planning. Well before the stock market crash John Dewey, Stuart Chase, Scott Nearing, Rexford Tugwell, and countless other American writers had hailed the Soviet planning experiment as an economic model of surpassing importance. But after 1929 Russian political and economic developments came to occupy an ever increasing part of the Left's attention. And in almost every case it was Russia's ambitious planning effort that most impressed American intellectuals.[2]

The American Left did not respond with unqualified fervor to the Russian experiment. While orthodox Marxists applauded almost uncritically every aim and accomplishment of the revolution, the response of the non-Marxian Left was more varied and complex. Closest to the Marxists were liberal "fellow travelers" like Corliss Lamont, Louis Fischer, the Moscow correspondent of the *Nation,* and Walter Duranty of the *New York Times,* writers who passed over or downplayed the repressive policies of Stalin's regime. Other non-Communist progressives like Carl Becker, Charles Beard, Oswald Garrison Villard, William Henry Chamberlain, and Horace Kallen, while sympathetic to Soviet planning, vehemently denounced the dictatorship. Between these two groups, but closer to the Beard-Becker position, were independent insurgents like Bingham, Stuart Chase, John T. Flynn, George Soule of the *New Republic,* and Bruce Bliven of the *Nation.* These "Soviet sympathizers," as Frank A. Warren has called them, while critical of the dictatorship, approved almost as unreservedly as the fellow travelers the sweeping material achievements of the Soviet planning effort. Even the Soviet sympathizers, however, differed in their reaction to the Soviet government. The editors of the *Nation* and the *New Republic* admitted that Stalin was a dictator; but they rarely carried their criticism deeper than this.[3] *Common Sense,* on the other hand, not only outrightly condemned the dictatorship, but attacked head-on, as neither of these journals did, the entire Communist assumption that democratic socialism could be achieved through a policy of repression and coercion. "The means chosen [to achieve socialism]," Bingham argued consistently, "cannot be divorced from the end sought."[4]

Bingham, of course, had not always been so unequivocally critical of the Soviet dictatorship. In Russia, in 1931 and 1932, he had sanctioned the curtailment of political and legal freedoms on the grounds that these were but temporary, stopgap policies. Shortly after returning to the United States, however, as the "temporary" dictatorship began to take on the ugly characteristics of a permanent control, he began to speak out strongly against the Communists' brutalitarian methods; and after 1933 he openly denounced every blatant extension of Stalin's power. By this time his magazine had become a rallying center for anti-Stalinist radicals.[5]

Yet Bingham's anti-Stalinism failed to dampen his enthusiasm for Soviet planning. Those who wrote regularly for *Common Sense,* including Chase, Flynn, and Douglas, shared his divided view of Soviet developments. None of these writers recommended that the United

States blindly follow the Soviet planning model. All agreed that America would have to pioneer an economic strategy expressly tailored to national realities.

Ardent for change yet fearful of class revolution, a number of these non-Marxian insurgents recommended economic planning not only as the aim of socialism but as the very means of achieving it. George Soule epitomized this cautious insurgency in his widely influential book *The Coming American Revolution* (1934). America, he argued, was already in the first throes of a social revolution, although not the kind of upheaval that had shaken Russia. In America the unwitting agent of revolution was the federal government. Slowly, yet inexorably, through its intrusion into economic life it was urging the nation in the direction of full collectivism. When this process was completed, America would be a socialist state, not in name perhaps, but most certainly in fact.[6] Stuart Chase, Paul Douglas, and a number of other independent progressives joined Soule in endorsing government planning as an orderly means to full production for use.

Beyond their common fear of class violence, most of the planning enthusiasts who wrote regularly for *Common Sense* agreed on a number of assumptions about the nature of American industrial society and how it might be transformed. All welcomed the emerging collective state, seeing in its institutional patterns glowing possibilities for material plenty, democracy, and community. And, curiously, none sought to eliminate the corporation, or to drastically curtail the scope of its economic activity. Through inspired and continuous public regulation the corporation, they agreed, could provide the economic abundance essential for expanded freedom and social well-being.

Advocacy of a new industrial collectivity based upon the reformed corporation meant enlarged public power for a rising class of men, the economic and technical officialdom charged with national planning and administration. Whether one looks at the Technocratic dream of a dictatorship of engineers, or the less frightening proposals of Bingham and Soule, there is at the heart of most of the 1930s planning arguments an often unstated but implicit belief in the desirability of a society directed by men of superior expertise. Many planning advocates—Bingham, Dewey, Douglas, Chase, and others—had been to the Soviet Union and there observed Communist economists, engineers, scientists, and educators actively fashioning a new society. Russian intellectuals seemed to be integrated into the life of the community as American intellectuals were not. They were an honored class enlisting their energies in the service of the nation. This sometimes submerged yearning on the part of American intellectuals for a society managed by men like themselves

surfaced again and again in their planning designs. Whether as disinterested advisors to men of power, or as managers of the new planning
and regulatory agencies, they envisioned for themselves a decisive role
in national decision making. The Technocracy movement was perhaps
the most brazenly authoritarian manifestation of this passion for expertise. Few of the decade's planning enthusiasts went this far. Most
non-Marxian intellectuals like Dewey, Bingham, Soule, Tugwell, and
Douglas recommended strong democratic checks on the powers of the
planners. But even these industrial democrats found it exceedingly
difficult to disguise their envy of the Soviet managers; their planning
proposals placed in the hands of selfless experts enormous powers for
public suasion and control.[7]

In advancing their ideas for expert administration, some of these
planning advocates gave oblique expression to a distrust of popular
democracy, or of any type of spontaneous political agitation that
did not issue from organized, officially sanctioned social groupings. This
was the same fear of mass activity that underlay their opposition to
class action. Suspicious of popular rule, of government actively responsive to the citizenry, certain of the more undemocratic collectivists
recommended that the more important functions of government be
turned over to experts capable, presumably, of making intelligent
policy free from the incessant pressures of an uninformed and capri-
cious electorate. In most cases this meant transferring the load of
decision making from the legislative to the administrative branch of
government, a movement already well underway. The acceleration of
this trend toward administrative rule would, they maintained, insure
a more rigorously honest and efficient state system. Politicians,
it was suggested, were too corrupt, ill trained, and sensitive to arbitrary
voter pressures to govern effectively. To the more zealous collectivist,
the coming corporate order demanded a new administrative officialdom,
thoroughly trained, scientifically oriented, consummately dedicated to
the national community, and alive to the manifest possibilities of the
technological revolution.[8]

Stuart Chase came close to this position in urging the creation of
"an industrial general staff with dictatorial powers covering the smooth
technical operation of all the major sources of raw material and supply."
As for democracy, that could remain; but only if it confined itself
"to all but economic matters." Where once Plato had called for philosopher kings, "the greatest need ... [now] ," Chase insisted, "is for
philosopher engineers."[9]

This line of argument, however, was carried to its most openly undemocratic extreme in the Technocracy movement. Howard Scott rarely

spoke publicly on political matters, but one of his early followers, Harold Loeb, published in 1933 a book called *Life in a Technocracy* which sharply portrayed the Technocrats' disdain for political democracy.

Loeb first met Scott in New York in 1919 and was immediately intrigued by his "logic of treating the production and distribution of wealth as an engineering problem. Most reformers," Loeb later noted, "are concerned in the first place with human and humanitarian values and thereby confuse their practical measures with emotional considerations. Scott's concentration on the mechanics of the thing seemed a more valid approach." When the depression Scott predicted hit in 1929, Loeb, who had spent the greater part of the 1920s in Europe editing *Broom,* a radical literary journal, and following Hemingway and his crowd around Paris (he was Robert Cohen in *The Sun Also Rises*), recalled Scott's ideas and returned to New York to secure his assistance in writing a glowing account of the Technocratic future.

Loeb's Technocratic utopia attests to the prominence of the corporation in collectivist thought. Ninety-two nationalized corporations have taken over the political functions of government. They are the state. All communal life radiates around them; no activity escapes their influence. Their boards of directors rule in the name of the "stockholders," or citizens, of the various regions, choosing representatives for the central coordinating board, whose chairman is the highest official in the land. The engineers, scientists, and production executives who administer the industrial conglomerates are chosen by the state, not the citizens, strictly on the basis of "fitness in their field." The institutional skeleton of the old political system remains, but politicians, a class of individuals Loeb referred to as "clowns," have been shorn of all effective power, their duties being merely ceremonial. Yet Loeb refused to be dogmatic about this. If there were a demand for it, he wrote, political officials could continue to be elected to office "thereby titillating the egos of those who like to think they are running things." But in a society that had reduced most political questions to technical decisions, it would be "stupid," he added, to decide an issue by popular vote when a "yardstick" could be used. "To trained minds in possession of complete information," the answer to nearly all technical problems "would be incontrovertible." Only nontechnical questions such as "what to produce and how much to produce" were left to "popular decision," although Loeb failed to describe in any detail the administrative mechanism through which citizens would register their opinion. Loeb freely admitted that this society was undemocratic by contemporary standards. But "with money abolished and every material want satisfied" the people would show little inclination for politics. Their unfailing loyalty would be secured by the continuous flood of products pouring from the assembly lines of the national corporations.[10]

The Technocrats were certainly not the first to raise the possibilities of a meritocratic corporate order. The key institution in Bellamy's utopia was, after all, the nationalized corporation, swept clean of rapacious businessmen and run by an administrative bureaucracy which had assumed most of the functions of the old legislature. Other progressive planners who followed in the tradition of Bellamy suggested even more imaginative variants of the administrative state. One of the most influential of these earlier planning enthusiasts, Herbert Croly, attempted to fashion a compromise between the growing movement toward participatory democracy that was taking place in the first years of the century and the impelling need for greater public expertise. What emerged was a kind of "plebician administocracy," a spirited administrative government manned by trained professionals and headed by a vigorously active chief executive capable of interpreting and implementing the public will as it became expressed through the new democratic techniques reformers were then enacting. Such an invigorated administrative government would, he believed, promote social harmony and heal the class divisions most progressives feared. Croly and his associates on the staff of the *New Republic* never urged the complete emasculation of the legislature, and most stopped short of advocating out-and-out socialism. But many of the outstanding tendencies of 1930s planning literature were clearly prefigured in the writings of these earlier collectivists.[11]

Technocratic intellectuals like Loeb inherited the best and the worst of this earlier planning faith. Their emphasis on science and social intelligence as indispensable instruments of human advance, their concern for economic equality and intelligent social planning, their insight into the need for a new cooperative ethic, spoke to what was finest in the intellectual heritage of collective planning. Yet like so many previous collectivists, often without abandoning the language of democracy they championed programs that were dangerously undemocratic and narrowly utilitarian, programs that later in the decade, when shorn of their socialist biases, would be turned to the defense of a fast emerging corporate capitalism. In their elaborate blueprints for the future, efficiency, technological and human synchronization, and sheer factory production too often took precedence over free expression, cultural diversity, and popular autonomy. Renegades against unregulated capitalism, these Technocrats advanced industrial designs that left little room for the kind of radical social dissent they saw themselves engaged in.[12]

Yet how radical were the Technocratic collectivists? Their relentless assault on capitalism was balanced by a conception of culture that mirrored rather than challenged the developing industrial order. Instead of conceiving a new idea of community, a cultural synthesis harmonizing collectivism and individuality, the best of the new industrial habits with the durable values of the past, the claims of imagination with those of rationality, they raised the mechanical values of the power age—productivity, rationality, and bloodless efficiency—to the level of a social ideology. Loyal heirs of the father of scientific management, they fashioned an industrial program that would have made Frederick Winslow Taylor glow. Like so many present-day social engineers, theirs was the dream of enriching the quality of life through public administration.

Undeniably, there is much to admire in the Technocratic vision. It calls on social aims sound and decent; its dream is a community governed by reason and intelligence, a society where none go hungry and all work for the general good. But Lewis Mumford, writing well before the depression of another group of social planners, struck to the heart of the Technocratic fallacy. Most industrial dreamers, Mumford observed, suffered from "the assumption that modern industrial society possessed all the materials essential to the good social order. . . . All that was necessary was a change in power and control: the Social Commonwealth would simply diffuse and extend all the existing values." Modern utopians like Bellamy and Upton Sinclair accepted the collectivized society and worked to extend it. Critics of capitalism, they

> could envisage only a bourgeois order of society in which every one would have the comforts and conveniences of the middle classes, without the suffering, toil, anxiety, and frustration known to the unskilled workers. . . . In attack, in criticism, they did able work; but when it came to offering a genuine alternative, their picture became a negative one: industry without millionaires, cities without graft, art without luxury. . . .

Having no idea of "other values, other modes, other forms of activity than those practiced by the society around them," their work failed to "lead out of the muddle."

Despite their noble intentions, these industrial utopians failed to appreciate that the good life involved more than a reordering of public institutions. What was equally necessary, Mumford insisted, was a transformation of the regimented style of life that had come to characterize all industrial societies, socialist and capitalist.[13] In his own way, then, Mumford offered the most thoroughgoing critique of the Technocratic utopians, challenging the very values and priorities that informed their work.

Bingham, we know, shared several of the directing assumptions of the Technocrats: their faith in technology and expertise, their dark fears of class disorder, their serene confidence in the reformed corporation. This is why he invited so many Technocrats to write for his magazine. Yet his utopian essays reveal a markedly different conception of the future from that of the Technocrats. The outstanding distinction between Technocrats like Loeb and independent radicals like Bingham, Mumford, and Dewey was that for the latter group democracy was the very fulfillment of collectivism. Collectivism, to Bingham, meant a political and economic system of genuine equality, a community in which all citizens had an active hand in the decisions that touched their lives and welfare. The Technocratic design for concentrating power in the hands of disinterested experts would, he believed, merely substitute one form of class society for another, with expert administrators replacing politicians and businessmen as arbiters of public policy. In the Technocratic future, moreover, it was the individual's relationship to the industrial system that finally mattered, whereas in Bingham's new society a regionalized and decentralized political system determined the social needs of the state. The planning administrators drew their power and were ultimately responsible to the electorate; they were not an autonomous ruling clique. It was this underlying emphasis on decentralization and participatory democracy that set Bingham apart from the Technocratic utopians.

Considered together, Bingham's early economic writings constitute a sustained effort to frame a new human ethic for the machine age, a social philosophy combining a realistic acceptance of industrialization and collective planning with a solicitous regard for man's individuality and his deepest spiritual and ethical ideals. Bingham was joined in this effort by two of the decade's premier moral philosophers, John Dewey and Lewis Mumford, writers whose work far surpassed his in creative reach and analytical power. While others emphasized the incompatibility between technology and humanistic values, collectivism and individuality, Dewey, Mumford, and Bingham suggested the groundwork of a philosophy harmonizing democracy and planning, humanism and the machine— a holistic conception of change emphasizing individual as well as societal regeneration.

Both Dewey and Mumford produced an extensive body of social criticism over the course of the decade; but two of their works in particular, Dewey's *Individualism Old and New* and Mumford's *Technics and Civilization,* stand witness to the kind of organic social ethic they favored. No two works of the period better illustrate the critical qualitative distinction between the democratic collectivists and the Technocratic collectivists.

In *Individualism Old and New* Dewey went straight at the problem Bingham had addressed in his "New Society" essays—the need for a new conception of individuality appropriate for a society growing increasingly more collectivized. Thus far, Dewey argued, the rapid "corporization of life was . . . still largely mechanical and qualitative"; it had not been accompanied by a transformation of fundamental ideas and habits. By and large, Americans still clung to the orthodoxy of an era already past, to the narrow individualism of the "pretechnological age." This older individualism, Dewey admitted, had opened the way for stupendous industrial advances. But it had also encouraged a deadening cultural conformity, produced economic instability and insecurity, and blocked the realization, ironically, of true individuality. It was, besides, dangerously inadequate in a society overwhelmingly corporate. Dewey blamed this stubborn cultural lag, this "maladjustment between individuals and the social conditions under which they live[d]," for much of the anxiety, frustration, and alienation that prevailed in current industrial society. Outwardly modern society might be smoothly ordered, but the inner man remained confused and bewildered, incapable of finding satisfaction in a world radically at variance with his values and working beliefs.[14]

A "truly human society" would emerge, Dewey claimed, only when men shook off the deadening burden of the old individualism, developed an "intellectual recognition of the realities of an industrial age," and utilized this new social intelligence to harness these forces for the "liberation and enrichment of human life." America, he insisted, was in "for some kind of socialism" no matter what people would choose to call it. "But there is a difference and a choice," he added, "between a blind, chaotic and unplanned determinism, issuing from business conducted for pecuniary profit, and the determinism of a socially planned and ordered development. It is the difference and the choice between a socialism that is public and one that is capitalistic." Under capitalism true individuality and democracy were impossible. Capitalist workers had little directing influence in the labor process; nor did their work give creative release to feelings and imagination. Under a system of cooperative sharing, however, "initiative and responsibility would be demanded and achieved," and creativity and imagination given free play. Human values would control economic values, not the reverse. And in the end only through democratic socialism would the "sound element of the older individualism—equality of opportunity—be made a reality."[15]

Dewey never depicted the precise form he expected the new individualism to take. This, he warned, was asking the impossible. For individualism was not a static construct, complete in itself. It was rather a "distinctive way of feeling the impacts of the world and of showing a preferential bias in response to these impacts." It developed "into shape . . . only through interaction with actual conditions." The only concrete advice Dewey could offer those sympathetic to the kind of integrated culture he favored was that they spurn the old individualism and begin to actively shape industrial society to human purposes.

Thus instead of separating self from society, Dewey insisted that inner fulfillment was possible only in a community of cooperative sharing. Democratic collectivism would nurture creativity and uniqueness precisely because men would feel themselves "sustaining and sustained members of a social whole." In this sense, Dewey's collectivism, like Bingham's, met the twin demands of ethical humanism and democracy. Collectivism, for both men, meant not only a refashioning of material institutions but the creation of a new democratic culture and a new democratic man. They agreed, moreover, that collectivism, as well as individuality, would have to be continually redefined in response to transformations in the material conditions of society. Out of this evergoing interaction between man and his outer world, Dewey concluded, "we, who are also parts of the moving present, create ourselves as we create an unknown future."[16]

While Dewey's overriding concern was the encouragement of a new individualism, Lewis Mumford stressed in his work the need for a philosophic synthesis reconciling the instinctual and the rational sides of human behavior, a balanced philosophy of life that would allow man to transcend the shaping discipline of the machine and redirect modern material forces for the enrichment of personal and community life. This, in large, was also Dewey's intention. Yet Mumford, who had always been critical of Dewey's excessive relativism, set down the specifics of a new social ethic and framework of living. In Mumford's work we also find an ecological perspective and an appreciation of the nonrational springs of human behavior absent from the work of most of the decade's other radical collectivists. More than Dewey or Bingham, he perceived the dangers of a careless overextension of economic growth.

The crux of the modern problem, in Mumford's analysis, was man's insanely passionate commitment to material progress. It was not science or technology themselves but their overexpansion and misapplication that were responsible for the confusions and dislocations of the modern age. In *Technics and Civilization* Mumford traced the rise and triumph of machine civilization in the West, copiously recording its debasing impact on imagination, free choice, and creative living. In Mumford's view, the machine swept over Western civilization in three successive but overlapping waves. The first machine epoch, the eotechnic era, lasted from the waning of feudalism until the dawn of the advanced industrial revolution. Although the eotechnic age introduced the factory system and wage labor, made life more specialized and regularized, exalted profit oftentimes over craftsmanship, and exhibited in some of its industry a diminished concern for "human standards," it was in the main an era of startling cultural diversity and sweeping practical achievement, an age that joined its material concerns with a passionate cultivation of the sensual and the spiritual. Unlike a later material civilization it did not exalt work over all other pursuits. In the Catholic countries there were one hundred complete holidays a year, and men used this leisure to enrich themselves in non-pecuniary ways. Society's standard of value was not power and economic success alone, "but a greater intensification of life: color, perfume, images, music, sexual ecstasy, as well as daring exploits in arms and thought and exploration." Here also in the rounded culture of the late Middle Ages machine technics were used directly "in the service of life." New technologies were employed to transform the "woods and swamps of northern Europe into a continuous vista of wood and field, village and garden," to build cities that were orderly, spacious, and beautiful and to construct a network of canals that immeasurably improved human communication. In a world where the spiritual and the mechanical, the aesthetic and the rational were valued equally and where work was balanced by creative leisure, men enjoyed fuller lives in harmony with themselves, with their natural surroundings, and with their fellow man.[17]

This balanced organic civilization, however, gave way eventually to the paleotechnic era, an age dominated by science, technology, and competitive capitalism. In the paleotechnic phase the promising scientific and mechanical gains of eotechnic man were multiplied, consolidated, and systematized; the whole rhythm of life was adjusted to the monotony of the machine process. Where eotechnic civilization aimed to balance the material and the spiritual, a vulgar paleotechnic culture heralded material progress as the sole key to the good life, reducing the passional and emotive aspects of experience to leisure pursuits. Two developments in particular brought on this age of mechanization, regimentation, and compulsive materialism: the relentless advance of physical science and the rise of commercial capitalism.

Eotechnic man had been vitally interested in science and mechanical technics; but paleotechnic man transformed this estimable concern into a determined effort to bring the whole of human experience under the direction of science and the machine. In its voracious urge to comprehend and master the natural world, the new science defined as "real" only those aspects of experience that were external and repeatable, that could be studied and verified by careful experimentation. Existence was separated into units that could be "weighed, measured or counted": all else was judged "unreal." Subjectivity, intuition, and feeling had no place in a framework of ideas which stressed organization, regularity, standardization, and control.

Capitalism further contributed to this process of cultural debasement by subordinating all values to profit and productivity. And like the new science, it glorified power as well as "abstraction, measurement and quantification." Driven by a life-damaging compulsion for wealth and power, paleotechnic man plundered the environment, transformed the city into a sprawling wasteland, and imprisoned its poor in factories and mines. Progress came to be reckoned by the amount of goods produced; and work, once considered merely "a necessary part of living," became an "all-important end." Not only this. The paleotechnic era witnessed as well the fragmentation of community living and the spread of a new individualism that proclaimed personal success in material pursuits as the summit of man's achievement.[18]

Yet the paleotechnic did not define the possibilities of the future. By the beginnings of the twentieth century, there had begun to appear the first signs of a new civilization and culture which promised to redirect science and the machine in the interests of freedom and social community. Mumford called the emergent age the neotechnic, but warned that it was still far from achieving full form. "Paleotechnic ideals," he noted, "still largely dominate the industry and politics of the Western World." But in certain of the dynamics and practices of his age he found indications of a fresh orientation. For one thing, large scale production itself was inherently cooperative in its operation and used materials with fine precision and skill. By encouraging cooperation and sound efficiency, machines were fostering habits of cooperative thought and action "in other spheres." The electric generator also promised a greater decentralization of industry, making ever more possible an organic regional culture that balanced manufacturing and agriculture. Then there was the fact that sophisticated neotechnics required of their operators greater alertness, intelligence, and technical expertise. If the more tedious work in industry were eliminated by automation, the remaining skilled professionals might be a proud and responsible work force, not a class of spiritless industrial conscripts.

Recalling the words of Matthew Arnold, Mumford described America as a nation "living . . . between two worlds, one dead, the other powerless to be born." The nation had at its disposal magnificent instruments for regeneration and renewal. Yet the persistence of outmoded paleotechnic habits prevented the utilization of these technics for human enrichment. At this point Mumford's analysis joined Dewey's. In thrall to capitalism and its pecuniary standard, Americans, they agreed, were employing neotechnic instruments for paleotechnic purposes, degrading culture and self in the name of profit.[19]

Yet neither blamed the machine itself for the modern problem. The machine, Mumford insisted, was "ambivalent." It could be "an instrument of life," or one of destruction and domination. The measure of the machine was man; it was the uses to which he put it that finally mattered. In the closing section of *Technics and Civilization* Mumford described the kind of community that might emerge from an intelligent mastery of the machine. His richly suggestive neotechnic society, which he called "basic communism," was a decentralized and regionalized community of material sufficiency, wide personal freedom, and warm community association. In contrast to Technocratic planners like Scott, Mumford urged sharp limitations on the scope of the national planning effort and the powers of the planners. Any collective effort, he insisted, must "leave a place for irrational and instinctive and traditional elements . . . which were flouted . . . by the narrow forms of rationalism that prevailed" in the paleotechnic phase. Only that part of the economy producing the basic necessities was to be centrally planned and managed. Here the capitalist market would give way to a communal distribution system based on human need rather than ability to pay, with complete equality of income in regard to basic commodities. All citizens would share in the work of the community "up to the amount required to furnish the basis." Above that standard "the desire for leisure would compete with the desire for more goods," and in this area "fashion, caprice, irrational choice, invention, special aims, would still perhaps have a part to play."[20]

In its economic phase Mumford's basic communism was strikingly similar to Bingham's industrial utopia, with one overriding difference. Whereas Bingham approached being an enthusiast for unlimited economic growth, Mumford entreated Americans to scrap the ideology of limitless material advance and to assimilate and consolidate the gains industry and science had already brought. This was not a call for an iron moratorium on growth. As much as any Technocrat, Mumford recognized that countless human problems could be mastered only by further scientific and economic progress. But after society had provided a decent standard of living for all its citizens he urged that it call a halt to those kinds of material changes antithetical to community and personal well-being. Yet this reemphasis need not be coercive. Once men's basic material needs were met, Mumford hoped for a profound revolution in interests and attitudes, away from the pecuniary goals of an economy of "acquisition" toward a cultivation of non-material ideals and values. When this occurred, when the acquisitive doctrine of increasing wants yielded to a "normalized standard of consumption," the production and distribution mechanism would be adjusted to the altered plane of consumption. The result would be an "economy of sufficiency," not an "economy of abundance."[21]

Technics and Civilization is an extraordinary intellectual achievement. It joins a searching critique of machine civilization with a complete program of human renewal. Mumford not only questioned a number of the sovereign assumptions of Western scientific and industrial development, but suggested the basics for a new culture and a new consciousness. Yet the sweep and richness of his argument is vitiated somewhat by his failure to offer a program to carry to fulfillment the basic communism he so suggestively describes. Even the most sympathetic reader leaves the book impressed, perhaps, by Mumford's vision of the emergent neotechnic age, but unsure as to how this age is to be brought to life. This curious failure to fashion a political or even a clear cultural strategy for the achievement of basic communism can be attributed largely to two factors: Mumford's faith in the primary importance of inner or personal reorientation; and his organic conception of human civilization.

Mumford never supported *Common Sense*'s third party drive; nor did he actively support any of the decade's other political movements. Unable to find a political party fully congruent with his views, he spent the decade largely isolated from practical politics. Neither liberalism nor socialism, in his estimation, had an authentic insight into the crisis of industrial society; and neither embraced the values essential for a rebirth of community. Focusing entirely on the outer world of science and industrial organization, both liberals and socialists, he argued, over-valued the material and the rational, serenely assuming that human satisfaction would issue from a constructive readjustment of the going technology and social forms. This abounding faith in the redemptive power of material reconstruction was, Mumford charged, both simplistic and badly misplaced. Its obdurate refusal to appreciate the importance of inner change was its outstanding fallacy. On this count,

Mumford found both Marxists and New Dealers, native radicals and independent progressives, equally at fault. All failed to discern the need for a prior and thoroughgoing transformation of the consciousness of industrial man. Such a change, Mumford claimed, would have to precede and lay the basis for any radical institutional reconstruction. Mumford did not have in mind here the kind of revolutionary consciousness Marxists expected to develop in the proletariat. The need, in his view, was to go beyond liberalism and socialism, to discard old ways of looking at society and man, and to forge a new philosophy aimed at transforming every dimension of community and personal life. Liberalism and socialism were ideologies of industrialization, intellectual offshoots of a scientific and technological revolution that sanctioned conquest rather than harmony with nature, that licensed technology as the instrument of that conquest. Both were narrowly utilitarian and dangerously materialistic; each emphasized industrial growth with little thought for its life-destructive consequences; neither offered a key to the restoration of man's shattered harmony with his natural environment. Most liberals and radicals, Mumford claimed, accepted the paleotechnic premise that the "effectiveness of a social system depends on the amount of work done and the quality of goods produced," when in fact the moral imperative of any economy was the "adjustment of the means of living to the needs of life."[22] While some intellectuals like Dewey and Bingham looked for such a value change to occur after the revolution, for Mumford this value change *was* the revolution.

Inner conversion came first in Mumford's logic of change. Rebirth was to begin in the minds and hearts of individual men. Industrial man would have to reexamine his priorities, reappraise his standard of values, alter his expectations, and redirect his interests. But this inner change would have to be confirmed by an outer, public one; only then would the new self spread and become universal. The social setting, the conduct of economic life and public administration, every social institution must be made to correspond to and support the reorientation of personal standards.

Mumford did not expect the majority of men to undergo at once this moral transformation. Only full and prolonged exposure to basic communism, to a social setting infused with the new ideals, would encourage neotechnic habits and attitudes in most men. But before such a social setting could be built, there would have to occur a value metamorphosis among those in the vanguard of change. If the intended agents of change themselves were in thrall to paleotechnic values, they could hardly be expected to introduce a wholly new life pattern once in power. All that could be expected from the success of such a radicalism was a redistribution of wealth and power, not a relentless challenge to the mechanized life standard of the paleotechnic. Writing in *Common Sense* in 1933, Mumford announced his unwillingness to support any movement for change that failed to present a positive philosophy of alternative values. To Mumford, only a conception of change that began with inner renewal and moved out to transform every part of culture and every person could bring to fulfillment a commonwealth of organic balance and human harmony.[23]

Mumford thus described an agenda for radical change—inner conversion leading to a total social reorganization. Yet he failed to specify how neotechnic consciousness was to be built into the life of the community. Even if, say, an enlightened vanguard were to acquire the kind of ethic he described, how were they to carry this ethic into institutional practice? This curious unwillingness to raise the issue of revolutionary strategy in a decade of explosive ideological controversy stems directly from Mumford's organic analysis of culture and civilization.

Instead of analyzing society from a class angle, as a structure organized in terms of productive relations and economic interests, Mumford, inspired by his master Patrick Geddes, compared society to a biological organism, whose health depended upon the harmonious cooperation and unity of purpose of its many components. In his organic view, socio-economic classes are not viewed as important in themselves; they are seen rather as vital and interdependent parts of an interlocking social organism. Classes, like the parts of the human body, are interlinked and function for the good of the entire organism. Harmony, balance, and internal cooperation, the keys to bodily health, are deemed essential to community health as well. This kind of inner harmony and unity of purpose, in Mumford's view, largely obtained in the late Middle Ages, when all classes and social groupings joined in the pursuit of universally agreed upon values; and men, even in their private moments, upheld the organic ideal of balance, fusing material concerns with the cultivation of the spiritual and the sensual.

Actually, Mumford's organic interpretation is less an analysis of change than an attitude toward it. While he brilliantly describes the course of human change in the West, nowhere do we find a comprehensive explanation of the dynamics of change. In his broad-reaching historical saga economic classes and powerful interests do not induce change, change just seems to happen. This is not surprising; for the organic view leads naturally to an emphasis on gradual assimilation and integration rather than on class or mass action. In the organic perspective, to quote James T. Farrell, "social problems are viewed as analogous to physical and/or mental illness. A social disease is the result of the mal-functioning of a member. If a part is out of gear, the whole is affected." The problem, then, becomes one of returning the ailing organism to its proper function in the larger design. Through such smooth assimilation integration and harmony are achieved.[24]

In addition to emphasizing the orderly and the evolutionary, the organic interpretation, at least as employed by Mumford, tends to mask the class character of society. This is most immediately apparent in Mumford's rapturous view of the late Middle Ages. What social cohesion and consensus he found in the eotechnic era was probably attributable less to the age's universal cultivation of the organic than to a religiously sanctioned, hierarchical class structure which kept the lid on social mobility and class tension. Mumford's organic view is thus inadequate not only because it conceals important kinds of class exploitation but, just as critically, because it offers little clue as to how certain classes come to social dominance. In *Technics and Civilization* one civilization seems to yield to another through the workings of a mysterious and unexplained cosmic determinism. Falling back on a formless and diffuse theory of change, a kind of shallow eschatology, his work, like that of the radical utopians he assailed, fails "to lead out of the muddle." This is not to denigrate his perceiving cultural design. But his insufficient attention to the class dynamics of social change make his proposals for renewal more visionary than he intended.

Working independently, but not unaware of each other's efforts, Mumford, Dewey, and Bingham searched for a form of community congruent with powerful advances in machine technics and social organization. Industrialism in the service of private profit had, they agreed, ripped apart the more ordered organic society of an earlier America, leaving in its place a world of cold impersonality, gross injustice, and deadening regimentation. Yet theirs was not an idealization of the pre-industrial past. Each in his own way welcomed the emergent era of industrial collectivism. The enemy of community was not industrialization but capitalism; until capitalism and the exploitive habits it encouraged gave way to a cooperative social system, real community would remain a distant ideal.

Yet how to inaugurate this transition? More than Mumford, who remained aloof from the stormy political disputes of the 1930s,

Bingham and Dewey recognized the need for a political movement expressly dedicated to democratic socialism. Yet no one knew better than Dewey the difficulty of organizing such a movement. Since 1928 he had been working with other independent insurgents in the League for Independent Political Action (LIPA) to encourage an independent socialist party. The league, however, had disappointed the expectations of its founders. With an executive committee dominated by intellectuals, and lacking the financial resources to hire a large staff of organizers, its appeal remained narrowly limited; by 1933 it was losing many of its members to the New Deal.

Bingham was aware of the LIPA when he launched *Common Sense,* but found its academic orientation ill suited to his revolutionary purposes. Yet by the late winter of 1933 he had made no progress toward organizing a party of his own. Nor were his ideas reaching the wide audience he had anticipated. He and Rodman had begun *Common Sense* with the expectation of achieving a newsstand circulation of 50,000. But by March, 1933, with sales fluctuating between 2,000 and 5,000, and finances running perilously low, they were forced to consider abandoning publication.[25]

It was this common experience of frustration and organizational failure that eventually drove Bingham and Dewey into active cooperation. In April, 1933, they announced that henceforth *Common Sense* and the LIPA would "cooperate vigorously" in an effort to build a "united people's party." *Common Sense* would become the unofficial organ of the league, carrying its News Bulletin as a regular feature, and in return Dewey sent letters to all LIPA members asking them to subscribe to *Common Sense* at a special discount rate of one dollar a year.

The merger of *Common Sense* and the LIPA was thus a marriage of convenience for both parties. Dewey's faltering organization welcomed a young publicist with money, a magazine, and a small but committed following, and placed Bingham on its executive committee, while Bingham was able to keep his magazine alive with the increase in subscriptions that resulted from the tie-in with the league.[26] More importantly, Bingham now had an organizational base from which to begin in earnest his new party drive. He would seek from this point on to refashion the league in the image of his own ideas, transforming it into a genuinely revolutionary organization.

5

CHALLENGE TO THE NEW DEAL

When Bingham broke into radical politics in early 1932, he announced his independence from all existing parties and programs. The New American Radicalism was to be a fresh and original expression of the social vision of a new generation of American insurgents. Certainly older radicals were welcomed to the cause. But Bingham looked to young dissidents like Rodman, Amlie, and Paul H. Douglas to lend the new radicalism its distinctive vigor. Like other generations of radicals before them, those who gathered around *Common Sense* proclaimed a clean break with the past; they assailed not only capitalism but the older radical parties as well, arguing the need for a movement and a program separate and distinct from all others on the national scene.

Yet their break with the past was not as complete as they thought. Much of the program of *Common Sense* was, as we have seen, strongly derivative, its ideas borrowed from the intellectual heritage of native dissent. And although Bingham was reluctant to admit it, there was also a close similarity between the kind of program and movement he favored and the kind of independent insurgency the League for Independent Political Action had been seeking to encourage. While Bingham refused at first to accept the league's unqualified adherence to peaceful change, convinced that some violence would be unavoidable in the drive to socialism, he shared its vision of a democratic collectivist future to be achieved largely through democratic political action. Both the league and *Common Sense,* moreover, had a pronounced middle class emphasis. In addition, many LIPA officials like Dewey, Douglas, and Howard Y. Williams endorsed Bingham's plan to convert the league into a broadly popular political organization. This important carry-over of ideas and leadership personnel makes some understanding of the early history of the LIPA essential for a full understanding of *Common Sense*'s third party drive.

The LIPA was a product of the advanced intellectual progressivism of the late 1920s. With neither of the major political parties committed to comprehensive change and the Socialist Party enfeebled by factionalism, a number of the country's outstanding reformers and socialists organized the league in late 1928 as an educational and promotional committee to clear the way for an independent radical party. John Dewey was elected national chairman, Oswald Garrison Villard of the *Nation*, treasurer, Howard Y. Williams, a Unitarian minister active in Minnesota farmer-labor politics, executive secretary, with James Maurer, a former Socialist Party candidate for vice president, Zona Gale, the novelist and radical critic, and Paul H. Douglas, a young University of Chicago economist, serving as vice-chairmen. Also on the league's executive committee were Stuart Chase, Reinhold Niebuhr, W. E. B. Du Bois, Robert Morss Lovett, Nathan Fine, Harry Laidler, and A. J. Muste.[1]

While the guidance and coordination of the league's day-to-day field work was delegated primarily to Howard Y. Williams, it was Paul Douglas and John Dewey who were most responsible for establishing its political orientation and organizational strategy. Dewey's outstanding contribution was his reform pragmatism, which became the adopted philosophy of the league, while Douglas reduced this inclusive reform philosophy to a detailed program for democratic socialism. In *The Coming of a New Party* (1932) Douglas described the league's argument for political and economic reconstruction, suggesting an organizational strategy that Bingham and *Common Sense* would later adopt almost in full.

Fashioning an analysis coincident with Dewey's *Individualism Old and New,* Douglas argued that the old economic individualism was inappropriate to the new collectivist-industrial reality. This defiant individualism might have been suitable to an age "when the mass of people were independent artisans, farmers, and merchants . . . [and] the success of every man did depend almost entirely upon the amount of energy and intelligence which he put into his business." But that age had passed irretrievably into history. No longer a balanced society of independent farmers and small entrepreneurs, America was now indisputably "a nation of employees," of men and women who worked in large economic organizations and depended on wages and salaries not prices, for their livelihood. To Douglas, the political implications of this organizational revolution were clear: American workers of the hand and brain would have to realize that their hopes for economic improvement were now "bound up not so much with the faint possibilities of individual economic success as with the improvement of the conditions of the class to which they belong[ed]." Organization, an ambitious counter-organization of the vast army of salaried employees, was the only realistic alternative to the capitalists' consolidation of productive enterprise. Only through such collective effort could America's laboring millions, both white and blue collar, gain their ends.[2]

To spearhead this organizational effort, Douglas called for a third party expressly dedicated to democratic economic planning.[3] While there were some who argued that it was possible to work for such changes through the old parties, Douglas dismissed this strategy as dangerously unrealistic. Both the Democratic and the Republican parties were securely in the grip of the monied classes, and "nothing short of a tidal wave" could break that dominance. Struggling to re-shape the priorities and policies of the old parties, moreover, would involve an inevitable series of political compromises, furtive backroom deals that would drain the fighting ardor of the reform faction. Insurgency would give way to expedience, and once impatient firebrands would soon find themselves temporizing liberals.[4]

Douglas pointed to Minnesota's flourishing Farmer-Labor Party, which had recently elected two United States senators, three congressmen, and a governor, as proof positive of the third party appeal, suggesting that the party become a model and rallying center for the national new party forces. Following its lead, the LIPA could begin organizing at the grassroots, patiently building a network of local party cells until sufficient support arose for a national party. In this way the league could avoid the mistake of the hastily assembled La Follette third party movement of 1924, which, lacking local and state roots, had collapsed after the national elections.[5]

Douglas also urged the exclusion of the Communists from the new party movement, citing their commitment to violent proletarian revolution and their organizational ties to the Kremlin. But the Socialist Party, with its "excellent . . . program and membership," would, he argued, make an invaluable political partner. Douglas even suggested a tentative strategy for LIPA-Socialist political cooperation. In areas where the party was strong, such as New York City and Milwaukee, he advised that it become "the agency for the new party"; whereas in areas where it was weak or non-existent the league could form its own organizations, hopefully with full Socialist support. And until the league had marshaled sufficient strength to run its own national ticket, Douglas asked its membership to endorse the national candidates of the Socialist Party.

Yet although Douglas envisioned a close working partnership with the Socialists (something the Socialists never accepted), he shared with Dewey and other active league spokesmen a reluctance to use the term "socialist" in connection with league organizational activities, for fear of alarming potential middle class supporters.[6] Dewey articulated this concern most succinctly: "This is a 'bourgeois' country; and an American appeal couched in language which the American people understand must start from this fact." Dewey believed that the depression's mounting toll on the middle classes would eventually draw them to the new party movement, provided the term "socialist" were kept out of league propaganda. But neither he nor Douglas suggested how the league, in an open electoral alliance with the Socialist Party, would be able to convince the middle class that its economic program was in any real way distinguishable from that of the Socialist Party.[7] Calling socialism by another name would hardly allay bourgeois suspicions of an avowedly anti-capitalist movement.

There were other reasons for the league's refusal to join a national coalition headed by the Socialist Party. While the aims of the Socialists were similar to those of the LIPA, the Bolshevik revolution, the split in the radical movement in 1919, and the Socialist Party's loose but nonetheless persistent identification with the international Marxist movement convinced Dewey, Douglas, and other league spokesmen that radical unity could never be achieved under the Party's standard. They were not the first to reach this conclusion. In the opening years of the 1920s, all over the Midwest, a host of radical farmer-labor parties burst into existence. There was an agrarian depression in the corn and wheat belt, but these were not simply disgruntled capitalist farmers seeking higher prices and currency inflation. Some of the insurgent organizations demanded thoroughgoing economic reorganization; a few came out openly for socialism. Several efforts were made before 1925 to unite these scattered state and local movements in a national organization embracing the trade unions and the Socialist Party. Radical agrarians, many of them veterans of the Debsian Socialist Party, had become convinced that radical unity could be achieved only by a new independent political party dressed in the familiar coat of farmer-laborism.

This radical unity obviously never materialized. Neither the Socialist Party nor organized labor gave it full support; the Socialists feared joining any movement they could not lead; while the trade unions, with only a few exceptions, backed off from any sweeping program of nationalization. Nonetheless, the appeal of militant farmer-laborism all over the Middle West indicates that economic radicalism was alive and widespread in these years. Radical anti-capitalism, as James Weinstein makes clear, did not disappear after 1919; there was simply no focal national organization to unite its disparate strains.[8] Beginning in earnest with the onset of the Great Depression in 1929, the LIPA set out to revive this pre-1925 farmer-labor agitation, to bolster its commitment to economic radicalism, and to transform this sectional outburst into a national production-for-use movement.

Under the spirited direction of Howard Y. Williams, the league first concentrated its efforts in the economically distressed corn and wheat belt. Yet while impatient with the old politics, farm and labor leaders were reluctant to align with a little-known and politically inconsequential organization headed by a group of radical intellectuals. Williams failed even to cement an alliance with his own state's Farmer-Labor Party, whose leader, Governor Floyd B. Olson, considered national third party action in early 1930 as precipitous.[9] Nor was the league successful in persuading the Midwest's leading progressive, Senator George W. Norris of Nebraska, to join its effort. Like his fellow progressives in Congress, Norris was unwilling to risk his political future and jeopardize what reform he could accomplish as an independent legislator on a commitment to a flimsily constructed third party movement.

The Norris overture, in the form of an open letter from John Dewey to the senator,[10] provoked a permanent split between the LIPA and several of its former socialist allies. A. J. Muste, for one, resigned from the league's executive committee, charging that the offer to Norris demonstrated the organization's commitment to a liberal, as opposed to a radical party. And Norman Thomas, under mounting pressure from his party's militant left wing, ceased from this point on to cooperate actively with the league in New York City politics.[11] Thus by the spring of 1932, with no major national politician in its camp and without the support of either the Socialists or the Minnesota Farmer-Laborites, the LIPA dropped its plans for a presidential ticket in the national elections and urged its membership to back Norman Thomas, while working for the election of state and local third party candidates.[12]

League hopes for a national party brightened somewhat after 1932. Norman Thomas received a disappointing 900,000 votes, but league officials interpreted Roosevelt's victory over Hoover as a standing mandate for economic change. In addition, two LIPA members and four Minnesota Farmer-Laborites had been elected to the United States Congress, while on the labor front the United Textile Workers and the American Federation of Hosiery Workers went on record for a national third party.[13] All the while the Midwest was ablaze with agrarian militancy.

As farm prices sank to a new low in the summer of 1932, agrarian radicalism again swept the Plains states. Milo Reno, the stormy leader of the Iowa Farmers' Union, took the lead with the formation of the National Farmers' Holiday Association. Reno's organization sought to dramatize the need for higher farm prices by halting the shipment of farm produce to market. All over Iowa in the scorching summer heat, angry farmers fought pitched battles with sheriffs and state troopers, smashing windshields, barricading roads with logs and spiked telegraph poles, and puncturing tires with pitchforks in a daring effort to close the highways to Sioux City markets. From Iowa the agitation fanned out to surrounding states; and soon it spread further north. In Wisconsin Walter Singler led the state's dairy farmers in an equally audacious product boycott. But declining farm prices were not the only burning issue in the Midwest. Like farmers all across America these were men engaged in a desperate struggle to keep their lands in the face of a ravenous foreclosure movement by banks and mortgage companies. Here also there was violence, or at least the threat of it. At Storm Lake, Iowa, a raging mob of rope-swinging farmers came perilously close to hanging a lawyer conducting a foreclosure; while similar, if less ominous incidents, were reported all over the Midwest. A leader of Nebraska's farm holiday movement aptly expressed the boiling insurgency of the Plains farmers: "If we don't get beneficial service from the Legislature," he warned, "200,000 of us are coming to Lincoln and we'll tear that new State Capitol Building to pieces."[14]

These farmers were by no means revolutionaries; few were ready to abandon their long-standing faith in capitalism. They were, however, angry, frustrated, and grievously disenchanted with their government, both state and federal. This in itself gave the LIPA something to work with. Williams and other league officials close to the midwestern scene were convinced that if the farm crisis deepened in the absence of massive government relief, this restive agrarian insurgency would explode into something more menacing to the status quo.

Bingham shared this view. When he joined the league in the spring of 1933, many of its liberal members had already deserted to the New Deal; while the split with the Socialists had cut further into the organization's strength. But those leaders who remained, like Williams and Douglas, were anxious to cooperate more closely with the farmer-labor movement. From this point on the league concentrated less on the intellectual elaboration of its position and worked more actively to encourage the establishment of farmer-labor parties in the Midwest. The league, frankly, had no alternative: the farmer-laborites were all they had to work with. And even this movement, as Bingham recognized, "represent[ed] merely a tendency, a blundering, somewhat timorous revolt, unaware of most of the fundamentals of the conditions which cause them to revolt." Yet, as he admitted in a letter to Senator Bronson Cutting, an LIPA ally, "There is no other group with a possibility on whom we can count."[15] Thus with a new consistency of strategy and purpose, the transformed league, under the active direction of Williams and Bingham, renewed and intensified its efforts to fashion a distinctly American radical challenge.

In the summer of 1933 Bingham and Williams acquired an invaluable political ally for their movement. Thomas R. Amlie, a brilliant young Wisconsin progressive, who had recently served a term in the United States Congress, had by this time shed his liberal reformism for a more audacious economic radicalism. A disciple of Thorstein Veblen, Amlie was impressed by the Technocrats' statistical indictment of capitalism and was actively searching for a political agency embodying their economic ideas. The Socialist Party was strong in his home state, but he desired a radicalism more expressive of his country's traditions and more attractive to the middle classes. The LIPA seemed more in line with his thinking, but its orientation struck him as excessively academic. Gradually, however, in a political metamorphosis much like Bingham's, he began to consider seriously the possibility of joining the league and using it as an organizational base for a radical new party effort.

Amlie had his baptism in politics as a Non-Partisan League organizer in the years immediately after World War 1. When the league collapsed, he went to law school, passed his bar exams, and divided his interest between a modestly successful Elkton, Wisconsin, law practice and a burgeoning career in local and state politics. All the while he read deeply in American and European social criticism. In the spring of 1933, following one term in Congress, he met Howard Y. Williams, who recommended him to Bingham as a promising new party leader. Bingham, aroused by Williams's glowing description, went that summer to Elkton to meet Amlie.[16]

Amlie was just the kind of leader Bingham had in mind for his movement, a radical with a sensitive and probing intellect, an expert on Veblen and Werner Sombart, a man who combined a command of advanced social theory and institutional economics with wide experience and some success in electoral politics. Tall, massively built, with sandy hair and rugged features, Amlie cut an impressive figure. While not a flamboyant or emotional leader, he had already developed a reputation for courage, integrity, and honesty that set him off from most politicians. His platform as well as his private manner was convincingly sincere and quietly persuasive. He had a dry, pungent wit and an impassioned concern for the underdog that proved hugely attractive to the small town, rural audiences he loved. Most importantly, his prestige and political contacts in the Midwest would be invaluable to the LIPA. "From that first talk with him," Bingham later recalled, "I felt a force of personality, a depth of intelligence, and an integrity of character that cannot be surpassed by any one in public life. In that small town law office, lined with dusty shelves, with its conventional pictures of Lincoln and Washington on the walls, I felt an almost instantaneous conviction that I was close to greatness." Amlie was equally impressed by Bingham and pledged his full support for the league's new party drive.[17]

Even before enlisting Amlie, Bingham and Williams had taken the first step toward establishing a more widely based national federation, issuing in the spring of 1933 a call for a national congress of all dissident organizations to be held in Washington in early June. The announcement of a league-initiated meeting, however, was preempted by the Socialist Party's call for a "Continental Congress" in that same city on May 6-7, 1933. The aim of the Socialist conference was to unite leading militant farm and labor groups behind an economic program more far-reaching than Roosevelt's. The LIPA urged its members to attend this conference but differentiated the goals of its upcoming meeting from those of the Continental Congress. "The Continental Congress," the league bulletin noted, "is called to formulate the demands of millions of hard-pressed, suffering workers and farmers. . . . The League congress is called to take definite steps for united political organization and action, and if the time is ripe, the definite formation of a united people's party."[18]

The Continental Congress was attended by over four thousand delegates, most of them representing radical farmer and labor organizations. The league sent Paul Douglas as its representative, hoping to encourage the delegates to go on record for a united party of the left. But Douglas's resolution to that effect was defeated by the Socialists, who saw a new third party as a threat to the legitimacy of their organization. In a final compromise gesture, empty of real meaning, the Socialist-dominated congress empowered its continuing organization, the National Committee of Correspondence and Action, to explore the possibilities of "independent political action" in the future.[19]

This was Bingham's first active contact with the Socialists, and he made no attempt to conceal his anger over what he saw as their narrowly sectarian tactics, their insensible determination, as he put it, to place "their own interests over the welfare of the people." The Socialists, he wrote in *Common Sense*, failed to see that "only a . . . united party of the great mass of people who are exploited under the present system can win to power. . . ." By blocking the Douglas resolution the party had squandered a magnificent opportunity "to further the winning of power by united action of the producing groups."[20]

Yet the LIPA did not see the Continental Congress as a complete failure. The surprisingly large turnout was an encouraging indicator of militant concern, causing the league to cancel its plans for a conference in June. "In view of the success of getting thousands to the Continental Congress," the league bulletin declared, "it seems both unnecessary and unwise to call another mass congress in the near future. The temper of the people is known. What is now demanded is organization." Accordingly, the league issued a call for a smaller meeting of progressive and radical leaders to "map out a plan for uniting their organizations in a mass party." This conference was scheduled for September in Chicago.[21]

In preparation for its Chicago convention the LIPA, in conjunction with *Common Sense*, launched the United Action Campaign, an organizational and educational effort to incite third party support. The overriding aim of the campaign was a mark of the dramatic turnabout in the national political situation; for by the summer of 1933 it had become abundantly clear to league officials that the enemy was now Franklin Roosevelt as much as capitalism. The continuing popularity of the New Deal would, they realized, destroy any hope for a new party. Until the New Deal was exposed as a failure and a sham, theirs would remain little more than a paper organization. It was to this end that the league dedicated its United Action Campaign.[22]

The sweep and vigor of the early New Deal took the entire nation by surprise. In March, 1933, Roosevelt inherited a country broken in spirit and desperate for clear leadership. Farm prices, factory production, and retail trade were all experiencing new lows. Unemployment had shot up from 1 or 2 million before the crisis to an astonishing

15 million. Some Americans were angrily calling the system itself into question; but the prevailing mood, as Bingham himself had realized, was one of bewilderment, resignation, and listless dissatisfaction. No one seemed to have an answer to the deepening crisis. Even Congress was dazed and directionless, unable to provide firm legislative leadership. Everyone seemed to be searching nervously for a plan, a program, or a leader to lift the nation out of the crisis. The playwright Robert Sherwood measured the public mood well. "No cosmic dramatist," he wrote, "could possibly devise a better entrance for a new President— or a new Dictator, or a new Messiah—than that accorded to Franklin Delano Roosevelt." Some must have caught the chilling resemblance between their own America and a discordant and confused Germany on the eve of Hitler's takeover. "I will do anything you ask," an Iowa congressman wrote to the new President. "You are my leader."[23]

This was the significance of the "Roosevelt revolution." Whatever its social and economic limitations, the sweeping legislative program of the first one hundred days was a brilliant psychological success. In barely four months Roosevelt had wrought a reversal of national morale that Walter Lippmann could only compare with the "second Battle of the Marne in the summer of 1916."[24] Poverty and unemployment remained; but under Roosevelt the nation at least regained the hope that the crisis would pass. Even liberals who had campaigned against him were now willing to give his administration a chance. The *Nation* and the *New Republic,* the senior organs of progressive opinion, had been lukewarm toward Roosevelt during the campaign. Now they saw in his new legislative enactments, particularly the Agricultural Adjustment Act and the National Industrial Recovery Act, a fitful but nonetheless significant movement toward national economic planning. Perhaps with liberal encouragement Roosevelt could be driven further leftward? Sensing the progressive possibilities of the new administration, both journals withheld serious criticism of its early legislative program.[25]

It was this subtle shift in liberal sentiment that most distressed LIPA officials. They were given an ominous reminder of Roosevelt's appeal to the Left when in July, 1933, their treasurer Oswald Garrison Villard announced his support for the President.[26] Coupled with the actions of the *Nation* and the *New Republic,* this seemed to portend a massive shift of progressive opinion to the administration. This explains the focus of the United Action Campaign. League offices were busy all through the summer of 1933 mobilizing a frontal assault on the New Deal recovery program. Anti-Roosevelt pamphlets were hastily assembled, league field organizers were instructed to concentrate on the inadequacies of the New Deal legislation, but it was in the pages of *Common Sense* that the most detailed and discerning analysis of the New Deal appeared. The two principal architects of that critique were Bingham and Dewey.

Bingham led off the assault with a searing indictment of the argument, advanced by a growing number of liberals, that the New Deal would eventually blaze the way to a fully planned economy. This analysis, he warned, was founded on an egregious misunderstanding of the nature and direction of the early New Deal initiative: its outstanding fallacy was its failure accurately to assess the character of Roosevelt's public philosophy. Bingham never disputed Roosevelt's commitment to reform. He consistently portrayed the President as a well-intentioned public leader with an engrossing concern for the common welfare. Roosevelt's problem, in Bingham's view, was of the head rather than of the heart. Whatever his sympathies for the unfortunate, he was intellectually committed to competitive capitalism. His intention was to strengthen and stabilize capitalism, not to replace it. At core he was an economic conservative suspicious of ambitious government planning and deficit spending. As yet, Bingham noted, he "has shown neither a desire for fundamental change nor an understanding of the necessity of it."[27] His New Deal was a blind, drifting attempt to patch up the worst defects of capitalism, an effort to erect a form of "state socialism" not unlike the "controlled capitalism of Mussolini and Hitler." Such a broadened welfare state might bring with it expanded social benefits, but would leave ultimate control of the economy in the hands of the very capitalists who had brought on the recent crisis, creating in the process a sprawling public bureaucracy heedless of the popular will. "At its best," Bingham wrote, "it will lead to a philanthropic or paternalistic government, providing bread and circuses for the populace, rather than a government 'of the people, for the people, and by the people.'" Worst of all, even these expanded controls and benefits would not bring full prosperity, for neither Roosevelt nor his principal advisors had grasped the root problem of the new economic era—capitalism's fatal inability to function efficiently in an age of potential plenty. The New Deal's failure to appreciate this and to move toward a cooperative system consonant with new material realities would, Bingham claimed, bring on an economic collapse "far worse than the last."[28]

As evidence of Roosevelt's intention to stabilize rather than fundamentally transform capitalism, Bingham cited the inadequacies of even the New Deal's most sweeping legislative triumphs. Mobilizing an indictment akin to that of many present-day Leftist historians of the New Deal, he emphasized the opportunities for radical action Roosevelt had squandered. Never, he argued, had a president assumed leadership of a Congress and a people more anxious for change. With enlightened resolute leadership the electorate might have supported a movement to recast the power relationships of American society. Yet Roosevelt had backed off from the challenge. This was the real tragedy of the one hundred days; at a time fraught with promise so little of real consequence was accomplished. Anti-business fervor, inflamed by a severe bank crisis, had peaked to a new intensity in the first months of 1933; a pliant Congress seemed primed for drastic banking reforms. Nationalization itself, Bingham suggested, might have been possible. Roosevelt's emergency banking bill, however, turned out to be a disturbingly conservative measure, drafted largely by private bankers and Hoover's treasury officers, a bill that returned control of the banks to their former owners. Roosevelt's farm program, in Bingham's estimation, was a similarly disappointing measure. Instead of going to the heart of the agrarian problem by introducing government cooperatives, controlling prices, and eliminating the middleman exploitation of producers and consumers through public ownership of processing and distributing factories, Roosevelt backed the Agricultural Adjustment Act, a "scarcity" program that artificially limited production at a time when millions went hungry. The AAA, in addition, left the administration of the farm program in the hands of the wealthiest and most politically powerful commercial farmers.[29]

What Roosevelt gave with one hand, moreover, he appeared to take back with the other. Pledging his administration to an enlarged program of federal relief and public works, he at the same time pushed through an Economy Act, cutting veterans' pensions and salaries of federal employees in an effort to reduce sharply the public deficit. To *Common Sense,* there was an inexplicable inconsistency to these policies, an uncertainty of purpose born of sheer intellectual confusion. "Having no plan and no objective," Bingham observed, ". . . [Roosevelt] drifts aimlessly, right, left, right, left—while the capitalist system flounders to its doom."[30]

Bingham reserved his most stinging reproval for the National Industrial Recovery Act, the most far-reaching of Roosevelt's early legislative enactments, and the bill, more than any other, that had persuaded liberals of the New Deal's commitment to national economic planning. The NRA was founded on the same kind of economic reasoning that underlay the Agricultural Adjustment Act. The problem in industry, as in agriculture, its sponsors claimed, was overproduction and anarchic price competition. Thus, under the NRA, trade associations in every industry were given the go-ahead to draft "codes of fair competition" which in effect, allowed industry to fix prices and production quotas free from the threat of court action. It was hoped that such a federally sanctioned cartel arrangement would restore stability and confidence in the industrial sector and open the way for a general economic recovery.[31]

Common Sense, however, vigorously disagreed; and throughout the summer of 1933 its writers hammered away at the NRA as the symbol of the administration's brazenly pro-business policies. The New Deal's most ambitious planning departure, the NRA was in their estimation the command agency of a new form of corporate capitalism, a system weighted heavily in favor of the rich and the powerful. Not only was there no social control of profits or production, but just as critically, business-dominated trade associations dictated the entire industrial planning process. Labor was conceded a measure of representation in the NRA, but businessmen had the upper hand in drafting the codes governing their industries, making the NRA little more than "a plaything of big manufacturers." John Flynn put the matter flatly: the NRA, he wrote, is simply a revivication of "the old Chamber of Commerce scheme for self-rule in industry—the self-rule done by the employers." Masquerading as "an assertion of the power of the . . . people over their own economic life," the New Deal, Flynn concluded, had "surrendered" economic government into the hands of the very interests most responsible for the depression.[32]

Labor and agriculture, to be sure, had been brought into an open alliance with government under the New Deal recovery initiative, but as the editors of *Common Sense* noted, only the larger and most consequential groups in the farm and labor sector had easy access to government. Sharecroppers, slum dwellers, and the unemployed, along with huge numbers of the unorganized middle class, were underrepresented or simply not represented at all in the new organizational partnership.[33]

Bingham assailed the aim as well as the scope and character of the New Deal recovery plan. Both the NRA and the AAA rested on the assumption that overproduction and falling prices were responsible for the economic downturn and that recovery could therefore be achieved by limiting production and keeping profits high. Bingham, on the other hand, saw the problem as one of underconsumption rather than overproduction, and recommended a redoubled federal spending effort to restore consumption power. The crisis, he insisted, called for an economics of abundance, not an economics of scarcity for business profits. Instead of curtailing production and maintaining high profits, "a real

New Deal," John Flynn agreed, "would be built on the effort toward lower prices, greater volume, wider distribution and smaller profits."[34]

To *Common Sense,* then, the chief constricting influence on the New Deal was its own ideology. Traditionally liberal, the New Deal could not be expected to advance an agenda of deep-going reform. This question of the limits of the New Deal's reform possibilities has been hotly debated by modern historians. Perhaps, as some have argued, Roosevelt was restrained from doing more by party and public pressures. The nation might not have backed a bolder initiative. Yet radicals like Bingham obviously thought otherwise. Reading the national mood in the blackest hours of the crisis, they sensed the faint beginnings of a genuinely radical discontent welling up in Americans of all classes and regions. An unsettled compound of anger and directionless frustration, this was not yet, they agreed, the stuff out of which successful revolutions were made; but this could change. Bingham took the first furious months of the Roosevelt presidency as vindication of his conviction that the shapeless public discord could be guided to a constructive movement for radical change. The vaunted "Roosevelt revolution," he claimed, had not yet tested the depths of the national discontent. Having called the stored energies of a once listless nation into action, Roosevelt had failed to sponsor the kind of radical changes the public might be persuaded to support.[35]

Bingham was joined in his assault on the New Deal by John Dewey, who differed from him politically only in the sense that Dewey continued to call himself a liberal. Dewey gave full intellectual expression to his unique conception of liberalism in *Liberalism and Social Action,* a book that, although not published until 1935, presented the essentials of a political philosophy he had been advancing since his first years in the LIPA. Bingham enthusiastically endorsed Dewey's "revitalized" liberalism, and he and Dewey hoped that *Liberalism and Social Action* would become the philosophic manifesto of their third party movement.[36] Here, and in a series of articles Dewey wrote earlier for *Common Sense* and the LIPA, we have the clearest summary of the league's opposition to the reform liberalism of Franklin Roosevelt, as well as the explanation as to how two men who called themselves liberals could differ so dramatically in their approach to the economic problem.

Liberalism arose, in Dewey's view, in the eighteenth and nineteenth centuries as an emancipating movement to release human energies from the grip of mercantile regulations and oligarchic government. The fighting creed and philosophic persuasion of the advancing bourgeoisie, it was directed at impositions upon economic as well as civil freedom. By the end of the nineteenth century, however, the very forces liberalism had freed and left unchecked had themselves become destructive of economic freedom and individuality. The centers of economic power had by then been secured by a new plutocracy who recklessly exploited them for their own selfish gain. And liberalism, once a great reforming creed, "hardened into the dogma of the freedom of the industrial entrepreneur from any organized social control," into an orthodoxy protective of the vested powers of the victorious bourgeoisie.[37]

The problem of this earlier liberalism, Dewey argued, was its intellectual "absolutism," its "lack of perception of historic relativity." For Dewey, liberalism was a relativistic and experimental social philosophy, a flexible reforming creed engaged in the "continuous reconstruction of the ideas of individuality and liberty in intimate connection with changes in social relations." Always its commanding concern was the corrosive impact of material institutions on full human freedom. But the dominant material threats to freedom and individuality, Dewey warned, were ceaselessly changing. Where once mercantile restrictions were seen as the principal barrier to effective liberty, by the tail end of the nineteenth century liberalism itself, in the form of an orthodoxy of laissez-faire and the capitalist order it sanctioned, had become socially oppressive for the mass of men who failed to share equally in the economic wealth they had a part in creating.[38]

Modern liberalism, Dewey acknowledged, had begun to meet these new challenges to individuality and freedom by moving to regulate and humanize industrial capitalism. But the methods of the progressive and the New Dealer, he argued, were not enough. As economic relations became the controlling forces in society, effective liberty for the majority of men demanded that they be democratically directed in the interests of the collective welfare. "The ends which liberalism has always professed," Dewey wrote, "can be attained only as control of the means of production and distribution is taken out of the hands of individuals who exercise powers created socially for narrow individual interests." Socialism thus became for Dewey the "ground and medium" for all he judged worthy in the liberal heritage, the all-important means to a genuinely liberal society.[39]

To Dewey, the proper mediums of social reconstruction were education and democratic political action. The purpose of "renascent liberalism" was first of all educational—to "aid in producing . . . [cooperative] habits of mind and character" suitable to the emergent age of material cooperation and consolidation. For this, education interpreted as mere "schooling" was not enough. All society's principal institutions, including the school, would have to be transformed; these, after all, were the major determinants of habit and character. The spearhead of this transformation would be a new political movement, which, once in power, would initiate an institutional reformation that would in gradual but significant ways foster among the citizenry the cooperative habits essential to the success of the cooperative commonwealth.[40]

Dewey never offered a detailed blueprint for change. He suggested merely an approach to socialism, not a complete politics of transition. Nor, as we have seen, did he give full expression to the kind of cooperative future he envisioned. But all reform, he believed, had to be set in motion and guided by specific ideals and ends, so that change, although it might unfold slowly, would always be directed toward a general restructuring of things, not a mere retooling or refinement of existing arrangements. This is why he could not support the New Deal. Its piecemeal, directionless reforms failed to meet his criterion for clear and specific social objectives. ". . . 'Reforms' that deal now with this abuse and now with that without having a social goal based upon an inclusive plan, differ entirely," he explained, "from effort at reforming, in the literal sense, the institutional scheme of things."[41]

Some of Dewey's contemporaries must have thought it ironic that his criticism of the New Deal was based upon its absence of clear reform direction and content; for this was precisely what they saw as the dominant flaw in his own social philosophy. Dewey had long argued that a philosophy had legitimacy only when it went at the task of moral criticism, only when it addressed itself relentlessly to the reconstruction of man and society. Yet while he was specific about the role of philosophy, he believed that the content of a philosophy had to relate to a particular age and place. His instrumentalism offered no final answers—no panaceas, no transcendent moral creed, no cosmic explanation for the drama of human progress. Elevating method, the method of intelligence, over all metaphysical and moral systems, it urged that all ideas and institutions be continually examined and revised to meet new historical situations. Dewey had begun his philosophic career in hot rebellion against the excessively formalistic thinking of the mid-nineteenth century, and he remained determined to keep his philosophy open and flexible, ever alive to new experiences. But as in the Greek sense of tragedy, where a man's unique excellence *(arete)* is identical with his tragic flaw *(hamartia),* the very strength of pragmatic liberalism, its resolute flexibility, was at once its tragic flaw. Always critical of intellectual absolutism, Dewey was often guilty of being too abstract and unspecific, of emphasizing pure method over intellectual and moral content. At times his instrumentalism, or at least the way he expressed it, seemed little more than a plea for the application of the scientific method to social problems. And for many of his critics, past and present, this simply was not enough.[42]

This line of criticism, however, applies more appropriately to an earlier Dewey. While his pre-depression pleas for change are often hopelessly vague, his depression era writings have a more sharply defined aim and focus. Targeting in on corporate capitalism, he threw his full support to a political movement committed to democratic collectivism. The depression deepened Dewey's political involvement, causing him to give greater specificity to his arguments for change. Now he cemented the method of intelligence to a clearly defined social objective, sponsoring with Bingham an agenda of carefully detailed proposals for social reconstruction, while never losing sight of the fact that a radical program, or "hypothesis," had to be constantly revised and reshaped in accordance with an ever changing material reality.

When asked late in life whether or not he was a socialist, Dewey replied that if he were permitted to define the terms "socialist" and "socialism" he would probably call himself a "democratic socialist." But, he added, "my experimentalism goes deeper than any other 'ism.'"[43] This concept of experimental intelligence formed the intellectual bedrock of both Bingham's and Dewey's social philosophy. As opposed to the extreme philosophic relativism of the *New Republic,* whose editors endorsed Dewey's renascent liberalism but committed themselves to little more than economic planning,[44] Bingham, with Dewey's full support, developed a coherent radical program and mobilized his magazine behind a political movement to realize it. Of the two, *Common Sense* approached more closely Dewey's idea of pragmatic experimentalism—the formulation of clear social hypotheses and the testing of these in experience. In the end it was this common allegiance to the pragmatic method that explained both Bingham and Dewey's opposition to the early New Deal.[45] Convinced that there was "no opposition between liberalism as social philosophy and radicalism in action," Dewey joined Bingham in urging America's non-Communist insurgents to bury their differences and unite in Chicago in September, 1933, to form a mass organization capable of launching the kind of thoroughgoing social revolution Roosevelt would never back.[46]

The United Conference for Progressive Political Action opened on September 2, 1933, with over two hundred delegates in attendance. The Farmers' Union, the United Farmers of America, Milo Reno's Farmers'

Holiday Association, the Minnesota Farmer-Labor Party, the Wisconsin Progressives, and the Non-Partisan League all sent representatives. Some lesser labor officials came, a few representatives of the newly formed National Unemployed League, several Technocrats, and a scattering of independent intellectuals; but essentially it was an agrarian gathering, dominated by the insurgent farm groups.

The meeting began inauspiciously with a round of speeches, most of them surprisingly moderate, by various farm and labor spokesmen. All the while the ubiquitous General Coxey drifted around the back of the hall handing out his familiar leaflets. It was by all odds a disorganized gathering. There was a good deal of shouting and confusion, and several bitter exchanges broke out on the convention floor. By the close of the morning session, nothing of real substance had been accomplished. There seemed no agreement among the delegates about a platform or a new party, and the consensus was that the meeting would end, as it had begun, in chaos and division.[47]

Then suddenly the atmosphere changed. On the evening of the first day, a badly splintered and listless delegation was brought to life by a ringing call to action from Thomas Amlie, chairman of the Platform Committee. It was fitting that Amlie's speech followed a cautiously worded address by Oswald Garrison Villard, for its very purpose was to convince the delegates of the obsolescence of the reformism of old progressives like Villard. Speaking slowly and with calm confidence, Amlie assured his audience, many of whom he knew intimately from his seventeen years in farmer-labor politics, that even the most advanced liberal program would not restore prosperity. Capitalism, he declared, was doomed; only the precise moment of its expiration remained in doubt. "Capitalism today . . . is like a man who is suffering from a fatal disease. A doctor can tell him that he will surely die, although it is unsafe for him to pick out the exact date when the man is going to die." Since the mission of liberalism had always been bound up with the fate of capitalism, the liberals laboring ceaselessly to curb its inhumane excesses, the collapse of capitalism signaled as well the end of liberalism. In a world without capitalism there was no place for its reforming counterpart. Amlie concluded with an appeal to the delegates to recognize the inevitability of collectivism by adopting a platform incorporating a constitutional amendment aimed at abolishing "absentee ownership" of the nation's natural resources and machinery of production.[48] Here was the spirit of Veblen alive again in American radicalism.

Amlie's speech galvanized the delegates into united action. From this point on the conference took on a decidedly more intransigent character as the delegates moved the following morning to adopt a radical platform and to organize the broad political federation Bingham had hoped for. Now for the first time, Bingham noted in a post-convention editorial, the nation's agrarian rebels seem "intent on the question of winning political power, not only to raise the price of wheat, but to bring a different kind of system out of the ruins of capitalism."

The convention platform echoed Amlie's conviction that capitalism was fast crumbling, demanding that it be replaced by a "scientifically planned system, based on production for use rather than profit." Then followed an agendum of specific demands, including public ownership of natural resources, basic industries, banks, and agencies for marketing farm produce; abolition of speculation and profiteering in food and other necessities of life; a national insurance system; soak-the-rich taxation; and a guaranteed job "for every worker on a high American standard of living." Amlie's constitutional amendment was referred to an ongoing committee for future consideration as a platform plank.[49]

The convention next moved to establish the Farmer-Labor Political Federation (FLPF), an organization to prepare the way for a national farmer-labor party. The FLPF was to assist in the formation of state farmer-labor parties and "to seek cooperation with and coordination of all progressive forces on the basis of its economic and political program." The new federation was a larger, more inclusive body than the old LIPA; and it had a more pronounced agrarian flavor. But its elected officers marked it as the intellectual and organizational heir of the LIPA. John Dewey was named honorary chairman, Thomas Amlie, chairman, Howard Y. Williams, national organizer, and Bingham, executive secretary. The other officers included Anthony Ramuglia, the tiny, outspoken leader of the Unemployed League, J. B. S. Hardman of the Amalgamated Clothing Workers, and Paul Douglas. A national committee of action was also formed to prepare for a mass convention to launch the new party, "preferably in time to make possible participation in the congressional elections of 1934."[50]

Only one serious dispute marred the conference; that erupted over the question of whether or not to admit Communists into the federation. Some in attendance looked toward a broad popular front of all radical groups; but Bingham, Amlie, and Douglas, fearing Communist disruption of their organization, gained acceptance for a resolution banning Party members from all federation organizations. The resolution, however, left the door open for Socialist participation. (The Socialist Party had been invited to Chicago but had refused, arguing that the time was not yet ripe for a mass people's party.)[51]

This issue settled, there remained only the question of the future relationship between the old LIPA and the new FLPF. This was resolved in a meeting held shortly after the convention. Fearing that many of its long-time liberal members would presently be unwilling to accept the advanced economic program of the FLPF, it was agreed to continue the LIPA for a time as a separate organization. Its functions, however, were to be strictly educational.[52]

Bingham was elated with the results of the Chicago conference. The conference had not, as he had originally feared, adopted a slate of "halfway," "populist" measures. The FLPF, moreover, was much more than a narrowly agrarian organization. Its purpose was to marshal a political coalition that included labor and the middle classes. Its platform was radical but included a number of short-range economic proposals to provide relief during the difficult transition to socialism, measures designed to appeal, in Amlie's words, to "Mr. Average American." There was no mention in the document of class struggle, violence, or wholesale confiscation of private property; nor were there any "funny-money" or crackpot inflationary schemes.[53] The convention, furthermore, had the sagacity to avoid any heady efforts to establish immediately a national party. The FLPF would build from the grassroots, organizing state third parties where they did not already exist and incorporating existing third parties into its institutional structure. Only when sufficient local and state support was mobilized would the call go out for a national party. For the next three years all Bingham's creative efforts were directed toward this end.

6

WINNING THE MIDDLE CLASSES

From September, 1933, Bingham as executive secretary and Amlie as chairman virtually ran the Farmer-Labor Political Federation. They were almost solely responsible for establishing the federation's policies, and along with Howard Y. Williams, the LIPA's chief field organizer, were the most active and important spokesmen for the production-for-use movement. While Amlie and Williams headed the federation efforts in the Midwest, Bingham directed the organizational drive in the East, seeking out labor, middle class, and Socialist support for a new party. As editor of *Common Sense,* Bingham was also the movement's leading publicist and theoretician. With the occasional assistance of Amlie he fashioned the political strategy and organizational program that distinguished the production-for-use movement from all other movements for change in the 1930s.

Immediately following the Chicago convention Bingham and Amlie began an active friendship and professional association that was to span the decade. In their capacity as federation leaders they confronted the problem of shaping a widely popular radicalism in a nation long suspicious of socialism. Here was the dilemma that had confounded all previous American movements for socialism: how to be both politically realistic and unvaryingly radical? To some, middle class America seemed well-nigh impervious to socialism, implacably hostile to even the most democratic forms of radicalism. Yet while history weighed heavily against them, Bingham and Amlie went at their organizational work with robust optimism, confident that they would succeed where others had failed. The freshness and originality of their response to this

challenge marks their new party effort as one of the most interesting
episodes in the history of the decade's political insurgency.

On one point Bingham and Amlie found themselves in early and
complete agreement: their movement would aim toward the kind of
cooperative commonwealth Bingham had sketched in the pages of
Common Sense.[1] Yet neither had yet worked out a political strategy
to realize this society. A successful political revolution, they agreed,
would have to precede and set the conditions for the revolution in
values essential to a working socialist cooperative. But how to convince the mass of Americans of the need for such a revolution?

The Chicago conference had reached a rough consensus on the
need for a planned economy and had authorized a loose federation
to prepare the way for a national third party. But little else of real
consequence had been accomplished. There had been no sustained
effort to address the exceedingly difficult problems of tactics and
strategy that arose from the convention's high-sounding platform
commitments. No one, for example, had come forward with a
political blueprint to secure the economic aims of the convention
document. The delegates had endorsed an inclusive political association of farmers, workers, and the aggrieved middle class. But nowhere
was it specified how this union was to be achieved. What forces or
common concerns would meld together the disparate elements of the
anticipated coalition? And what groups would spearhead the new
alliance? Most critically of all, how would the new party overcome
that long-standing American aversion to socialism? How, with its avowedly
anti-capitalist platform, could it hope to secure an electoral victory in
middle class, capitalist America? What would distinguish its program and
appeal from those of other radical parties, past and present? On these
and other crucial matters of policy and strategy, the convention fell
silent, leaving the movement's intellectual and organizational direction
largely in the hands of Bingham and Amlie.

As the federation's chief theoretician, Bingham took on the responsibility of developing a political strategy for the movement, a program
identifying the expected agents of change and the means by which change
would take place. He would attempt to accomplish for American radicalism (and he did not discourage the comparison) what Marx had done for
European insurgency, articulating a theory of revolution congruent with
the ascendant currents of material reality.

Bingham had, of course, long viewed the middle class as the key to
social change. In a prevailingly middle class nation it seemed axiomatic

to him that no political movement could win power with large numbers of this class in the opposition. Yet he had still not worked out a clear strategy to recruit the middle class, the pivotal class, for socialism. This was the aim of *Insurgent America: The Revolt of the Middle Classes,* his first and most important book. Although not published until 1935, *Insurgent America* called together ideas and organizational strategies Bingham had been emphasizing since his return from Russia, tactics he used extensively in his early new party efforts. This book brings together in nearly complete form the matured political strategy of the production-for-use movement and is one of the decade's only comprehensive attempts to assess the radical possibilities of the middle classes.[2]

The preeminent question Bingham addressed in *Insurgent America* is the larger historical question we still live with: why has socialism failed in America? And the answer he gave to it was determined by his own understanding of socialism's previous inability to amass an American majority.

The history of American radicalism before the Great Depression had been a history of repeated frustration and failure. Certainly radicalism had its proud moments, its inspirational heroes, and its share of public influence. For a time, even, socialism appeared destined to become a permanently consequential force in American politics. In the opening two decades of the twentieth century, the American Socialist Party recorded impressive organizational and electoral gains, marshaling an inclusive coalition of workers, farmers, and middle class intellectuals. But government suppression during and immediately following World War 1 and a fierce intra-party dispute over the Bolshevik revolution divided and crippled this promising radical movement. Even during the first years of the depression, with capitalism fearfully vulnerable, neither the Socialists nor the Communists nor any other of the American radical groups had been able to inspire a mass national following. America into the age of Roosevelt remained, as it remains today, "the great exception"—the only advanced industrial nation in the world without a considerable socialist movement.

Writing well before the 1930s, the German political economist Werner Sombart provided what many of Bingham's contemporaries still considered the most convincing explanation for socialism's minimal influence. It was America's unexampled material abundance, with the multiplying opportunities it opened for social mobility, that had frustrated the development of a powerful socialist movement. This ever expanding prosperity, together with the inviting vision of a free-landed frontier in the West, had caused most Americans to spurn socialism in the race for a fuller share of capitalism's largesse. Even for those denied immediate access to this wealth, the dream of material advancement in a nation so richly endowed—whether it was the dream of free land or the expectation of a better wage—subverted the appeal of socialism. "All socialist utopias," as Sombart engagingly put it, "have come to grief on roast beef and apple pie."[3]

Most of those who followed Sombart expanded upon rather than challenged his analysis. To the abundance factor Selig Perlman, the labor historian, added the "free gift of the ballot" denied to most European workers in the first throes of industrialization, causing them to turn to more class-conscious labor movements for social relief. Perlman also pointed to America's massive immigration movement, which divided labor along ethnic, linguistic, religious, and cultural lines, preventing the establishment of a cohesive trade union movement, let alone a strong and united Socialist Party. Also, the majority of these recently arrived workers were Catholics for whom socialism represented a hated variant of atheism. Given the religious character and heterogeneous makeup of this work force "to make socialism or communism the official 'ism' of the movement," Perlman concluded, "would mean . . . deliberately driving the Catholics . . . out of the labor movement. . . . Consequently, the only acceptable 'consciousness' for American labor as a whole is a 'job consciousness' with a 'limited' objective of 'wage and job control. . . .'"[4]

A later and perhaps more astute analysis of the "psychology" of the American worker, Leon Sampson's *Toward a United Front* (1934),[5] explained the anti-socialist bias of native workers in terms of their spirited attachment to "Americanism"—the term Sampson gave to what he considered the prevailing national ideology. This Americanism served as a substitute or spurious form of socialism, draining off energies that were essentially socialistic. While America might be an avowedly capitalist country, most Americans, Sampson argued, held distinctly socialistic attitudes. The socialist ideals of equality, classlessness, the creation of wealth for all, equal opportunity, economic "fair play," self-emancipation, liberty, and full democracy—even the glorification of the "mass" and the suspicion of the state—were part of the official American "doctrine" extolled in every public school. "Every concept of socialism," Sampson shrewdly noted, "has its substitutive counterconcept in Americanism, and that is why the socialist argument falls so fruitlessly on the American ear." Americanism *was* the socialism of native workers, its slogans and ideals so closely approximating those of socialism that they thought they enjoyed the advantages of socialism without its odium.[6]

Other observers in the 1930s saw America's two-party system as an unbridgeable obstacle to socialism, insisting that the decentralized, non-ideological character of the national parties, with their preponderant concern with electoral success rather than principle, made it virtually impossible for an aroused ideological faction to capture and control them. History had also shown these two parties to be amazingly adept at absorbing the more popular causes of the various protest parties that rose to challenge them. Then there were the innumerable legal obstacles third parties faced in getting on the ballot in the various states.[7] Finally, radicals cited government suppression of their activities, dramatized by the ugly red hunt of 1919.

These were by no means the only reasons given for socialism's failure; but they were in the early 1930s the principal ones.[8] And beyond their obvious dissimilarities they shared a single unifying assumption. All emphasized structural factors—material and ideological conditions peculiar to American development—as the leading reason for socialism's inability to command wider support. The radical Left, in this view, struggled against an environment either hostile or massively indifferent to its revolutionary vision and program.

Bingham, however, could not agree. While not discounting these crucial external factors, he located the cause of socialism's failure primarily within the movement itself. The American Left, he insisted, had committed, and continued to commit, countless judgmental, ideological, and strategic errors which grievously damaged its standing and influence among its potential following. Implicit in his analysis was the unmistakable assumption that if radicals had acted differently they would have enjoyed considerably greater organizational success and public impact. It was this assumption that gave Bingham's radicalism so much of its animating optimism.

The commanding problem of American radicalism, in Bingham's view, was that it was not American enough. The nation's radicals had for too long looked to revolutionary Marxism for tactical and intellectual guidance, ignoring their country's unique historic development. To Bingham, Marxism's outstanding failing was its disregard of the "exceptional" character of American civilization. America was indisputably different from Europe; and this explained the failure of Marxism here. Yet, unlike so many others, Bingham refused to consider America's distinctness as a permanent impediment to socialism. Without disagreeing with either Sombart or Perlman, he insisted that America was "ripe for socialism," that it already possessed the structural and ideological prerequisites for a successful radical movement, although obviously not the kind of radical movement Marxists had long anticipated.[9]

Along with Perlman, Bingham saw labor as a decidedly non-revolutionary force, its membership concerned primarily with short-term goals related to wages and job security, its leadership often hostile to reform outside labor's immediate domain. Recent advances in mass production and mass advertising had further blunted labor's revolutionary potential by placing before the workers a seemingly endless array of consumer products that they now believed were within their reach. Consumer capitalism had not eliminated poverty, but it had tied the laboring classes psychologically to the middle classes. In temperament and outlook, if not in actual economic circumstance, labor was indissolubly part of the middle class. The average American worker, Bingham observed, was "too profoundly bourgeoisified . . . to want to join a 'proletarian' movement."

Bingham did not deny labor a role in social change. "As the largest and most exploited class, and the class with the most powerful organization for action on the economic and political fields," labor would, he predicted, play a formidable role in any future radical action. "But neither as a class nor as a class movement will labor play the leading role." If labor was to be radicalized, it would be in ways Marx had not foreseen. Workers would be radicalized "along with, and no faster than" the middle classes with which they so fiercely identified.[10]

Not only had Marxism inaccurately gauged the developing political character and strength of industrial labor, but it had failed as well to take into account the phenomenal growth of the middle classes, particularly the rise of a new white collar stratum in the professions, services, and industry. While Marx had anticipated the eventual extinction of the middle classes and the rise to power of the proletariat, in the United States corporate capitalism was steadily increasing the size and influence of the middle classes while depleting the ranks of industrial labor. This trend would continue and accelerate, Bingham predicted, with salaried white collar workers increasingly outnumbering blue collar laborers.

But other factors were enhancing the importance of the new middle classes far out of proportion to their growing numbers. With the decline of the old individualistic entrepreneurs and the separation of ownership from control in the modern corporation, the "active direction and administration" of the corporation, and of the economy as a whole, was shifting inexorably to salaried managers, administrators, and skilled professionals. These groups were already the chief repositories of the skills and expertise essential to a high production economy; they would also be essential in any system that might replace capitalism. For this reason alone no intelligent radicalism could afford to leave them in the opposition. Their functional dominance magnified their political importance.[11]

Bingham thus attributed the political failure of American Marxists largely to their inability to seize on this, the critical structural transformation of twentieth-century capitalism. Yet he did not hold Marx himself fully accountable for this oversight. Marx's class analysis and encompassing weltanschauung were, he intimated, essentially faithful to the state of productive forces as he found them in Europe in the fervid beginnings of accelerated industrialization. The unleashing of new productive and class forces since then, however, had invalidated many of his most telling insights. For this Marx could not be held accountable; he was, after all, a social scientist, not a seer. Instead, Bingham blamed the sterility of modern Marxism on its twentieth-century Communist practitioners, who had abandoned the "scientific spirit" of the master for a worshipful orthodoxy Marx himself would have scorned. Frozen by the requirements of an ideology of their own making, they stubbornly refused to expand Marx's searching sociology of change to incorporate new class and productive circumstances. Theirs was a theology rather than a science of revolution.[12]

"A scientific revolutionist," Bingham explained, "must recognize that there is tremendous social force inherent in the middle-classes. . . . The most egregious error committed by the Marxist theorists is in misunderstanding and under-rating this force. And probably *it is the chief reason for their failure*."[13] No approach to the social problem in the United States that was not founded upon a close inquiry into the habits, ideas, and political inclinations of this class could pretend to be adequate or hope to be successful.

Bingham admitted that the middle classes—the managers as well as the clerks—were presently a politically docile lot, confused, deeply anxious about their economic security, and politically divided, seemingly incapable of coalescing for common action. But this could change. Economically the middle and lower ranks of the white collar classes were like labor, "wage slaves" with low incomes and with no real property stake in capitalism. On this basis alone they could be radicalized. Bingham insisted, however, that there was little hope that the middle classes could be mobilized with labor as a "new working class," as some Marxists believed. While their economic plight might be similar to labor's, even the most exploited members of the lower middle class refused to consider themselves a "new proletariat." Their mentality, like that of organized labor itself, remained implacably bourgeois.[14]

Here Bingham hit upon one of the crucial determinants of modern American political dynamics; and here he made perhaps his most important contribution to class analysis. It was the "psychology" of a class, its mental perception of its economic and social standing, more than its actual material circumstance, that determined its political consciousness and direction. In decided contrast to the Marxian organizational approach, which rests on the presumption that material factors determine political consciousness, Bingham developed what amounted to a psychological theory of radical organization, a mode of analysis geared not to the actual material situation of labor and the middle classes but to their shared "middle class ideology."

To Bingham, property was not the sole or even the paramount objective determinant of class consciousness. Nor did he perceive a direct correlation between material position and ideological consciousness. If there were such a clear correlation, why, he asked, had neither labor nor the lower middle classes, both of which were propertyless, exploited, and financially insecure, not already acquired a proletarian consciousness? No narrowly material explanation, Bingham argued, could explain this seeming paradox; for it was "psychology," in America at least, that was the essence of politics. In the end Americans identified with the class they *thought* they belonged to, not to the class some political sociologist assigned them to. Radicals would have to learn, he wrote, that "for purposes of social or political action classes are entirely a matter of psychology." In a self-consciously middle class nation the need then was for a radicalism respectful of middle class values and aspirations, a radicalism keyed to the prevailing middle class mind. It was to this ubiquitous "middle class mind" rather than strictly to the middle income groups that Bingham directed his radical appeal.[15]

At this point Bingham's analysis paralleled Leon Sampson's. What Sampson referred to as "Americanism" Bingham called the "middle class mind." And both saw this middle class mind as "naturally inclined and ready for the classless society." Bingham argued that the average American "behaves more as one would expect a member of a cooperative socialist community than of an individual in a competitive acquisitive society." Inwardly he preferred a classless society; his only mistake was in thinking he already lived in one. Bingham also saw the "average American" as a consummate "joiner," a community booster with a "strong social consciousness as a member of his group." His hopes and aspirations for full democracy, for social order, "for peace and security, for a mounting standard of living, . . . for the full development of the human personality, physical and spiritual," were, moreover, the motivating ideals of democratic socialism. These and other classless and collectivist instincts could, Bingham argued, be exploited for socialist advantage.[16]

Yet where Sampson proposed that the middle class be drawn to an avowedly Marxist labor party, Bingham called instead for a movement with a distinctly middle class emphasis. Most Americans, he observed, considered Marxism a menace to everything they held sacred—freedom, family, church, nation, competition, individualism, democracy, security of property, and more. The new radicalism, therefore, would have to be a "one-hundred-percent American" radicalism, a radicalism "defending the home, the family, the church and the nation," a radicalism respectful of the "patriotism" and "puritanism" of the middle classes. There could be no "emphasis on revolution, civil war, domestic turmoil, class struggle, confiscation, expropriation, destruction." The new radicalism would promise instead an orderly democratic transition through a constitutionally elected party. Above all, the new radicalism would make clear its paramount aim of economic security for all. The promise of universal abundance would be the keynote of its appeal.[17]

While Bingham supported Sombart's contention that abundance had in the past acted as a deterrent to socialism, he was convinced that the depression signaled the end of the historic era of capitalist expansion. Capitalism had reached its breaking point; and as the crisis deepened more and more Americans would grasp that reality. Bingham thus assumed that the middle classes, along with the rest of the population, would be drawn to radicalism by the force of their own economic self-interest, by the promise of an economic prosperity capitalism could no longer insure. The vaunted middle class "stake" in capitalism was, he argued, largely "illusionary." In America the actual ownership of the means of production was narrowly concentrated in a tiny capitalist class. No longer predominately a class of small property owners and independently employed entrepreneurs, the middle class was now largely a "salariat," dependent on labor markets rather than access to property for its income. Its stake in the going economic order was, in other words, a job stake, not a property stake. It was its desire for material security, not an unreserved allegiance to capitalism, that underpinned its opposition to radical change. If radicalism was to gain headway among these people, therefore, it would have to convince them that a socialization of productive facilities would not jeopardize their jobs or their hard-earned property, that far from endangering their coveted economic security, a socialist economy run at peak capacity would introduce an era of unmatched material affluence, guaranteeing most Americans a purchasing power far in excess of present standards. For full and "irrefutable" proof of these claims, Bingham cited the recent findings of the National Survey of Potential Production Capacity, a New Deal-funded study of the national economy, and urged that the survey's findings form the cornerstone of a new radical strategy to win the middle classes.[18]

The National Survey of Potential Production Capacity (NSPPC) grew out of the earlier effort by Howard Scott's group to undertake a study of the nation's productive potential. When mounting public criticism of the accuracy of the group's findings, and disputes between Scott and several of his colleagues, combined to break up the survey, the Technocrats split into two factions, one under Scott's leadership called Technocracy, Inc., and the other the Continental Committee on Technocracy, headed by Harold Loeb. In January, 1934, Loeb approached Bingham with the idea of reviving the original Technocrat survey and employing its findings in behalf of the production-for-use movement. With Amlie's assistance Bingham and Loeb convinced Aubrey Williams, then Harry Hopkins's chief assistant in the Civil Works Administration (CWA), to underwrite the project. From the start, however, there was a misunderstanding between Loeb and Williams about the aim of the survey. Williams assumed that the group's findings would lend support to the New Deal's work relief program, while Loeb set out with the express intention of demonstrating the wastefulness and gross inefficiency of capitalism.[19]

Loeb began his study in March, 1934, assisted by a team of sixty-four researchers headed by former Technocrat Felix Frazer. The sovereign question guiding their research was this: Exactly how much could the nation produce and distribute if it applied its full economic might to satisfy the basic needs and reasonable wants of its entire citizenry? What, in other words, were the precise material possibilities of a production-for-use economy? Considerations of profit, either as stimulus or impediment to production, were strictly excluded. The survey was to measure physical factors alone.

Seven months later the group announced its findings. An exhaustive "scientific" survey had convincingly demonstrated, Loeb asserted, that if the nation's *present* productive plant were utilized to full capacity the entire population could have a standard of living twice that which 90 percent of Americans enjoyed in 1929. *The Chart of Plenty*, the survey's official report and statistical manifesto, claimed that the economy now had the potential to provide every American family an annual

income of $4,370 in goods and services measured by 1929 retail prices.
Only capitalism, a system geared to scarcity conditions, held America
back from an era of universal plenty.[20]

The Loeb survey provided exactly the body of evidence Bingham
had been looking for: framed by "experts," ardently "scientific,"
and explosively radical. *The Chart of Plenty,* he rejoiced, "blasts the
foundations out from under our capitalist system in a way that no
book has ever done before. . . . This . . . may turn out to be the most
important book of the twentieth century. The survey it describes will
become the basis of any planned society we may achieve."[21] Bingham
hoped that the publication of this impressive statistical brief would
finally awaken Americans to the fatal inadequacies of capitalism. The
Loeb survey, he wrote, proves that we have abundance, "and the
corollary is not far behind. *If* production for profit can't work, then
production-for-use must replace it." Already production-for-use had
become a fighting slogan in states like California and Washington,
where the influence of Technocracy was most pronounced. Equally
encouraging to Bingham was "the spread of the 'abundance' psychology
to the midwestern third party revolt." Even Huey Long and Father
Charles Coughlin, the radio priest, were exploiting the explosive potential of the abundance argument. Whatever their differences, all these
movements were asking the same pressing question: Why must there
be poverty in a nation so richly endowed?

> It is in the conviction that underlies that question [Bingham wrote]
> that we may find the key to middle class action in America of
> these critical years. For it is a conviction that America is indeed
> a land of plenty, and . . . that the present system sabotages that
> plenty. Veblen and his followers among the modern "Abundance
> Men" are the unconscious preachers of the new gospel of Ameri-
> can radicalism. . . .a radicalism that is bound to appeal to the
> middle class person more than the Marxist emphasis on unjust
> exploitation of labor.[22]

Bingham thus realized that the drawing power of Long, Coughlin,
Upton Sinclair, and others who were raising this question symbolized
the lower middle classes' faith in the nation's limitless economic potential and in their right to a fair portion of this wealth. It was raw economic self-interest, he acknowledged, that was the catalyzing force of
middle class insurgency; and it was on this hard-headed conviction, not
on any over-idealization of the socialist inclinations of the middle classes,
that he founded his radical hopes.

Although altered to the circumstances of depression America, Bingham's abundance approach was wholly in character with a persistent tendency in the heritage of American economic insurgency. Rather than emphasizing class engagement or massive redistribution of existing wealth as the instruments of social justice, Bingham urged the expansion and more efficient utilization of the nation's productive facilities. Like Edward Bellamy, Upton Sinclair, Thorstein Veblen, Simon Patten, Stuart Chase, and an endless number of other abundance men, he claimed that technology's powers and nature's rich endowment would allow America to purchase economic justice without a brutalizing class upheaval. Certainly there would be some compulsory division of existing wealth; there would be no plutocracy in the society of plenty. But Bingham's undeniable emphasis was upon expansion rather than forced divison. By increasing the overall output all could be comfortable with only certain minimal sacrifices for the hugely wealthy. Here was an economics quintessentially American, resting on that radiant faith in the nation's inexhaustible plenty.

Yet Bingham realized that the new radicalism must do more than convince the middle classes that capitalist prosperity was a baseless dream. A successful radical party would have to assure security-conscious Americans not only of the superior efficiency of a production-for-use system but of the feasibility of moving from capitalism to the new economy in an altogether orderly and democratic manner. In drafting such an economic "plan of transition" and presenting it, first in *Common Sense* and later in *Insurgent America,* Bingham rounded out his agenda for a middle class radicalism.

Bingham's transition plan was an update and revision of a strategy first suggested by Edward Bellamy in *Equality* and later incorporated by Upton Sinclair in his EPIC campaign for the governorship of California. Bingham simply took Sinclair's scheme to start California's unemployed producing for their own use, added a few technocratic features, and expanded the program to encompass the entire national economy. Instead of attacking capitalism head-on by moving immediately and forcibly to nationalize all productive facilities, Bingham proposed to "outflank" it by having the government take over a "vertical cross section" of the economy and operate it on a production-for-use basis. At first only the unemployed were to be admitted to the new economy. But after one year it was to be opened on a voluntary basis to all. The commonwealth's resources and industrial plant were to be leased by the federal government from the owners of factories and lands left idle by the depression, thus making it possible to begin the experiment "with a minimum of confiscation or compulsion."[23]

The socialist economy would for a time co-exist with capitalism, but eventually, through the persuasive power of its superior efficiency, it would absorb the individuals, properties, and businesses of the private sector, leaving the old capitalist sector an "empty shell."[24]

Bingham argued that the real advantage of this plan over quicker and more audacious measures was that it did not jeopardize the economic security or political freedoms of the vast majority of the population. Little or no outright property confiscation was involved. Only the leasing or purchase of properties no longer utilized to peak capacity by capitalism was to be compulsory. Certain vital corporate monopolies were marked for immediate nationalization, but with full financial compensation to their former owners. Furthermore, businesses dealing in luxuries, custom goods, and other scarce items would be allowed to remain in private hands. Membership in the commonwealth, moreover, was to be on a strictly voluntary basis. And within the community complete freedom of consumer choice would prevail. It was to be a society "freely chosen and freely built."[25]

Bingham admitted that there were huge dangers and risks in appealing to the middle class on the basis of its material instincts. Such a party might easily take on the ugly characteristics of a native fascism. The lower middle classes, especially, were a stormy and volatile social grouping, fully capable of assuming a "rough anti-labor attitude" and quick to rush to the defense of "private property" and "Americanism" against alien influences. But this susceptibility to fascism made it all the more important that they be captured for socialism. In the absence of a radicalism attractive to them, their deteriorating economic circumstances and dark fears of a proletarian upheaval could drive them to a proto-fascist movement for the economic security and social discipline they demanded.[26]

Unlike the Marxists, who defined fascism as a last-ditch effort by big business to save a collapsing capitalism,[27] Bingham saw fascism as a middle class revolt precipitated by economic crisis and democratic ineptitude. Capitalist businessmen had, he agreed, subsidized the fascist parties in both Germany and Italy; but they had not funded and directed these movements from the start. Instead, fascism had risen to power in these countries on the crest of a middle class upsurge set in motion by the failure of capitalism and the fear of a workers' revolution. Originally it was a depression phenomenon, a revolt rooted in real economic grievances and capable of extensive social reconstruction. These positive tendencies, however, were soon buried under an avalanche of hatred and destructive fury. Frightened by the class militancy of Marxist labor, yet contemptuous of the ineffectuality of parliamentary liberalism, the middle classes settled eventually for the easy answers of the fascist strong man. To a considerable extent, then, fascism was an inevitable outcome of the failure of German Marxists to seize on the constructive potential of this middle class revolt.[28]

Fascism also resulted from the fear and confusion that plagued the "middle class mind." On the one hand, the middle classes hated the "uncertainty and insecurity and anarchy" of competitive capitalism. Yet they were held back from radicalism by their terrible fears of "disorder and violent change, an upsetting of the habitual mode of life." They demanded, in other words, the benefits of economic security without any disruption of the settled framework; they wanted "the advantages of economic planning and control, without wanting to give up the capitalist system." This social schizophrenia drove them in the end to a strong-arm government promising a restoration of civic order and economic prosperity, a state socialism pledged to public planning as a way of saving capitalism. Abundance and security were to be had even at the price of a menacing absolutism. What originated, in part, as a frenzied outburst for economic change thus degenerated into a state socialism that undergirded an economic arrangement it gave early promise of challenging and transforming.[29]

Bingham was one of the few radicals of his day to underscore the strong positive appeal of fascism for the German middle class. After a brief stay in Germany in 1935, he reported "millions of healthy, normal . . . [Germans] acquiescing cheerfully and even eagerly in the new regime." National socialism had obviously spoken to certain of these people's deepest needs, to their yearnings for civil order and economic prosperity, to their fierce nationalism, to their anxious concern for security of person and property. Bingham detected in many Germans an exuberant pride of accomplishment in the new government that few outsiders were willing to admit. "The street fighting and the bitter political squabbling and uncertainty of the old days are gone," he observed, "and the great stolid well-behaved middle-class German people is heartily glad of it."[30]

This made fascism all the more terrifying. Taking up a line of argument later more richly developed by Erich Fromm in *Escape from Freedom,* Bingham saw in fascism the hysterical politics of a people reluctant to take on the risks and burdens of freedom. Confronted with economic collapse, shifting governments, and radical threats to private property, the middle classes bargained away their democratic freedoms for the disciplined authoritarianism and mendacious *Gemeinschaft* of the fascist imperium.[31]

For Bingham there was a fearful lesson for American radicals emblazoned in the recent histories of Germany and Italy. Fascism had come to power in these countries by exploiting for its own sinister purposes the revolt of the middle classes. Shunted aside by the Marxian left, the middle classes had turned to National Socialism for the achievement of their political purposes. If fascism came to America, it would not emerge from the twisted paranoid charlatans of the various colored-shirt movements, nor from the reactionary businessmen of the Liberty League. Instead, it would arise from the dispossessed and uncertain lower middle classes; and in its beginnings it would resemble a popular upsurge against finance capitalism. It was to the populist Left, Bingham warned, to the followers of men like Huey Long and Father Coughlin, that radicals should look "for the signs of distorted idealism and restless desperation" that marked fascism in embryo. With the emergence of a "strong man" promising a quick and easy way to prosperity, these bewildered millions could easily become the sturdy recruits of a native fascism.[32]

Convinced of the imminent likelihood of total economic collapse, Bingham saw the survival of democracy bound up with the political fate of the middle classes. And he closed *Insurgent America* with an urgent plea that this class join with labor and the farm community to form the united people's party that would stand as the one sure guarantee against the menace of fascism.

Insurgent America was received with almost universal approval by independent radical and liberal reviewers. John Dewey hailed it as "a genuinely original and first hand diagnosis and prognosis of our social situation," while Harry Elmer Barnes judged it the "ablest historical and economic analysis of the need for a radical third party in the United States." Dewey, Barnes, and others were especially approving of Bingham's critique of the Communist approach to social change.[33] Yet ironically, almost simultaneously with the appearance of *Insurgent America,* an American Marxist economist published an analysis that in important ways paralleled Bingham's. With a refreshing spirit of independence from official Communist ideology, Lewis Corey set out to reverse American Marxism's long-standing disregard of the middle classes in *The Crisis of the Middle Class.*[34]

Corey was a familiar figure on the radical scene, yet few knew him by this name. Early in the century, as Louis Fraina, an impoverished, self-educated Italian immigrant, he had joined the New York section of the Socialist Party at the ripe age of fifteen. A brilliant theoretician and a commanding orator, he soon rose to influence as the fiery leader

of the party's immigrant-dominated militant wing. Thrilled by the
Bolshevik upheaval, Fraina took the lead in demanding that the
party prepare for the expected world proletarian struggle. Unable to
sway Victor Berger and the moderates to his view, Fraina in 1919
marched his insurgents out of the Socialist Party to found the
Communist Party of America. Three years later, however, at the
age of twenty-eight, he abruptly quit the party after repeated but
unsubstantiated charges that he had mishandled party funds. His
ideological independence and quickness to question organizational
directives from the Comintern had made him expendable. Fraina
nonetheless remained a Marxist and in 1926 began to write articles
on politics and economics for the *New Republic* under the name
"Lewis Corey." Still an independent Marxist, in 1934 he published
The Decline of American Capitalism, a ponderously complex indictment of corporate capitalism; one year later *The Crisis of the Middle
Class* appeared.[35]

Corey argued that the long-awaited disappearance of the middle
classes had not taken place, nor was it likely to. Instead, capitalist
collectivism had spawned a new white collar class of salaried employees, a class wedded to capitalism by a job rather than a property
stake. Like Bingham he saw the economic condition of the majority
of white collar workers as almost indistinguishable from that of industrial labor. As the economic crisis worsened and capitalism moved
in full career toward a final smash-up, this class would, he predicted,
become further proletarianized; its wages would be drastically reduced,
it would lose title to its minimal property, and it would acquire a
heightened awareness of its common plight with labor, joining eventually with the industrial working class in a revolution for the planned
abundance of socialism.

Sheer political and economic realism dictated that this sinking middle
class be mobilized for socialism. Since they had an indispensable functional role in "capitalist collectivism," they would, Corey claimed, be
essential to the successful operation of a "communist collectivism."
Also, unless they were attracted to socialism an economic collapse
would drive them in desperation to a native form of fascism, swelling
the ranks of the sworn enemies of revolutionary labor. In the absence
of an intelligent radical strategy, socialism's loss would be fascism's
gain, a loss that in middle class America would surely presage the doom
of socialist revolution.[36]

There were ample and obvious parallels between Corey's work and
Insurgent America. Both books were inspired by the failure of the
American Left to recruit the middle classes for change; both stressed

the pivotal role of the new white collar classes; and both argued that unless the middle classes aligned with labor for a socialist collectivism they would be drawn to an Americanized fascism. Finally, both Bingham and Corey urged revolution for a classless democratic commonwealth. Yet transcending these immediately apparent points of agreement were a number of fundamental divergencies in their analysis of social forces, as well as in the political strategies they suggested to achieve socialism. Almost every one of these points of contention derived from the fact that Corey was a Marxist and Bingham was not.

In *Insurgent America* Bingham stressed the deteriorating importance of organized labor as an agency for change, pointing to the workers' psychological "bourgeoisification" as evidence for his view that radical action had to be geared to the "dominant middle class mind." Corey, on the other hand, denied that labor was becoming an insignificant revolutionary force, indistinguishable in psychological makeup from the middle classes. The lower middle classes, he claimed, were being inexorably pressed by the weight of economic pressures into the growing ranks of the working class. In the process they were acquiring a sharpened sense of their proletarianization, the first stirrings of a radical consciousness that could eventuate in revolutionary action. Corey, the Marxist, simply broadened the definition of the proletariat to encompass the exploited lower middle classes; his class analysis and appeal still rested on the idea that men could best be organized on the basis of their actual economic condition.[37] Bingham, on the other hand, countered Marxism with a psychological explanation of social action, a theory founded on the idea that the middle classes and labor were knit together by a shared "middle class ideology." To Bingham, the critical fact was not that the lower middle classes and labor were together an exploited proletariat, but that they refused to see themselves in these terms. Corey and Bingham thus agreed on the need to unite labor and the lower middle classes; they divided on the question of how this common front could best be achieved. In the end their disagreement reduced itself to this simple fact: whereas Corey believed that the lower middle classes could be made to follow the leadership of radical labor, Bingham did not.

Corey was not the only American Marxist in the 1930s to stress cooperation with the middle classes. A. J. Muste's American Workers Party, organized in 1933 out of the Conference for Progressive Labor Action, originally announced its intention to build an "Americanized" radical movement, a party encouraging middle class membership. But like Corey, Muste looked to the middle classes to follow the leadership of industrial labor. And his Workers Party was to be a disciplined revolutionary organization, as opposed to the broad democratic federation Bingham had in mind.[38] Similarly, V. F. Calverton's *Modern Monthly*, a lively organ of independent Marxism, repeatedly cautioned radicals not to dismiss the middle class as insignificant in the revolutionary process. "To prevent Fascism from getting a stranglehold on this country," Calverton insisted, "it is . . . necessary . . . to prevent the little man [the forgotten lower middle classes] . . . from going over en masse to the Fascist cause."[39] Corey, Muste, Calverton, and Bingham all recognized the need for a uniquely American radicalism; all appealed for a united front of labor, farmers, and the middle classes. Yet for Corey, Muste, and Calverton this translated itself into a concerted effort to shape Marxism to the American situation. All three regarded Bingham's efforts to fashion a middle class radicalism as impossibly unrealistic.

It is hardly surprising that most Marxists dismissed *Insurgent America* as an historically inaccurate assessment of revolutionary change. Yet there were several prominent non-Marxist radicals who expressed grave reservations about a socialism appealing to the values and pecuniary concerns of the middle classes. Perhaps the most searching critique of Bingham's middle class strategy was advanced by Lewis Mumford in the summer of 1934, fully a year before the publication of *Insurgent America*.

Mumford never actively joined Bingham's production-for-use movement; yet he was attracted to its economic analysis, and he attended several FLPF meetings in New York City. At one of these gatherings he was taken aback by Bingham's suggestion that the movement seek out lower middle class support, and immediately afterwards he wrote to Bingham warning him of the hazards of such a strategy.[40] This set off a heated correspondence in which both men laid bare their respective theories of political action. In this acerbic and sometimes coldly hostile exchange, Bingham also gave a revealing indication of the complex amalgam of social, economic, and intensely personal considerations that drove him to make cause with the middle classes.

Mumford accused Bingham of overreacting to the "Marxists"

> foolish over-idealization of labor into an equally foolish justification of the . . . white collar classes. . . . The notion of labor, that is that everyone should have a function and an economic responsibility, is a sounder basis for organization and for ideological and practical change, than is the belief that the middle classes,

as they have existed in the comfortable past, must be preserved and extended. . . . The fact is, your Farmer-Labor-Progressivism is merely an early form of Fascism, unless you cease to accept the middle-classes at their own self-evaluation, and work for a profound remoralization on a basis which will abolish their present notions of their moral and intellectual distinction in relation to the farmer and the manual worker.

There was little place for the salesman or the accountant in Mumford's theory of social action. "The honest writer or technician would rather share a poor standard of living" with the worker, he told Bingham, "than a high standard with suburban snobs in the salariat." Mumford rested his hopes for change upon a "reapproachment and understanding between the intellectuals and professionals, and the more self-conscious wings of the workers and farmers. . . . There is," he added, "something better in store for America than the triumph of the middle classes. . . . We had a taste of a society of equals, organically united a century ago; and we may yet have the full meal if we have the heart to work for it."[41]

Bingham replied that while a "pure workers'" revolution would unquestionably be "more thorough" than a revolt of the "white collar workers," such a revolution was presently impossible. At the final crisis of capitalism the "dominant 'middle class' . . . will take things into its own hands. . . . Either it will be Fascism, or it will be something new, which I believe can be born out of Farmer-Labor Progressivism." Certainly there were risks in such an approach; violence, racism and unreasoning patriotism could easily overtake the cause, transforming it into an ugly facsimile of national socialism. But with capitalism in collapse there was simply no other choice open to the realistic radical. Finally, Bingham made it clear to Mumford that he had never pressed for a movement drawing solely on the middle classes; nor did he stand for "the triumph of the middle classes." His aim rather was "a classless movement of workers, farmers, and white collar and professional workers" and eventually a classless commonwealth.

Bingham, however, made no effort to mask his personal bias toward the middle classes. "I have worked in a factory," he told Mumford, "and I have seen plenty of white-collar and professional types. There is no question in my mind which class I would rather have ruling this country and which class I would like to see liquidated. Wage labor at the monotonous and stultifying grind of factory jobs is something to get rid of. If we can't find any better ideal than suburbia to take its place then we have no imagination."[42]

Mumford was not alone in the belief that Bingham exaggerated the radical tendencies of the middle classes. Even Amlie warned him repeatedly against allowing his enthusiasm for the middle classes to blind him to the growing radicalism of farmers and industrial workers, the groups Amlie expected to spearhead the coming social transformation. Amlie's personal sympathies had always been with the manual worker and the struggling dirt farmer. "Emotionally," he confessed to Bingham, "I still continue to live in the miserable frame building where I was born on a North Dakota farm." Amlie supported Bingham's efforts to draw the middle classes to the new party movement, not because he expected them to lead the struggle for radical change, but rather because he felt them too "strategically" important to be left in opposition. As he told Bingham: "Basically you and I differ in that I am willing to make concessions [to the middle classes] for strategic reasons, while you believe that these groups will furnish the shock troops."[43]

Amlie's statement, however, vastly exaggerates his differences with Bingham over the future political role of the middle classes. It is also a misrepresentation of Bingham's political philosophy. Bingham never claimed that the middle income groups, the dentists, shopkeepers and lawyers, would furnish the "shock troops" for social revolution. By the middle class, as we have seen, he referred to a "more or less all-pervasive middle class mind" that predominated in America, in the factory, and in the field, as well as in suburbia. Moreover, in his more private moments Bingham never doubted that labor would be ready for revolution "long before" the middle income groups. Yet he stressed the theme of middle class radicalism in his published writing because he, like Amlie, recognized that it would be suicidal to leave them "in opposition." As he explained to Amlie, he felt

> so certain that labor will come along in any effective radical movement that I am willing to take some risk there. On the other hand, I am inclined to believe that the whole future of civilization may depend on the ability of this country to solve the economic problem, and that the whole political problem depends on how to prevent the middle classes from going Fascist— or, stated positively, how to insure that they as a social force will move in the direction we want them to go.[44]

As his correspondence with Mumford and his Russian diary make clear, Bingham was also responding to a strong personal identification with the middle classes, an attachment abetted by his fear of proletarian revolution. But it would be wrong to attribute his political strategy entirely to these factors. Bingham's core values and ideals may have been similar to those of the liberal middle class, yet he did not consider himself *of* that class. His background, he once remarked, was "strictly ruling class with equal mixtures of feudal aristocracy and capitalism."[45] Writing to Mumford in 1934 he denied that a "petty bourgeois background" in any way colored his attitudes toward labor and the middle classes. "Whether for good or ill my background is not 'petty bourgeoisie.' The white collar worker is just about as alien to my background as the manual worker. I am as nearly of the top ruling classes as I could be."[46] Bingham was convinced that this allowed him to evaluate dispassionately, as few other radicals could, the middle class character of American life. "Most American radicals," he told Amlie, "come from the middle classes themselves, and the all-pervasive middle class atmosphere which they breathe is not something they can observe from outside, as I was able to. My background, I believe, enables me to see the social structure in some ways more clearly than other people."[47] Perhaps. But the irrepressible influence of Bingham's upper crust, Prospect Hill background powerfully influenced his approach to radicalism. As we have seen, both the program he advanced for the achievement of his social ideals and those ideals themselves were profoundly shaped by family and personal considerations.

Here also we confront the continuing importance of his family's missionary inclination. Bingham's Calvinist ancestors, secure in their faith, were righteously driven to carry it to others "less fortunate." As a youth, Bingham was moved by this same pious reformism, in a more secularized form. At Yale he burned with the urge to find a suitable calling, a life's career morally responsible and inwardly satisfying. When he found in Russia the secular faith and life mission he had been seeking, he returned to America determined to carry this message, as his ancestors had carried Christ's word, to those "less enlightened." He was possessed of a deeply personal vision of the future, a conception of the good society as strongly marked by his Prospect Hill youth as by what he had witnessed in Russia; and he was committed to the spread of this ideal in industrial America.

For this he would need a movement large enough to win power. Given his fears of the proletariat and his insight into the prevailing character of American society, the middle class seemed the critical class to win to this struggle. The same sureness of belief, the same compelling inclination to shape the world to the requirements of a deeply felt ideal, the same proselytizing zeal that guided his missionary grandparents was ever alive in the radicalism of Alfred Bingham. The middle class strategy of *Insurgent America* was the all-important means to the new commonwealth, but a commitment to a very personal conception of the future, and the urge to participate in the shaping of the world tomorrow, was the wellspring and catalyzing force of Bingham's radicalism.

Unlike Bingham, Mumford never made explicit the role he expected the middle classes to play in the anticipated social transformation. Were they to be shunted aside by the radicals to become human fodder for an enterprising demagogue? Or would they be driven by the force of accelerating economic pressures into the expanding army of alienated labor? Or would they, perhaps, be listless bystanders, unable to choose sides in any future social struggle? Mumford never specified. Nor did he suggest how a "reapproachment" between the intellectuals, the honest technicians, and industrial labor might be accomplished. Yet, in the end, he did raise a profoundly disturbing question concerning the advisability of approaching socialism via the middle classes.

Mumford wisely perceived that a radicalism that accepted the middle classes "at their own self-evaluation," catering to their pecuniary values and narrow prejudices, ran the risk of undermining its own proclaimed ends.[48] The real danger, however, was not that a movement addressed to the lower middle classes would evolve into an ugly variant of fascism, as Mumford feared; but that in the process of capitalizing on prevailing middle class values and instincts the party might eventually lose sight of the very social aims its founders had set for it. Instead of challenging and seeking to transform the most unappealing and narrowly stultifying characteristics of the middle classes—their hollow boosterism, their rampant materialism, their unthinking patriotism—Bingham suggested that they be exploited for radical purposes. The organizational strategy of *Insurgent America* was, at heart, a manipulative one, founded on the implied suspicion that the middle classes could never be drawn to an unreservedly radical program and party. If they ever accepted socialism, Bingham implied, it would be a socialism resplendent in the uniform of "one-hundred-percent Americanism." Only prosperity and patriotism, the lure (and Bingham acknowledged this) of the fascist, would rally them to the standard of revolutionary change.[49]

Bingham, as his utopian essays make clear, never looked to socialism as a movement for mere material gain. His was the thrilling vision of radical humanism, to shape a social fabric consonant with man's aspirant emotions, a community befitting his loftiest ideals. Yet the political strategy of *Insurgent America,* the tactical means to democratic socialism, was dangerously inconsistent with these generous ends. Seizing upon the predominant theme of "abundance for all," those who might have gathered to such a movement could easily have made it into a shabby crusade for economic gain. Bingham was undoubtedly aware of this; yet he was convinced that only such a blatantly nationalistic and unabashedly material appeal would succeed in middle class America. Tactical realism dictated a transitional program rooted in the liberal, middle class consensus, a strategy that ironically used many of the ideals of capitalism for socialist purposes. Just as importantly, he feared that there was insufficient time for the kind of patient, long-term value reorientation Mumford and others advised as a prelude to socialism. This would have to await the turn to socialism; for economic crisis was fast approaching, and unless radicals were prepared with a program immediately attractive to the middle classes they would, in the impending crisis, throw their support to the henchmen of reaction. Hopes for such a crisis reinforced the belief in its likelihood, giving Bingham's radicalism a millennial quality, an urgency and impassioned certainty that sustained him through the arduous business of mobilizing a new party challenge. Yet there were dangers in such millennialism.

In the end Bingham's radicalism suffered from two crippling flaws: a naive optimism about the likelihood of a socialist triumph; and, related to this, an inadequate appreciation of the recuperative powers of American capitalism. Bingham confidently assumed that Roosevelt would be unable to stop the economic decline, and that when the final crisis broke the production-for-use movement would reap the harvest of middle class discontent. But the crisis never came. Both capitalism and liberalism responded with a vigor Bingham had thought impossible. And the casualty was not only his political movement but, as we shall see, his very commitment to radicalism as well. His failure to appreciate the adaptive abilities of corporate capitalism and to develop a correspondingly resilient and less millennial radicalism, a radicalism for the long term, made it easier for him later in the decade to abandon socialism for New Deal liberalism. But this was not simply Bingham's failure. The record of the decade indicates that a host of other radicals, Marxian and non-Marxian, entertained similar misconceptions and eventually beat a similar political retreat.

Yet the larger significance of this theoretical flaw does not inhere in its personal meaning for the radical intellectual. Bingham and other radicals were waging a battle for the minds and support of the American public; and their millennial assumptions also armed them inadequately for this fight. The problem with Bingham's economic radicalism was that it went at capitalism where it was strongest. Corporate capitalism's major source of strength has been its ability to provide, with periodic interruptions, a rich flood of products and services and to convince Americans that their consumption *is* the good life. Americans are thus unlikely to rally to a radicalism promising them what they have been convinced capitalism can best guarantee. The depression, it is true, shook people's confidence in capitalism. But not to the extent Bingham hoped for; and not for long. And the reason, of course, was Roosevelt. His New Deal shored up an economic system Bingham and other radicals were certain would soon collapse, restoring enough prosperity to revive a buckled but still resolute national faith in capitalism's superior productive capacities.

It was not until late 1937 that Bingham conceded the unlikelihood of a radical movement unseating Roosevelt. Yet instead of adjusting his vision and working, say, for the long-term value reorientation Mumford advised, he moved rapidly toward an accommodation with the New Deal. This shift to liberalism proceeded directly from the nature of his radical faith. Impatient and excessively optimistic, armed with an inadequate appreciation of the resourcefulness of the political economy he assailed, Bingham was simply unwilling to tolerate for long the bitter frustration and lonely defeat that have been the hallmarks of the American radical quest.

But this was a later Bingham. Earlier in the decade, when everything seemed possible, he remained sublimely confident that if he organized his movement in time it would sweep to power with the final crisis of capitalism. For Bingham, the radical theorizing of *Insurgent America* was merely an essential prelude to the revolutionary political struggle he expected to lead.

7

TOWARD A NEW NATIONAL PARTY

In his early theoretical writings Bingham attempted to fashion a social program and a politics of transition for a new kind of democratic radicalism. Yet the essential and immediate task was to make this program manifest in political action. This, he knew, would be an enormously difficult undertaking, for the FLPF was in 1933 a powerless and ineffectual alliance without adequate funds or organizational support. The responsibility for transforming this loose paper alignment into an effective political coalition fell largely to Bingham, Amlie, and Howard Y. Williams. Under their spirited direction the FLPF dedicated itself to three paramount objectives: the promotion of farmer-labor parties in as many states as possible; the conversion of existing state third parties to a more radical position; and, ultimately, their alignment by 1936 in a national production-for-use party.

In view of the popularity of the Roosevelt administration, the federation decided to avoid any precipitous attempts to form a national party and to concentrate first on those middle western states—Minnesota, Wisconsin, Iowa, and the Dakotas—where the revolt against economic conditions had reached its most advanced stage. Actually, the federation had no other choice but to concentrate on the farm movement. "Whether we like it or not . . . ," Amlie confessed to Bingham, "the only way that we can get an expression on national affairs is to organize a third party movement in these various [middle western] states. . . . Our leaders may not be the type of leaders that would be approved of by intellectuals but they are the best we have. There is nothing else available."[1]

Always, of course, there was the possibility that this midwestern insurgency would turn out to be merely another in a familiar succession of farm revolts for currency inflation and price supports. Yet Bingham and Amlie sensed in the current unrest a radical promise absent from previous agrarian outbursts. This farm upsurge, Amlie assured Bingham, differed considerably from the populist movement of the 1890s. "The capitalist system then had fifty years ahead of it. Today we are definitely coming to the end of that period."[2] When the final crisis broke, Amlie remained confident that these aggrieved farmers and their working class allies would raise the cry for sweeping change. He and Bingham thus pinned their hopes on the likelihood of a continuing economic downslide, culminating in the complete collapse of capitalism. With the New Deal helpless to stem the decline, farmer-labor progressivism would, they expected, give way to demands for a party of radical change; and with the Middle West in the vanguard, other sections and movements would surge to the new party standard. From the start, then, the federation tied its political fortunes to national events wholly beyond its control, never doubting that capitalism would fail or that Roosevelt would be unable to avert that failure. In the absence of a national demand for socialism, and without any real organizational power of its own, there was little else the federation could do. "So long as the Roosevelt boom lasts," Bingham admitted in 1934, "interest [in a new party] will be sporadic and local." Only with the final recognition of the New Deal's inability to save capitalism would the corn and wheat belt witness the upsurge of a "conscious revolutionary radicalism."[3]

Yet when the crisis came, how would the movement take power? In its organizational work in the Midwest and elsewhere, the federation emphasized its commitment to orderly democratic change. Privately, however, Bingham and Amlie doubted that their party would be able to capture control in an altogether peaceful and constitutional manner. In their confidential correspondence immediately after the Chicago convention, both remained skeptical about the willingness of the dominant interests to hand over power to a democratically elected radical party. Extra-legal methods might, therefore, be necessary. "I am firmly convinced," Amlie told Bingham, ". . . that the change which we hope to aid in bringing about will not be effectuated by orderly procedure."[4] Bingham wrote back that he was "completely in agreement" concerning the limitations of a movement solely "orientated toward casting ballots."[5] As he told a friend one year later: "Acts of illegality and shows of force" would probably be "inevitable" in any revolutionary transformation.[6] Bingham and Amlie were not questioning here the ability of their movement to carry a national election; they simply doubted that the capitalist class would acquiesce peacefully to its own extinction. In this event, the party of change would have to be prepared to take "genuinely revolutionary action." "A . . . realistic political party . . .," Bingham announced in *Common Sense,* "must continually affirm its absolute faith in the democratic procedure and at the same time be prepared for its renunciation by the other side."[7]

An additional factor in Bingham and Amlie's reluctance to bank entirely on electoral tactics was their shared belief in the likelihood of a total economic breakdown, a crisis that would afford a disciplined revolutionary organization an ideal chance to seize the government. Bingham was more confident than Amlie about the immediate prospects of such a collapse; and he, more than Amlie, looked to economic ruin as an opportunity to power. When this crisis came, a forceable takeover might be necessary, he claimed, in order to prevent the establishment of a proto-fascist regime by the Right. "When civilization itself is at stake we cannot be too timid about questions of legality, and constitutionality, and if force is made necessary by the opposition we must be prepared to meet it."[8]

But how? Bingham and Amlie realized that it would be politically suicidal to sanction violence openly, even as a retaliatory measure. Therefore in late 1933 and into 1934 they explored the possibility of creating within the FLPF a secret "corps" of leaders trained to engineer a political coup. This would be, Amlie told Bingham, "a revolutionary movement within a political movement," an inner group that Bingham likened to the "disciplined revolutionary party membership of the C.P. [Communist Party]." At the same time Bingham also suggested the establishment of a "semi-military fighting organization of young people," a militant cadre "trained to secrecy" and prepared to use force against the agents of counter-revolution.[9]

In the end nothing came of this extravagant plan for a secret revolutionary cadre. There was simply never sufficient support within the FLPF for it. After 1934 Bingham and Amlie dropped the proposal entirely. The idea of a fighting youth corps, however, was partially realized in December, 1933, when Selden Rodman (who had always been more impatient with electoral tactics than Bingham) announced the formation of Young America, an organization he was instrumental in creating. The crowning purpose of Young America was to enroll discontented youth in the battle for radical change. Rodman and Bingham also expected it to play a critical role in the coming struggle for power. Its local community cells were to help prepare the plans and "operating personnel" for the drive to socialism; and when the final crisis of capitalism arrived, Young America would not shrink from genuinely revolutionary action. Just as "an army trained through months and years for the business of fighting, eventually becomes tired of mock manoeuvres and blank cartridges . . . , an army trained for taking over and operating a new society will not," Rodman declared, "be content to stand idle for long."[10]

Young America never fulfilled Rodman's exuberant expectations. Like the idea of an "inner core," it drew little support and played almost no part in the federation's day-to-day activities. Yet Bingham and Amlie's brief commitment to these ideas points up their genuinely revolutionary intentions. For a short time, at least, they showed themselves more willing than most of their fellow independent radicals to sanction revolutionary counterforce as a tactic of change.

Even while considering the question of violence, however, Bingham and Amlie concentrated their energies primarily on the more practical business of encouraging an electoral coalition through patient grass-roots organizing and a spirited educational campaign. The activities of Young America were always segregated from those of the more politically oriented FLPF; and federation organizers were instructed to avoid any mention of violence in their new party activities. In his *Common Sense* editorials Bingham himself made it clear that violence would be resorted to only in the event of a violation of democratic procedure by the opposition.[11] He and Amlie knew that their hopes for socialism were bound up with the agrarian militancy that was then sweeping the Middle West; and it was there that they centered their organizing efforts.

The two pivotal states in the federation's middle western strategy were Minnesota and Wisconsin. Minnesota already had a strong Farmer-Labor Party, while in Wisconsin there was mounting sentiment among Progressive Republicans for a reformist third party. Moreover, in Amlie of Wisconsin and Williams of Minnesota the federation had two seasoned organizers with wide contacts and support in the area. If the FLPF had any hope of amassing support in the Middle West, it was in these two critical states.

Since early in the century Wisconsin had been the staunchly Republican bastion of the La Follette family. Almost all important political struggles were waged within the Old Party between the La Follette Progressives and the conservative Stalwart faction, with the Progressives usually in the ascendancy. After the death in 1925 of Senator Robert M. La Follette, Sr., the founder and unquestioned leader of the Wisconsin

Progressives, party leadership passed to his sons Robert, Jr., who succeeded to his father's senate seat, and Philip, who gained the governorship in 1930. This Progressive Republican dominance, however, was broken in the 1932 primary by a successful Stalwart challenge. Then, that November, the long moribund Democratic Party, capitalizing on deteriorating economic conditions, swept the governorship and gained considerable power in the legislature, leaving Wisconsin Progressives in a state of confusion and disarray.[12]

This stunning setback prompted a number of Progressives to explore the possibility of forming a separate state party. For in the future, with their control of the Republican machine no longer secure, Progressives would be forced to run a costly and fractious primary campaign merely to qualify for the right to meet the revived Democrats in the general elections.[13]

It was at this point that the FLPF began in earnest its midwestern drive. In Wisconsin Amlie led the way. Over the next three years he almost singlehandedly directed the FLPF's campaign to swing Wisconsin's Progressives into the production-for-use movement. His aim, actually, was threefold: to speed the movement in Wisconsin toward a third party; to commit that party to a production-for-use platform; and to prod Wisconsin Progressives into taking command of the drive for a national third party.[14]

Working feverishly through the winter of 1933–34, Amlie traversed the state, contacting hundreds of reform leaders in an effort to encourage the movement for a new party. In the end, however, he knew that the fate of the new party drive in Wisconsin rested in the hands of two men, Philip and Robert La Follette. Philip, more impetuous and politically flamboyant than Robert, appeared cautiously receptive to a state third party, but remained officially neutral in deference to his brother's fear of waging a reelection campaign in 1934 on a new party ticket. The La Follettes also avoided announcing for a new party until they had sounded out Progressive opinion across the state.

Finally pressure from militant farm and labor organizations forced their hand. In the spring of 1934 the Wisconsin State Federation of Labor, the Cooperative Milk Pool, and the Wisconsin Farmers' Holiday Association, infuriated by the state government's economic inaction, declared for a farmer-labor party. That May, with the La Follettes' blessing, a special Progressive convention met at Fond du Lac and created the Wisconsin Progressive Party.[15]

It was not, however, the radical party Amlie had hoped for. At the convention Amlie had urged the adoption of a radical statement of principles "distinguishing the new party from the 'old La Follette

Progressives.'" But the La Follette machine, firmly in command of the proceedings, crushed the proposal and, seeking to avoid a divisive floor fight, put off adoption of a party platform until the regular Progressive convention in September. "The fight has just started here in Wisconsin," Amlie informed Bingham. "We have formed a new party, but without any platform or principle."[16]

Amlie aimed to transform the new Progressive Party into an avowedly radical agency with power lodged in the rank and file membership and with a platform demanding state ownership of major industries and public utilities. To accomplish this he realized that he would have to break the hold of the La Follettes' Madison ring over party platform and direction. This was the purpose of the Farmer-Labor and Progressive League (FLPL), a membership organization he and other radical Progressives formed in late June, 1934. The FLPL was to operate in association with, but independent of, the Progressive Party, seeking to raise support for a more thoroughgoing economic platform. Its larger and long-range aim was to wrest control of the party from the Madison ring.[17]

The creation of the Farmer-Labor and Progressive League signaled the apogee of FLPF influence in Wisconsin in 1934. But even this organization was unable to amass sufficient strength to influence the determination of official Progressive Party policy. At its convention in September, 1934, the Progressive Party adopted a mildly reformist platform, ignoring the demands of Amlie and the FLPL for a radical anti-capitalist document. The FLPL, moreover, drew its membership primarily from those interested in statewide reform; few shared Amlie's consuming passion for a national third party. Philip La Follette remained on amiable terms with Amlie, promising his eventual support for a national party. But hard and fast commitments never followed. In 1934 Wisconsin politics dominated his and Robert's attention.[18] They kept on good terms with Amlie because they feared the loss of his organization's support. Amlie nevertheless remained convinced that Philip would soon tie in with the production-for-use movement. Bingham was more skeptical about the sincerity of Philip's radical convictions, but even he admitted that the "achievement of prying the La Follette movement loose from Republicanism in a comparatively short time was, in itself, a great one."[19] Perhaps there was hope for a general radicalization of the party? The resounding Progressive victory in the 1934 elections gave the FLPF further cause for optimism. Philip took the governorship, Robert, Jr., retained his Senate seat, and the Progressives gained a plurality in the state assembly. More importantly for the FLPF, Amlie won election to the United States House of Representatives, along with six other Progressives. With the Progressive Party now in virtual control of the state government, and with Amlie in a stronger position to influence party policy, the federation concluded 1934 confident that Wisconsin would soon align with its national movement.[20]

But it was in the neighboring state of Minnesota that the most encouraging third-party developments occurred in 1934. Minnesota was already governed by a third party, the Minnesota Farmer-Labor Party, which had its origins in a political coalition of the farmers' Nonpartisan League and the Minnesota State Federation of Labor.[21] Behind the intrepid leadership of Governor Floyd B. Olson, the Minnesota party was growing increasingly impatient with the New Deal's domestic initiative. With Olson threatening bolder measures to meet the depression in his state and hinting publicly of his interest in a national third party, the Minnesota Farmer Laborites looked like they might become the first state party officially to join the production-for-use movement.

Bingham and Amlie realized that their federation's fortunes in Minnesota depended ultimately on the sincerity of Floyd Olson's commitment to national third party action; and they assiduously courted his favor. Born of Scandinavian immigrants in a Jewish neighborhood in Minneapolis in 1891, Olson was one of the most colorful and controversial figures on the national political scene, a former member of the Industrial Workers of the World and an avowed economic radical. Elected to the governorship in 1930, he had begun his first term cautiously, convinced that Minnesota's traditionally Republican farmers were not yet prepared for a radical assault on the economic problem. Olson also faced a hostile conservative legislature eager to block any but the most minimal reform program. But as the depression deepened and farm militancy redoubled, he came forward as the radical champion of the debt-ridden farmers and workers of his state. Speaking in Cleveland in the late summer of 1933, he shocked his audience with the suggestion that Roosevelt move in the future to nationalize the nation's critical industries. But that was just the beginning. By the winter of 1933 he was urging a national production-for-use system, and the FLPF was eagerly seeking him out as a possible third party presidential candidate.

Olson was a hugely attractive political figure. Tall, granite-featured, and muscular, a charming and robust platform speaker, with a flair for practical joking and convivial small talk, he conveyed a mixture of character, principle, and human warmth rarely found in a politician. A man of inexhaustible energy, he was vigilantly alert to the everyday concerns of his constituents. He made it his business to know their problems and their needs. And in immigrant Minnesota he knew their

languages and customs as well; his wife was Czech, and he spoke
Norwegian, Swedish, Danish, and Yiddish. Nor was he polished and
well born. He knew poverty; he had experienced the class struggle.
Yet although a self-proclaimed radical, Olson spurned Marxism for
an insurgency that had its roots in the native soil of the Midwest.
Like Amlie's his radicalism was more of the heart than of the head,
a militancy forged from first-hand experience with the economic realities of his state and region. Olson was exceedingly intelligent; yet he
cared little for theory or utopian speculation. His incessant concern
was with the active struggle for immediate change. Yet he was no
mere progressive. The depression had transformed his rebellious
populism into a strongly felt radicalism that set him apart from most
other midwestern farmer-labor leaders.[22]

Howard Y. Williams had been working since 1929, first with the
LIPA and then with the FLPF, to cement an alliance with Olson's
party. But Olson would not commit his party to national action until
surrounding states had formed successful farmer-labor movements.
Without the active cooperation of other strong state movements, he felt
certain a national new party effort would flounder and fail. Olson also
regarded Williams, a Unitarian minister, as hopelessly naive and dangerously doctrinaire, and refused to cooperate closely with him. Working largely independent of Olson, Williams nonetheless succeeded in
building up considerable support in the Minnesota party for the FLPF
program. And in the spring of 1934 he was inspirational in committing
the Farmer-Laborites to the most radical platform ever put forward
by an American political party in actual control of a state.[23]

For months prior to the March, 1934, Farmer-Labor convention,
Williams had been busy packing the platform committee with delegates
sympathetic to the federation's program. Still, he anticipated a bitter
floor fight for a radical platform. But when the convention convened,
the insurgents were given an unexpectedly easy avenue to influence by
the Governor's stirring keynote address. Speaking with characteristic
audacity, Olson announced that in the future the aim of the Farmer-
Labor Party would be nothing less than a cooperative economic order.
Then, rising to the aroused mood of the delegates, he declared: "I
am frank to say that I am not a liberal. I enjoy working on a common
basis with liberals for their platforms . . . ; but I am not a liberal. I am
what I want to be. I am a radical."[24] Williams, who had captured the
chairmanship of the platform committee, read Olson's remarks as an
official party indictment of capitalism and directed his committee
to draft an openly socialist document. The platform that emerged from
his committee proclaimed the death of capitalism and urged that

immediate steps be taken to reorganize "the social structure into a cooperative commonwealth." A sweeping public ownership plank proposed government ownership and operation of the state's mines, public utilities, transportation, banks, and monopolistic industries. On March 29, after Olson had left the convention for a trip to Washington, D.C., the delegates approved the platform overwhelmingly. The radicals had carried the convention; perhaps Minnesota would become the rallying center for a new national party? Minnesota is historic testimony, Bingham wrote excitedly in *Common Sense*, that "Progressivism does in fact become radicalism."[25]

The radicals' victory, however, was short-lived. Almost immediately the convention platform ran headlong into a storm of criticism from regular party leaders. It would, they feared, precipitate a flood of farmer-labor defections in the conservative rural areas where socialism was still terribly suspect. Even Olson conceded that the delegates had gone too far; and in the months following the convention he agreed to tone down the document by narrowing the scope of its public ownership clause. He also temporized. On several occasions he argued that the public ownership of factories referred only to idle plants which would be handed over to the unemployed to produce goods for their own use. When this failed to quiet mounting public criticism, the state committee, with Olson's quiet consent, revised the platform, segregating the controversial public ownership plank under a separate section entitled "Ultimate Aims."[26]

In the exercise of his official duties, Olson, it is evident, was a decidedly cautious politician. His speeches could be defiantly radical; but rarely in action did he stray far to the left of party regulars. As Governor he appointed conservatives to several high state positions, and he preferred to spend his leisure hours drinking and playing poker with bankers and industrialists. And always his radicalism was tempered by a concern for the politically possible. He fought mightily for his ideals, but when one legislative battle was lost he generally conceded defeat and moved on to another. He hated diehards and 100 percenters. In the interests of immediate and concrete economic improvements, he was ever ready to mediate his radical aims. Studying Olson's career, one cannot help suspecting that his assaults on capitalism and his repeated threats to form a national party were part of an artfully conceived con game to squeeze economic aid out of the New Deal bureaucracy. With the Minnesota Democrats divided and out of office, Roosevelt quietly cultivated the support of the Farmer-Laborites; and Olson exploited this advantage to the fullest.

Once, in a debate with the British socialist John Strachey, Olson admitted to being an opportunist. But he defined an opportunist as "one who will use any agency he finds at hand—whether he believes in the entire program—to translate into action such part of his own program as is possible."[27] This unrelenting attention to the politics of the possible was the defining characteristic of Floyd Olson's insurgent commitment.

The Minnesota party's reversal on the Williams platform had been a setback for the FLPF. But the leadership remained confident about the Minnesota situation in late 1934. The November elections bolstered their enthusiasm, as the Farmer-Labor Party retained control of the state government, Olson being elected by a convincing margin. The party did lose two of its five congressional seats, but the old farmer-labor stalwart Henrik Shipstead was reelected to the U.S. Senate. Olson, moreover, seemed more serious than ever about national third party action. In the fall of 1934 he accepted the honorary vice chairmanship of the FLPF, and in private meetings with Bingham and Amlie he gave his assurance that he would soon head the struggle for a national progressive alliance. However genuine his new party convictions, Amlie and Bingham counted Olson as a friend and expected him to bring his party into their movement in the near future.[28]

Outside Minnesota and Wisconsin the FLPF experienced little success in 1934. Agrarian insurgency was aflame in the Midwest, but discontented farmers generally looked to the New Deal rather than to a new party for economic relief. Their intensely sectional outlook and their concern for strictly agrarian issues made them doubly suspicious of the broadly radical program of the FLPF. The federation, in addition, lacked the funds and manpower to inspire a significant following. What minimal impact it had on midwestern farmer-labor politics in states other than Minnesota and Wisconsin was due almost solely to the exhaustive organizational efforts of Howard Y. Williams.

Williams was a one-man organizing committee; his efforts on behalf of the movement were Herculean. In early 1934 he converted his St. Paul, Minnesota, LIPA offices into the midwestern center of the FLPF and launched a furious effort to mobilize new party support in the corn and wheat belt. With the assistance of FLPF committeemen John F. Wirds of the United Farmers and Jessie Sickler of the Farmers' Holiday Association, he called a series of conferences in Iowa that led to the establishment of a state Farmer-Labor Party in July, 1934. The following November the new party ran a slate of candidates in the statewide elections but polled less than five percent of the vote. Yet it was a beginning. In South Dakota, one of the states hardest hit by the depression, a Farmer-Labor Economic Federation was created, with a platform similar to that of the Wisconsin Progressive Party. Williams hoped that this organization would evolve into a full-fledged farmer-labor party. But plagued by "inadequate preparation and organization," it was unable to muster sufficient support to run an independent ticket in 1934. In neighboring North Dakota the script was much the same. There FLPF committeemen Alfred Dale, the state treasurer, and E. E. Green of the Farmers' Union were prevented from forming a third party by a factional struggle within the renascent Nonpartisan League. Further east, in Illinois and Michigan, state FLPF branches were established. Not much more was accomplished in Illinois, but in Michigan Amlie and Williams helped to organize a state Farmer-Labor Party with a collectivist platform demanding public ownership and democratic operation of the state's public utilities, transportation, communications, banking, and monopolistic industries. As in Iowa, however, the Michigan party registered an insignificant vote in the fall elections.[29]

In the East the production-for-use movement lacked any real organizational power or political clout. Bingham headed the federation's eastern offices and did manage to organize an FLPF section in New York City. But this remained little more than a committee of radical intellectuals "watching for opportunities for action."[30] Small FLPF branches were also formed in New Jersey, Massachusetts, Pennsylvania, Ohio, and Washington, D.C. Without a large membership, however, these clubs could be counted upon as only nuclei for effective action once the national party was launched. As Bingham himself admitted, not much would be accomplished in the East until "the movement . . . gathered momentum in the West."[31]

Third party possibilities appeared more promising in the Far West. Organized eastern radicalism was largely confined to the Marxist parties or to the more class-conscious labor unions. West Coast radicalism, however, was uniquely indigenous, a baffling compound of utopian socialism and the pseudoscientific theology of Technocracy. Bellamyite clubs, utopian societies, and Technocratic organizations sprang up all over the West early in the depression, attracting the confused middle classes as well as aggrieved farmers and workers. Yet most western radicals had not given up on the Democratic Party, even in their own states. This was vividly evident in California and Washington, where the West's two most powerful radical organizations, Upton Sinclair's End Poverty in California movement (EPIC) and the Washington Commonwealth Builders, sought to win control of the Democratic Party organizations of their respective states.

Early in the spring of 1934 Bingham traveled to the Pacific Coast to assess the possibilities of bringing that section's scattered radical forces into the FLPF. The trip was a disappointment. The radicalism he encountered seemed directed to sectional and state rather than national problems. Here also local insurgent leaders were suspicious of outside organizers. Their narrow sectional concerns, their reluctance to join a flimsily constructed national organization, and their hopes of capturing the Democratic Party made these western radicals indifferent to Bingham's overtures. In California, especially, Bingham complained in a letter to Oswald Garrison Villard, there was "little immediate chance of third party action as Upton Sinclair has captured the unattached radicals."[32]

Sinclair's rise to influence had been as sudden as it was unexpected. Sickened by the depression and convinced he had a solution, he registered as a Democrat and in the fall of 1933 launched a whirlwind campaign for the governorship. Several months later he published his campaign document, *I, Governor of California and How I Ended Poverty: A True Story of the Future.* The book, which proposed a statewide production-for-use system, was an instant popular success. Hundreds of EPIC clubs were organized, and Sinclair was besieged by letters of support. In the spring of 1934 he shocked the nation, and many of his own followers, by winning the Democratic nomination for governor over George Creel.[33]

In view of EPIC's advanced economic platform and its success within the Democratic Party, Bingham and Amlie decided to work for Sinclair's election rather than push for a separate production-for-use party in California. But when Sinclair was defeated in November, 1934, by the reactionary Republican Frank Merriam, having received almost no support from Roosevelt and the national Democratic Committee, Bingham pleaded with him to admit the futility of working through the regular Democratic Party and to declare for a national production-for-use party. Sinclair refused. He would not abandon the New Deal; instead, he would seek to move it further leftward.[34]

In the states of Washington and Oregon, the FLPF had organizers in the field, but here, as in California, the movement lacked real political influence. Washington possessed all the raw ingredients for a radical third party. Technocracy was a flourishing movement in the state, and there were, in addition, a number of militant farm and labor groups. But most state insurgents rallied to the Commonwealth Builders, a production-for-use organization resembling EPIC in its determination to work through the regular Democratic Party. With some FLPF assistance the Commonwealth Builders elected their candidate Lewis B. Schwellenbach to the U.S. Senate in 1934, while in Oregon an independent political movement led by state Senator Peter Zimmerman and backed by the FLPF polled 100,000 in the elections. Elsewhere in the country federation influence was virtually non-existent. Occasionally organizers were sent into the South and the Southwest, but no permanent organizations resulted from these limited and sporadic efforts.[35]

At the end of 1934, a full year after its formation in Chicago, the FLPF stood far from its goal of a national third party. It had helped to initiate state party organizations in several states; its educational campaign had aroused further interest in the idea of production-for-use; and in Minnesota and Wisconsin, Amlie and Williams had won some radical support for the federation's program. Still, the more strongly established state radical and progressive movements were holding back from national action; nor had the federation attracted a national political figure of consequence. Without adequate financing or a wide rank-and-file membership, the FLPF, Bingham admitted, was "little more than [a] committee working in different parties of the country."[36] Yet he and Amlie remained convinced of the possibilities of organizing a new party by 1936. The 1934 elections, Bingham wrote in *Common Sense,* "emphasized the potentiality of a new party." The Progressives and Farmer-Laborites had won critical contests in Wisconsin and Minnesota, Upton Sinclair had run surprisingly well in California, and several FLPF-backed candidates had won election to the U.S. Senate, including Bronson Cutting of New Mexico, a close personal friend of Bingham's, Schwellenbach of Washington, and Lynn Frazier of North Dakota. Although the newly organized farmer-labor parties in the Midwest had fared poorly, their mere existence, Bingham believed, symbolized that section's swelling disillusionment with the old politics.[37] And while the Democrats had swept the recent elections, all across America in the winter of 1934–35 there was evidence of rising discontent with Roosevelt and the New Deal.

The New Deal had by 1935 stopped the downward spiral of the economy. The national income was up by almost 25 percent over 1933, employment had increased by over 2.5 million and, perhaps most significantly, hope had replaced despair as the prevailing national mood. Yet while Roosevelt had restored the confidence of millions of Americans the economic depression still remained, a harrowing daily reality for the poor and the unemployed. Roosevelt, a master political psychologist, had in his first year of office conveyed to the nation an image of boldly decisive leadership. His legislative initiatives, it was widely believed, would soon induce a general recovery. But in early

1935, with unemployment still hovering near 20 percent of the work force, his administration seemed to be drifting aimlessly, without clear purpose or direction. The heralded New Deal, some critics began to insist, had run its course.

The flood tide of radicalism is generally a time of expanded expectations, when a people recover from the doldrums of collective despair, awake to the possibilities of a better tomorrow, and move vigorously and often angrily to carry through their demands. Roosevelt, by buoying the confidence of millions of depression victims, ironically set in motion a confused popular insurgency deeply critical of his own economic programs. For when the New Deal seemed to have lost its reform momentum in early 1935, some of the very groups that had hailed its first initiatives were left disappointed and disillusioned. The New Deal had not met their expectations; and they began to look elsewhere for economic relief and inspired leadership.

Everywhere in 1935 there were rumblings of discontent with Roosevelt. In late April Milo Reno's Farmers' Holiday Association, embittered by the administration's failure to replace the AAA with a thoroughgoing program of farm support, announced for a national third party, while on the labor front some of the smaller unions, angered by Roosevelt's unwillingness to come to the support of the Wagner Fair Labor Practices bill in Congress, sounded the call for new party action. All the while the demagogues of the Left, Huey Long and Father Charles E. Coughlin, drew to their movements countless thousands of desperate Americans. And from its meager beginnings in southern California Dr. Francis Townsend's old-age crusade swept the country with a visionary and simplistic plan to end the depression and bring financial relief to America's cruelly ignored elder citizens.[38]

Third party rumors filled the air in the spring of 1935. In Congress Vito Marcantonio of New York, George J. Schneider of Wisconsin, Ernest Lundeen of Minnesota, and Byron Scott of California were all hinting at the possibility of a new party.[39] Then, in dramatic fashion, Floyd Olson urged in the April, 1935, issue of *Common Sense* that "*a third party* arise and preach the gospel of government and collective ownership of the means of production and distribution."[40]

While few of these political dissidents, including Olson, were prepared to take definite steps to form the new party, their rhetorical support for a new politics aroused Bingham and Amlie's hopes and impressed upon them the need for a larger and more inclusive third party organization, a federation with a less pronounced sectional bias.

Prompt action was imperative, Bingham believed, for in the absence of a responsible third party challenge Coughlin and other demagogues would attract the impatient lower middle classes to a proto-fascist movement. Bingham had already been laying plans for a new federation prior to the 1934 elections. "I think it urgent at this moment to make a move," he wrote Amlie on November 6, 1934, "before we find ourselves in the wake of somebody's bandwagon." Sinclair, Philip La Follette, and New York's fiery Mayor Fiorello La Guardia were, he told Amlie, all leaning toward the "third party idea" while the labor movement, Milo Reno's Farmers' Holiday Association, and "the funny money boys" were losing patience with the New Deal. Finally, "the old guard Socialists" appeared "ready to assume 'leadership' of a party 'of the workers by hand and brain.'" United, these groups "might constitute a fairly sound party, but if any one of them . . . takes the initiative," Bingham warned, "we might as well migrate to Fiji."[41]

Preparatory to calling a wider new party conference, the federation brought together a group of middle western farmer-laborites to gauge their interest in a production-for-use party. In December, 1934, delegates from ten states met in St. Paul, Minnesota, at the Mid-Western Legislative Conference to "discuss the feasibility of calling a national conference to launch . . . [a] party on a national scale . . . [and] to formulate legislation for immediate state action." Olson addressed the conference, reaffirming his support for the FLPF program. A radical statement of principles embodying the "ultimate aims of production-for-use" was then adopted; and on the final day of the meeting the delegates resolved to advise the section's farmer-labor organizations to cooperate in calling a convention to form a national party as soon as possible.[42] The following April, after a series of preliminary conferences in Washington, D.C., with progressive legislators and labor leaders, Congressmen Marcantonio, Amlie, Scott, Lundeen, and Schneider, speaking for the FLPF, issued the call for a production-for-use convention in Chicago in early July, 1935.[43]

The Chicago meeting was being convened, Amlie announced in a pre-convention declaration, not to launch the new party, but to form a wider coalition "so that if a third party is inevitable in 1936 we will have the leadership ready."[44] Yet aside from Senator Gerald P. Nye, only a few important national leaders attended. The La Follettes stayed away from the conference for fear of jeopardizing their political position in Wisconsin; while "speaking engagements" in his home state forced Olson to cancel out at the last minute. Olson did send Amlie his assurance that he was "ready to follow any movement which is designed to bring about a change from the present system to a production-for-use and service system."[45] But Amlie and Bingham had expected a more concrete commitment. Upton Sinclair also sent the convention a message; only, he advised against the creation of a new party for 1936, claiming it would only insure the election of Herbert Hoover, which he argued would be "the greatest calamity in American history."[46] Then, in a lengthy convention address, Senator Nye echoed Sinclair's plea. The forces of reform must "stand ready to make a third party if and when the time comes for it," Nye declared. But any precipitous movement against Roosevelt would, he warned, throw the election to a reactionary. "Don't look to next year," he cautioned, "look ahead five, ten, or twenty years."[47]

Nye spoke for himself, not his audience. Most of the 250 delegates had not come to Chicago to be regaled by pleas for caution and political restraint. "There was . . . an urgency about the conference," one observer noted, "a sense of immediate peril to be thwarted, a demand that forces be mobilized for action, which proved disconcerting to some of its sponsors."[48] The delegates, Bingham told a *New York Times* reporter, represented "a cross section of the native American radical movement without the benefit of the European ideas." Attending were Paul Douglas of Illinois, Harold Loeb and Felix Frazer of the Continental Committee, farm leader John Bosch of Minnesota, Congressmen Marcantonio and Scott, along with representatives of the Minnesota Farmer-Labor Party, the Wisconsin Progressives, the EPIC Democrats, the Farmers' Holiday Association, the Railroad Brotherhoods, and various state farm and labor organizations. To these insurgents, Williams proclaimed, production-for-use was an issue "greater than slavery."[49] When Nye urged that the convention "build for the future," a delegate from Michigan shouted from the floor that it was fine for a senator making $10,000 a year to advise restraint, but "What if you were starving?" "The conference" the *New Republic*'s Robert Morss Lovett observed, "was not in a Fabian mood."[50]

By all accounts, the convention seemed primed for bold, immediate action. When Amlie's organization committee reported in favor of convening a conference to form a production-for-use party in time for the 1936 elections, the delegates approved overwhelmingly. The convention next moved to replace the FLPF with a new third party agency, the American Commonwealth Political Federation (ACF). Howard Y. Williams led the fight for the retention of the name "farmer-labor" on the grounds that its absence would "rob the movement of considerable momentum" in the Midwest. But Bingham and other eastern delegates argued that the term "farmer-labor" would needlessly alienate potential middle class supporters. As a concession to Williams, Amlie and Bingham agreed to continue the old FLPF as the midwestern branch of the ACF.[51]

Then finally came the explosive issue of Communist participation in the movement. Bingham and Amlie remained adamant against admitting Communists into the ACF; and they had no trouble pushing through a resolution affirming the federation's "belief in the democratic process and in the achievement of its ends through peaceful means." Only those supporting these principles were to be admitted to membership. But when Ray McKaig of Idaho proposed a motion explicitly excluding the Communists, a rancorous debate ensued. The gain of one Communist, McKaig declared, would result in the loss of 100,000 votes. But other delegates, including Williams, disagreed. One of the several Communists in attendance noted that it would be senseless to ban the party since all those who attacked Wall Street would be labeled as Communists anyway. In the end, McKaig's motion was tabled. But the question of Communist participation would continue to haunt the federation. Bingham, Amlie, and Douglas interpreted their resolution as excluding the Communists outright from the ACF. But they had little power to enforce it. And in the following months Williams and other federation organizers openly welcomed Communist cooperation.[52]

Before adjourning, the convention agreed on a platform inspired by the economic program of *Common Sense*. The document opened with a ringing plea for a production-for-use economy and went on to mark out a long list of immediate demands, including comprehensive health insurance, a "cost of production" program for farmers, heavy taxation on large incomes, and federal ownership and operation of the nation's banking system. Rounding out the platform was Amlie's proposal for a constitutional amendment empowering Congress "to make all laws which in its judgment will be necessary to provide for the general welfare of the people." Amlie was then elected chairman of the ACF, John Bosch, vice chairman, Paul Douglas, treasurer, Bingham, executive secretary, and Williams, national organizer. John Dewey and Floyd Olson remained as honorary chairman and vice chairman of the movement.[53]

The Chicago conference resulted in no decisive changes in the program or organizational strategy of the production-for-use movement. Bingham and Amlie had hoped to form a more inclusive federation with closer working agreements between the various affiliates. But the ACF was really the old FLPF in new dress. A number of new organizations joined the movement, but essentially it remained little more than a loose alliance of progressives and radicals with a decidedly agrarian character. Olson and the La Follettes had not yet joined the struggle, and even Congressman Marcantonio, who had signed the invitation to the Chicago meeting, withdrew from the conference after the first day, because, in his words, "its action taken toward the formation of a new party at this time is not only premature, but also wrong."[54] Despite the growing discontent, the Roosevelt administration still remained widely popular in the summer of 1935, and most reform politicians were wary of endangering their base of support by aligning with a stridently anti–New Deal movement. New party action was made doubly difficult by the fact that both the Minnesota Farmer-Laborites and the Wisconsin Progressives enjoyed the quiet support of the national Democratic Party in return for their loyalty to certain New Deal reforms. They were, as a result, unlikely to declare for a national party until the movement commanded massive popular and organizational support.[55] Thus the very organizations and leaders that the ACF counted upon to spearhead the national struggle were themselves reluctant to move until other equally powerful organizations and political leaders had prepared the way.

Still, Bingham and Amlie were hopeful of getting a new party in the field by 1936. Just after the Chicago convention they hired a full-time experienced organizer, Nathan Fine, who was a labor expert from the Rand School of Social Science, and from the new ACF offices in Washington, D.C., he initiated a last-ditch organizational and educational push. Bingham, Rodman, Loeb, Henry Pratt Fairchild, and other federation intellectuals combined to put out a series of inexpensive pamphlets explaining the aims of the organization. Copies of *Insurgent America,* Loeb's *Production for Use,* and Amlie's *The Forgotten Man's Handbook,* a campaign pamphlet he had used successfully in Wisconsin, were distributed at cut-rate prices. Speeches and articles by Olson and Congressman Lundeen calling for new party action were also reprinted and circulated.[56] But the focal point of the movement's educational drive continued to be *Common Sense.*

Bingham and Rodman had begun *Common Sense* with the hope of gaining a large newsstand circulation; it was to be a radical magazine for the everyday American. Yet throughout its history *Common Sense* appealed almost exclusively to intellectuals and the interested middle class. A large newsstand sale proved unfeasible without heavy financial backing. As a result the editors relied almost entirely on growth through mail subscriptions, secured by extensive promotional campaigns. Using these methods, they were able to expand circulation from 2,000 in early 1933, when Bingham seriously considered stopping publication, to nearly 10,000 in late 1935. By paying little or nothing to their staff or to their contributors, Bingham and Rodman were also able to keep their deficit down to a manageable figure and to continue publication on a regular monthly basis.[57] *Common Sense* was never, then, in a position to influence grassroots radical sentiment directly. As Amlie once remarked to Bingham, *Common Sense* was "far beyond the [movement's] rank and file . . . [and] would never appeal to anyone, except a person with considerable background and intelligence."[58] Still, it remained the movement's most important and influential publicity organ, scrupulously reporting its political progress, publicizing its activities, and elucidating its political and económic program, a program it had done so much to shape.

The ACF complemented its final educational drive with a frenzied national organizational effort. Bingham, Amlie, Williams, and other federation leaders spoke throughout the country in the fall and early winter of 1935, blasting away at the New Deal and urging a third party as the only answer to the economic problem. In the East, where there were few centers of organized production-for-use radicalism, the federation moved to encourage Commonwealth Clubs, small neighborhood discussion and promotional groups designed to serve as nuclei for future political organizations. Bingham had first suggested these clubs as a means of carrying the production-for-use program to the middle classes. With the help of Fine and Fred Gram, Amlie's legislative assistant, he attempted to establish a network of clubs in the late summer of 1935. Literature suggesting procedures to organize clubs was sent out to all ACF members. They were then urged to hold "house meetings" at which the ACF program would be introduced as a topic for discussion. Those interested in the aims and ideas of the federation would then meet regularly to plan other ways of spreading its message to the local community. The Commonwealth Clubs, Bingham believed, were the federation's "only chance of building . . . rank and file organized demand for a new party." Yet while the idea of neighborhood units might have been a sound one, here also the movement was stymied by an absence of money and manpower. With only a handful of full-time organizers in the field and a tiny active membership, the ACF was hardly in a position to reach the American middle class.[59]

While Bingham concentrated on the Commonwealth Clubs, Amlie crisscrossed the Middle West and Far West in a final desperate attempt to swing the insurgent groups of these areas to the new party struggle. In Washington production-for-use enthusiasts were united in the Washington Commonwealth Builders, a political pressure group that had emerged in the summer of 1935 out of the old Commonwealth Builders. Led by Howard Costigan, the WCB aligned organized labor, Technocrats, the unemployed, Townsend Clubs, and reformist Democrats into a reform coalition which captured the state Democratic Party and committed it to public ownership of natural resources, munitions plants, and public utilities. The party's platform also declared a national plan of production-for-use "urgent and vital." Amlie, however, found Washington radical leaders still cool to the ACF, as yet unwilling to break with the Democratic Party. Similarly, in California Sinclair and his EPIC followers refused to leave the party they had come so close to capturing.[60]

By mid-winter of 1935–36 the ACF's slender hopes for a new party convention had come to rest entirely on developments in Wisconsin and Minnesota. With the failure of the struggle elsewhere, these states *were* in effect the third party movement. In Wisconsin the La Follettes were still holding firm against national action; but the creation of a new Socialist-Progressive alignment, the Wisconsin Farmer-Labor Progressive Federation, kept the ACF cause alive for a time in the state. Amlie had been instrumental in bringing the Socialists and Progressives together. After the 1934 elections he opened discussions with the state Socialist Party and the Wisconsin Federation of Labor for the purpose of uniting them behind his efforts to transform the Progressive Party into an instrument of economic reconstruction. While at first reluctant to cooperate, by the early winter of 1935 these groups buried their differences and combined with seven other state farm and labor organizations, including Amlie's Farmer-Labor Progressive League, to form a militant alliance for change. The aims of the new federation matched those of the old Farmer-Labor Progressive League: it would be a pressure group aimed at radicalizing the larger Progressive Party. Yet unlike the FLPL the Progressive Federation, with a solid front of established power groups, could be expected to wield considerable political influence in the Wisconsin party. Just as importantly, with state Socialists and radical Progressives united, the ACF could bypass the La Follettes and focus on the single task of persuading the new federation to support a third party convention. The Progressive Federation, Amlie knew, was first of all an organization for state action; its affiliates were not yet prepared to take national action. But if Minnesota seized the initiative, he and Bingham were confident that Wisconsin's insurgent Progressives could be galvanized into active cooperation.[61] Everything then depended on Minnesota.

Bingham and Amlie had good reason to believe that the Minnesota Farmer-Labor Party would issue the call for a national third party at its March, 1936, convention. In November, 1935, Floyd Olson, appearing at an ACF rally in New York City, privately assured Bingham that his Farmer-Labor Association would soon affiliate with the ACF and that he would personally work to encourage this tie-up. Olson's control of the association was complete, and with his endorsement the party would certainly call a national conference. Just before the Farmer-Labor convention Bingham wrote to Olson reminding him of his November pledge: "The danger of not taking advantage of latent possibilities this year," he told Olson, "is that the national third party movement, having no dramatic center or head, will remain impotent for several years more, during which time the forces of fascism and reaction will be organizing."[62] What Bingham did not realize, however, was that Olson had already determined to back Roosevelt in 1936; and with this decision had destroyed the possibility of a new party well in advance of the Farmer-Labor convention.[63]

Olson did announce at the Minnesota convention his willingness to form a national third party. He told the delegates that while he would prefer that the new party confine itself to running congressional candidates, the final decision on a presidential ticket would be left entirely up to them. Yet this was sheer political hypocrisy; he knew that the party rank and file would not override his wishes. Predictably, the convention passed a cautiously worded resolution affirming the need for a national Farmer-Labor party and setting up a committee to cooperate with other progressive organizations in calling a conference to "explore" the possibilities of putting candidates in the field in 1936.[64] Few party regulars took this resolution seriously. After the convention Olson's men in the Farmer-Labor Association made it plain to Amlie and Fine that they were "not vitally interested" in a third party in 1936. "I do not entertain a great deal of hope about the Minnesota situation," Amlie reported dejectedly back to Bingham, as the Farmer-Labor candidates believed it necessary to cooperate with the liberal "Wolfe" faction of the state Democratic Party in order to be elected. The liberal Democrats were supporting Farmer-Laborites in state contests in return for their endorsement of the President. Thus, for narrow political reasons alone, Amlie doubted that Olson's party would "take the militant and active leadership necessary to translate the resolution adopted into political action."[65]

The announcement of the creation of Labor's Non-Partisan League for Roosevelt in early April, 1936, closed down the ACF's already tottering third party campaign. Organized by John L. Lewis of the United Mine Workers, Sidney Hillman of the Amalgamated Clothing Workers, and George L. Berry, head of the AFL's Printing Pressman's Union, Labor's Non-Partisan League set as its single aim the reelection of Franklin Delano Roosevelt, who Lewis hailed as "the greatest statesman of modern times." "We know that the defeat of the Roosevelt Administration means no labor legislation for decades to come," Hillman added, in a statement that concisely evoked the raison d'étre of the new league.[66] Bingham and Amlie had never banked heavily on organized labor joining a new party movement in 1936, but they had expected some limited support from the smaller radical unions, and had hoped that the larger, more established unions would at least remain neutral in the presidential election. Now with nineteen state federations of labor and nine huge international unions massed solidly behind Roosevelt, and with Minnesota and Wisconsin apparently pledged to the President, all hopes for running an independent candidate were scotched. Labor's Non-Partisan League, Bingham conceded in *Common Sense,* has given the "final coup de grace [to] . . . third party hopes." Amlie agreed; and when Nathan Fine's dubious scheme to gain the endorsement of the old guard Socialists for an ACF-sponsored third party convention collapsed, he too admitted the futility of pressing the fight for a new party in 1936.[67]

Williams, however, refused to concede. Without ACF approval, he pressured the special committee created by the Farmer-Labor convention to call a conference in Chicago in late May to explore the possibilities of a national third party. But at Olson's insistence the question of a third party presidential nominee was not to be considered.[68]

Bingham and Amlie, convinced now that a national farmer-labor party was impossible in 1936, boycotted the Chicago conference. They were also angered by the Farmer-Labor Association's decision to invite a number of leading Communists, including Clarence Hathaway of the *Daily Worker* and Earl Browder, the party chairman. ACF participation in this conference would, they agreed, irreparably damage the organization's "standing and influence."[69] "Past experience had demonstrated," Amlie added in a pre-convention statement, "that the Communists are out of sympathy with our program and philosophy and that they seek admittance to our councils not to work with us . . . but to gain control of our organization for their own purposes."[70]

Williams, however, had never accepted the ACF's hard line on Communist participation. Always resentful of the control exercised over the movement by Bingham and other eastern radicals, he kept only the loosest ties with the ACF national offices. This wide autonomy allowed him to accept financial support from the party and to admit Communists to important positions in his midwestern organization. Williams admired the energy and relentless zeal of the Communists he worked with, and he never feared that they might subvert his organization for party purposes.[71] As late as May, 1936, he pleaded with Amlie to cooperate with Minnesota in its upcoming conference. "If this conference is a flop," he warned, "it would mean that Minnesota would wash its hands of the national scene." When Amlie ignored his letter, Williams attended the convention on his own.[72]

Eighty-five delegates from twenty-three states attended the Minnesota-sponsored conference. The Socialist Party and the Wisconsin Progressives refused to send representatives for reasons similar to the ACF's, leaving the Communists and the Minnesota Farmer-Laborites to dominate the proceedings. The conference went on record for a "national party of farmers, labor, liberal middle class and professional and unemployed workers' organizations," but left the calling of a national convention in the hands of the Minnesota organization and an advisory committee of twenty-five. As in the past, no concrete measures were taken toward building the organizational machinery for a new party. The delegates passed a number of high-sounding radical resolutions, adopted an audacious convention platform, and returned to their home states to work for the election of Franklin Roosevelt. With Olson dying from pancreatic cancer and the Minnesota Farmer-Laborites concentrating on the state elections, no one seriously expected a new party in 1936.[73]

After the Minnesota conference even the previously indomitable Williams conceded defeat. The federation had lost its progressive support to Roosevelt, and most of its remaining affiliates had been infiltrated by Communists. Under the name "Knickerbocker Democrats" the Communists had secured a voting bloc on the executive committee of the New York Commonwealth Federation, the most active eastern affiliate of the ACF. The party had also infiltrated ACF organizations in Colorado, South Dakota, Connecticut, and a number of other states and had gained considerable influence within Williams's FLPF and the Minnesota Farmer-Labor Association. It would play a major part in the destruction of the Minnesota party after 1936. The dispute over Communist participation in the federation had, moreover, wrecked any chances for future close cooperation between Williams and the other national officers of the ACF.[74]

Without any real support or influence, crippled by Communist infiltration, and shaken by an internal leadership schism, the ACF in the early summer of 1936 was merely the shadow of a political organization. Bingham, however, remained determined to keep the organization alive beyond 1936. While willing to concede the election to the Democrats, he still believed the future belonged to the third party forces. In the summer of 1936, working with a fierce sense of urgency and desperation, he fought to piece together the scattered remains of his production-for-use movement. More politically isolated than ever, confused and grievously disappointed, he searched frantically for some way to salvage a measure of influence in national politics for himself and his federation. This frenzied drive for political influence drove him dangerously close to a merger with Father Coughlin's proto-fascist Union Party.

In the summer of 1936 Gerald L. K. Smith, the evangelical leader of the assassinated Huey Long's Share Our Wealth crusade, Father Charles Coughlin, and Dr. Francis Townsend joined with Congressman William Lemke to form the Union Party. Coughlin's coalition entertained no visions of electoral victory; its aim was the embarrassment and political defeat of "Franklin Double-crossing Roosevelt." The party's platform, with its crackpot inflationary schemes, spoke to the simpler populism of an earlier century. And with Coughlin, a virulent anti-Semite and red baiter, as the power behind the alliance, the Union Party evoked the specter of a native American fascism. The Reverend Gerald L. K. Smith gave alarming credence to these fears when, speaking before a Townsend convention in Cleveland, he proposed the mobilization of 100,000 young storm troopers to guard the polls on Election Day.[75]

Although quick to recognize the fascist tendencies in the movement, Bingham and Amlie were at first reluctant to denounce the Union Party outright. Its aggrieved farmer-labor and lower middle class supporters were among those the ACF hoped to convert to radical change. As Bingham had anticipated, many of these groups, in the absence of a constructive American radical party, had gravitated to the economic lunacy of men like Townsend and Coughlin. Then there was Lemke, a long-time leader of the Non-Partisan League in his state, a man with an absorbing commitment to the debt-ridden farmers of the Plains. His dogged advocacy of a succession of radical farm and currency bills in the Congress had endeared him to midwestern insurgents, who valued him as one of the most relentless critics of the New Deal farm program.

On learning of the Coughlin alliance, Bingham at first considered cooperating with the party in the hopes of radicalizing its platform and widening its base of support. The Lemke movement, he wrote to Williams, "is so dangerous that we must risk a good deal to swing it in our direction."[76] With its appeal cast in narrowly agrarian terms and without labor representation, Bingham feared that it might provoke a "cleavage . . . between the agrarian radicals and the labor radicals which may never be healed," a split that could also lead to "Hitlerism" in this country. Perhaps by cooperating with the Union Party the ACF could give it a stronger labor orientation, keeping alive the possibilities of a national farmer-labor party after the 1936 elections. Finally, there was always the remote possibility that the announcement of Lemke's party might start a landslide of discontented groups into a third party, "in which case," Bingham told Amlie, "it would be imperative for us to be near the controls."[77]

Bingham, however, never considered joining the Union Party as it was then constituted. The party's "reformist" platform, its suspicious connections with notorious anti-Semites like Chicago's Newton Jenkins, and the undemocratic circumstances behind its formation (the party was simply "announced" by Lemke after a secret meeting with Coughlin, Smith, and Townsend) held him back from open cooperation. His plan instead was to persuade Lemke to submit the Union platform to a "democratically elected and managed convention" which he hoped would endorse a platform much like the ACF's.[78] But this reckless scheme failed when in late July Lemke notified the ACF that he would under no circumstances submit the Union Party platform to an open convention.[79]

One month later, having exhausted every political alternative, Bingham urged his *Common Sense* readers to vote for Roosevelt. There was, he conceded, no other realistic choice. He advised, however, that "this be a support limited only to the next few weeks and withdrawn the day after Election Day." For the ACF would begin then a new drive for a national production-for-use party.[80] Yet while Bingham would not yet acknowledge the obvious, his crumbling political alliance had already become what he had long secretly feared it might, a monument to the triumph of New Deal liberalism.

8

RETREAT TO THE NEW DEAL

Roosevelt's landslide victory in 1936 left the ACF leadership profoundly troubled about their organization's future. Aside from some limited gains in Wisconsin and Minnesota, including Amlie's reelection to Congress, the third party forces were soundly routed at the polls. Bankrupt and more politically isolated than ever, the ACF was not even in a position to pull together the scattered remnants of its once promising insurgent alliance.[1] Yet the collapse of the federation's new party drive failed to dampen Bingham's determination to influence the direction of progressive opinion; nor did it kill his hopes for a new politics. Still convinced that a third party would emerge in the near future, he was, however, forced to concede the need to revise the strategy and timetable for its realization. Rather than moving at once to build a wider new party federation, Bingham joined Amlie in early 1937 in a less ambitious effort to amass a coalition of advanced progressive congressmen behind an agenda of radical economic legislation prepared by ACF intellectuals. Both Bingham and Amlie realized that there was little hope that Congress would approve any such program of comprehensive economic reform. Yet the mere existence of a legislative vanguard fighting in Washington for a policy of planned abundance would, they believed, expose the inadequacies of the Roosevelt recovery effort and provide a sorely needed rallying center for the nation's disassembled progressive forces. Here also was a way of keeping the new party idea alive and before the public.[2]

The foundations for the kind of congressional alliance Amlie and Bingham envisioned had already been laid in the Seventy-fourth Congress, considered by many the most radical Congress since Reconstruction.

The elections of 1934 brought to the House of Representatives a spirited company of reform enthusiasts who banded together in an informal caucus to frame and promote progressive legislation. By March, 1935, there were thirty-five congressional dissidents in the bipartisan "Progressive Open Forum Discussion Group," including Amlie, Gerald J. Boileau and Henry Teigan of Wisconsin, Minnesota Farmer-Laborites John Kuale and Ernest Lundeen, reform Democrats Robert G. Allen of Pennsylvania and H. Jerry Voorhis and Byron Scott of California, along with intransigent Republicans like William Lemke and New York's Vito Marcantonio. Amlie was the group's most astute policy maker and its most intensely militant spokesman. But its inspirational leader was an irascible young Texas Democrat named Maury Maverick.

A successful San Antonio lawyer and businessman, Maverick came to Washington in 1934 with a reputation as a fierce partisan of the oppressed blacks, Mexican-Americans, and poor whites of his district. Yet while he liked to call himself a "radical," Maverick's eclectic "radicalism" was deeply rooted in the populism of his state and region. Passionately anti-ideological, he labored incessantly in Congress for the immediately possible; and like so many of his fellow insurgents in the congressional bloc, Maverick was a determined supporter of Franklin Roosevelt. Early in the Seventy-fourth Congress his caucus issued a legislative manifesto incorporating suggestions for a government policy of "planned abundance." Yet while often to the left of the President on domestic policy, Maverick and most others in the congressional bloc never considered their caucus the spearhead of a new party; theirs was the more limited aim of driving the New Deal toward a bolder assault on the economic problem.[3]

The 1936 elections left the progressive bloc virtually intact; and when Congress convened in early 1937 they reopened the battle for an enlarged program of relief and recovery. Yet "the Mavericks," as the press liked to call them, were stymied in their efforts by their own lack of ideological consistency or political unity. As a group they cut across the spectrum of dissident opinion, from the closely reasoned production-for-use radicalism of Amlie, to the iconoclastic populism of Maverick. They were, moreover, held together by only the flimsiest organizational ties. More an ad hoc discussion forum than a hard and fast union for common change, outside the doors of their caucus, on the floor of Congress, they often worked at cross purposes, championing a baffling array of contradictory social policies. Amlie, as much as anyone, realized how difficult it would be to marshal them behind a coordinated legislative program. Yet he and Bingham were determined to try.

In April, 1937, Bingham called together the Commonwealth Congress for Progressive Social Legislation to draft legislation for the congressional "Mavericks." At the conference Bingham, Stuart Chase, Harold Loeb, Henry Pratt Fairchild, and other ACF intellectuals, assisted by several members of the congressional bloc, put together a package of bills calling for, among other things, government ownership of the banking system, natural resources, and railroads, expanded federal aid to tenant farmers, an invigorated work relief program, a comprehensive housing bill, and a special "Human Rights Amendment," prepared by Amlie, giving Congress the legal authority to establish a cooperative economic order. The heart of the program, however, was an ingenious scheme for coordinated economic production, the Industrial Expansion Act, the brainchild of Mordecai Ezekiel, a quiet, scholarly economist employed by the United States Department of Agriculture. More than any other measure, Ezekiel's Industrial Expansion Act defined the revised economic policy and strategy of the post-1936 ACF.[4]

Ezekiel had first submitted his industrial plan to Secretary of Agriculture Henry Wallace in late 1934 as an alternative to the "scarcity" planning of the National Industrial Recovery Administration. This original plan was then revised and refined in two controversial books, *$2,500 a Year: From Scarcity to Abundance* (1936) and *Jobs for All through Industrial Expansion* (1939). The plan's predominating idea was what Ezekiel called the "AAA in reverse." Under the Agricultural Adjustment Administration the government had set out to induce farm recovery by restricting production, with an offer of benefit payments, financed by a processing tax, to farmers who agreed to limit output. Ezekiel simply urged the application of these same techniques—the voluntary contract with the producer and the benefit payment—to manufacturing to expand rather than restrict production. The remainder of the plan simply described the machinery for unleashing production. A central coordinating agency, the "industrial expansion administration," was to authorize all strategic industries to form NRA-type code authorities made up of representatives from management, labor, and the principal consumer groups. These semi-autonomous authorities would devise tentative plans for enlarging production in their respective industries and then forward them to the industrial expansion administration, which would dovetail them into a master plan for coordinated industrial expansion. Participation in the program was to be entirely voluntary. But as an incentive Ezekiel recommended that participating firms receive federal benefit payments similar to those granted to farmers under the AAA.[5]

To some, the industrial expansion act looked like the NRA reincarnated. General Hugh Johnson, the former administrator of the NRA, read the plan and liked it. It was, he boomed, "the Blue Eagle . . . with as many teeth as an alligator."[6] Yet the plan's sponsors denied the connection. As Ezekiel noted, the industrial expansion act posited a radically different approach to economic recovery, substituting a planned economic expansion for the "planned scarcity" of the NRA. It also had as its aim more than the enlargement of industrial production. Embodied in the bill were provisions for raising workers' salaries as a way of insuring the purchasing power adequate to the expected increase in material output. If implemented, the plan would supposedly within a few years eliminate unemployment and provide all industrial workers a minimum guaranteed income of $2,500 a year. Unlike the NRA, moreover, Ezekiel's agency would, he claimed, never become the instrument of the corporate giants. Democratic planning was its keynote. Labor and consumer representatives were to be guaranteed equal status with management in the planning of production, wages, and conditions of work.

Ezekiel was not a socialist: his plan abjured nationalization of the industrial plant for a policy of aggressive government planning and direction of economic life. Prosperity and economic democracy, he insisted, could be had short of socialism. Earlier in the decade Bingham would have strenuously opposed such a program. Now, however, he was convinced that the Ezekiel plan "[with] its ability to win various class . . . and group interests and antagonizing few . . . [was] politically" preferable to the "EPIC-type" program he had urged in 1935 and 1936. Combined in a legislative package with other Commonwealth Congress measures, it would, he felt certain, bring the "essential prerogatives of the businessman under public control." Its passage, moreover, might set in motion a gradual movement toward a full production-for-use pattern.[7]

Following the Commonwealth Congress, the ACF launched a national educational campaign to promote its legislative agenda.[8] Meanwhile, in Congress Amlie worked to align the "Mavericks" behind the program. By late April he had persuaded Maverick, Robert Allen of Pennsylvania, and Jerry Voorhis of California to join him in co-sponsoring the Ezekiel bill on the floor of the House. "We have framed this act," Congressman Allen announced in support of the bill, "to make a reality of the dream of plenty glimpsed by Veblen thirty years ago, dramatized by Loeb and his associates in *The Chart of Plenty* and brought down to earth by Ezekiel." This bill, Maverick added, "while it would exercise government guidance of industry," would do so without sacrificing democratic freedoms. "For a government to exercise guidance in order to bring an end to the fears of businessmen that if they produce they will not be able to sell, seems to us a means of preserving political democracy rather than destroying it." Strong words; but that was all. For Allen, Maverick, and Voorhis made no further efforts to support or publicize the bill. It was almost as if they had agreed to introduce it as a courtesy to Amlie. Nor could Amlie enlist the support of others in the caucus. The Ezekiel bill apparently reached considerably beyond the limits of the congressional bloc's commitment to economic reconstruction.[9]

The congressional insurgents never achieved the coordination and ideological consistency Bingham and Amlie had hoped for. But even if they had united behind a program of economic planning it is doubtful that such a program would have passed the Congress, for the whole New Deal was in trouble after 1936. Roosevelt's abortive effort to pack the Supreme Court and rising opposition to social legislation by conservative Democrats split the Seventy-fifth Congress, blocking the entire national reform effort. Congress passed a limited federal housing law, a pitifully inadequate measure to aid sharecroppers and tenant farmers, but all other attempts at meaningful reform failed. It was the beginning of the end of the New Deal.[10]

The congressional checkmate of the New Deal and the collapse of the ACF's slender hopes for an integrated progressive bloc finally convinced Amlie and Bingham to abandon the fight for a new party. The nation appeared to be entering a decidedly more conservative phase, and the most that progressives could realistically hope for was a reinvigorated and expanded New Deal. Amlie reached this conclusion first. Writing to Howard Y. Williams in August, 1937, he predicted that the significant political struggles of the foreseeable future would be waged within the Democratic Party between its New Deal and conservative factions, for the 1936 elections had virtually eliminated the Republicans as a consequential force in national politics. Amlie then invited Williams to join him in supporting Roosevelt's drive to liberalize the Democracy.

Amlie made his retreat to the New Deal without remorse or regret, convinced it was the only alternative open to the realistic reformer. "I am interested in a political strategy," he told Williams, "where my troops will have a chance and where I will not be forced to turn over command to the opposition." One year later Amlie's political career was brought to an abrupt end when, after being dumped by the regular Progressive Party leadership, he was defeated in an independent bid for the United States Senate by the old-line Progressive Herman Ekern. Unfailingly principled to the end, his advocacy of the industrial expansion act hurt him dearly at the polls. There was a final and bitter irony in Amlie's defeat, an irony fraught with meaning for the political future. The

Progressive Party's decision to drop this long-time dissident coincided almost perfectly with his decision to jettison third party radicalism for a tamer liberal reformism. In this sense at least, Amlie had proved prophetic; a new political age approached, an age that augured ill for the spirited insurgency he had voiced. Not surprisingly, he was one of the first casualties of the new national direction.[11]

In September, 1937, less than a month after Amlie's fateful letter to Williams, Bingham, too, announced his support of the New Deal. *Common Sense*, he told his readership, had long advocated a national third party. But now there was no need for such a party: the New Deal was "becoming all that the third party forces . . . could hope for." Roosevelt's court-packing plan and his post-election promise of a massive assault on economic want signaled his determination to carry the New Deal further leftward. Bingham conceded that the President had not yet come forward with a clear agenda for economic recovery. But he had pledged his administration to the aims of full employment and full abundance and to a policy of social planning for the broader welfare. Moreover, by uniting labor, farmers, and the middle classes in a powerful electoral alliance he had realized the dream of the third party forces, constructing all the while an iron guarantee against domestic fascism.[12]

Roosevelt was obviously not yet the kind of president Bingham could support uncritically. The September editorial was more an expression of optimistic expectation than a statement of unqualified support or complete candor, an effort to make the best of a bleak political situation. From the perspective of late 1937 Roosevelt's New Deal struck Bingham as the last remaining bastion of democratic progressivism, the radical movement having been divided and defeated by the very administration he now urged his readers to support. Thus, while Roosevelt's apparent move to a more militant liberalism contributed to, and provided a measure of justification for, Bingham's turn to the New Deal, the determining impulse of that political metamorphosis was the collapse of his own movement for comprehensive change.[13]

Bingham was also deeply alarmed by the revolt of the congressional conservatives. The defeat of Roosevelt's court-packing plan, the shelving of an important wages and hours bill, and other liberal reverses in the Seventy-fifth Congress were, he was convinced, merely the opening sorties of a concerted campaign by southern Democrats and reactionary Republicans to dismantle the entire New Deal achievement. In the face of this threat, Bingham called on all progressives to "cement their ties to the New Deal." The existence of such a determined reform alliance might also force the southern conservatives out of the Democratic Party, clearing the way for a new political alignment of sharply defined ideological choice.

With the reactionaries purged from the party, the political battles of the future could then be waged between a conservative Republican and a progressive New Deal party. Thus, with even Roosevelt's moderate liberalism on the defensive, Bingham rallied to the New Deal, accepting it for the time being as the "practical limit of effective progressivism."[14]

International developments also influenced Bingham's turn to the New Deal. The ugly atrocities of the Soviet regime, ruthlessly brought to light by the Moscow trials, along with the rising power of Hitler's Germany and Mussolini's Italy, rekindled his fears of sudden or violent transfers of power. Perhaps the idea of a radical third party had been wrong from the beginning? The "moral corruption" of the Soviet dictatorship, Bingham wrote in 1938, gave renewed evidence that democratic change must always be sought "by democratic methods whatever the cost in slowness and indecision."[15]

Against this menacing background of communist and fascist totalitarianism, with democratic governments on the slide all over the world, the New Deal took on special significance for disillusioned radicals like Bingham. It was, they reasoned, the world's "last best hope" for democratic reform. "I am convinced," Bingham noted in 1939, "that the New Deal, in its left potentialities, is the nearest thing that has yet appeared in any country to reconcile democracy and socialism, to provide an interim or transitional stage, to work out the techniques (by trial and error) for refashioning our social institutions."[16] Until his retirement from journalism in 1944, Bingham would support the New Deal as the surest democratic alternative to fascist and communist dictatorship. It was always, however, a support based more on the New Deal's promise than on its concrete accomplishments.

The internal evolution of fascism in Italy and Germany also left Bingham with a new appreciation of America's two-party system as a powerful safeguard of democracy. In Weimar, Germany, especially, the numerous and ideologically distinct political parties had produced shifting, unstable governments, without sufficient power to restore prosperity and civil order. This paralysis of parliamentary government had smoothed the way for fascism. In America, however, with the two dominant parties separated by only the slightest ideological differences, each acted as a check on the other, and transfers of power were made without seriously disrupting the continuity of national policy. "So long as the two parties are Tweedledum and Tweedledee," Bingham wrote in 1940, in a statement that announced the extent of his disillusionment with third party action, "our democracy will be reasonably safe."[17]

Personal and career considerations beyond political strategy or philosophic bias also influenced Bingham's turn to liberalism. Only by recalling the psychological impulses that drove him to radicalism and sustained that commitment in the face of staggering odds can we fully understand his eventual political retreat. Such an understanding gives sharper meaning not only to Bingham's public biography but also to the tortuously difficult position of the radical intellectual in American political culture.

For Bingham, radicalism had always been a calling as well as a career, a way of carrying into public life the animating ethical vision of his youth. He had always wanted desperately not only to live correctly but to impress his ideals on the prevailing culture: to be worthy and to serve well. Convinced in Russia that capitalism would not survive the current economic crisis, he turned to radicalism as a way of achieving personal fulfillment through principled labor for the community good. As a revolutionary publicist and theoretician he would have an active hand in building the socialist future. Here was a career that answered perfectly his inner needs.

Yet, however idealistic, Bingham aimed always at what he perceived to be immediately possible. In the face of a massive economic failure, he offered his revolutionary community design as the platform for a movement he fully expected to win power by the end of the decade. When capitalism collapsed completely, and Bingham never doubted that it would, he would be waiting with a plan and a program for a new human arrangement. This expectation of imminent economic ruin was the sustaining force of Bingham's radical faith. "A radical conversion means nothing," he wrote in 1934, "if it does not rest on the logical conviction of the possibility of accomplishment, here and now. More than that, there must be a conviction of imminent necessity; not only that the capitalist system be replaced by a better system, but it must. For it is doomed."[18] Unless one was convinced of the likelihood of such a breakdown, he came close to saying, there was really no reason to be a radical.

In the first flush of radical activity, as an editor and political organizer, Bingham felt himself part of a vanguard of destiny and high significance. Radicalism in the turbulent beginnings of the decade gave men that feeling. To its most committed enthusiasts, socialism *was* the future. Of course, Bingham sometimes questioned his competence and public impact as a radical. Were his ideas and organizational efforts really making a difference? If not, would they ever? These are the doubts all radicals feel. Yet for a time feverish involvement in the movement allowed him to fight off nagging suspicions about his public effectiveness. And then he had invested so much of himself in the cause. The feelings of inadequacy and stagnation he had felt at Yale had given way to an exhilarating sense of personal and social significance. No longer an isolated moral enthusiast, he was hooked to a larger cause, in motion with others he admired, working arm in arm for a new kind of world. Yet this heavy emotional investment in radical work and the feelings of social worth and personal rootedness it encouraged also distorted Bingham's sense of political proportion, leading him to an excessive optimism about his chances for success. The sure confidence that America would soon have socialism sustained him through the arduous work of organizing a new party challenge. But it made it exceedingly difficult for him to confront the fact of his own public ineffectiveness.

Even when his movement came apart in the spring of 1936, Bingham refused to concede defeat. It was only the collapse of the Commonwealth Congress strategy over one year later that finally convinced him of the futility of continuing the new party fight. This reluctant concession was doubly painful, for the end of the production-for-use campaign was for Bingham more than a political setback; it was a shattering personal reversal as well, the end of an ethical quest he had set upon with radiant optimism just five years before.

The radical commitment involves untold personal frustrations. It is a life work fraught with anxieties. Perhaps the most troubling of these is the uncomfortable awareness that one's ideas are not gaining a hearing —that one is addressing an audience that isn't there. To continue in radical work for any length of time, the intellectual especially, must either be convinced that his work is genuinely making a difference or that immediate success is unimportant, that his ideas will prevail in the long term. These beliefs help to shield the radical from the incessant uncertainties that beset all who challenge the orthodoxy. By 1937 Bingham had arrived at the painful realization that his work was not making a difference. The New Deal, he was now certain, had staved off the economic crisis he had seen as the prerequisite antecedent to socialism. Liberalism, not socialism, would be the dominant political force of the foreseeable future. Bingham thus found himself confronted with a crucial career decision: to continue as a radical publicist, alive to the unlikelihood of influencing national policy in the near future; or to abandon radicalism for what appeared to be a politically more practical reformism. Certainly there were other alternatives. Yet this is how he saw the issue. And he chose an accommodation with the New Deal not simply because he believed a socialist victory impossible in the near future, but also because he could no longer endure the isolation and alienation of radical work. "Creative work," as he confessed some years later, ". . . cannot be done in a vacuum. It needs to be combined with love and the sense of belonging. That is, it must be valued. The creative artist may, perhaps, carry on without appreciation, but only exceptionally and at great cost."[19]

This impelling urge for public recognition and influence, so important in his conversion to radicalism, drove Bingham eventually to liberalism. Tired of drafting proposals that were never heard outside his small circle of readers, he now confessed "that the most any one of us can do is to deflect the course of events a shade from the direction they are taking anyway."[20] By tying in with the New Deal he hoped to gain the public effectiveness and influence to do just that.

Yet, while Bingham refused to see his move to the New Deal as an abandonment of his primary ideals, his support of Roosevelt brought with it a steady erosion of expectations, a less imaginative approach to the social issue, and an appreciably diminished audacity. A loyal enthusiast of the New Deal, by the end of the decade he had ceased to be a socialist.

Jettisoning the role of radical propagandist and ideologue, Bingham moved after 1937 to make *Common Sense* the unofficial organ of the New Deal wing of the Democratic Party. Articles by A. A. Berle, Thurman Arnold, Louis Bean, and other New Deal intellectuals began to appear regularly in its pages; Eleanor Roosevelt and Henry Wallace spoke at *Common Sense*'s fund-raising banquets in New York; and Bingham and Rodman faithfully reported the ideas and activities of leading administration-based reformers. Whenever a New Deal brain truster needed public exposure and progressive backing for a reform proposal, he usually got it in *Common Sense*. Yet *Common Sense* aspired to be more than a chronicler and publicist of New Deal developments. Bingham wanted to influence the New Deal as well as record its accomplishments by fashioning a progressive program Roosevelt could turn to "when the pressure of events . . . [made] it necessary and practicable that he act."[21]

Bingham, however, never accepted the New Deal uncritically. While lauding Roosevelt's pragmatic experimentalism, he remained sternly critical of the President's unwillingness to press for a coherent policy of expanded public spending and national economic planning. Only an ambitious spending initiative, combined with the Ezekiel industrial expansion plan, could, he insisted, spark a full recovery. But whereas Bingham had previously viewed the Ezekiel bill as a transitional measure on the road to full socialism, he now recommended it, in conjunction with an accelerated public investment program, as the solution to the economic problem.[22] Demands for the abolition of the market system and for nationalization of industrial property disappeared from *Common Sense* after 1937, replaced by a sobered emphasis on "strategic planning," Keynesian monetary and fiscal policy, and administered prices. Even Roosevelt's failure to act on these economic suggestions, however, failed to sour Bingham on the New Deal. Ignored by administrative policy makers, Bingham could still wax confident in 1939 that Roosevelt was "launching America on profound changes with a speed and effectiveness that has been extraordinary."[23] Bingham traced the development of his new economic perspective and described his new liberal politics in two important books, *Man's Estate: Adventures in Economic Discovery* (1939) and *The Techniques of Democracy* (1942). Considered together, these works record his disillusionment with utopian planning and radical politics. They also address in copious detail the crucial public question of freedom versus collectivism, perhaps the single most important domestic concern on the democratic left after 1936.

Alarmed by the spread of totalitarianism, a growing number of American intellectuals began after 1936 to denounce all efforts at collective economic planning, opening a debate on the relationship between planning and freedom that was to have inestimable consequences for the future of American liberalism. Public planning, it was increasingly argued, led inexorably to the barracks state, to sweeping abridgments of human freedoms, to the authoritarian centralism of fascism and communism. Even former planning enthusiasts like John Chamberlain and the ex-Trotskyite James Burnham joined the assault on collectivism.[24] But it was the sagelike Walter Lippmann, himself a former socialist, who most eloquently expressed the new mood. Lippmann had given cautious support to the New Deal's first planning initiatives; but by the late 1930s he stood adamantly opposed to economic planning, arguing his indictment piercingly in a most influential book, *The Good Society,* which appeared in 1937. There was, Lippmann insisted, no possible compromise between freedom and planning, no such thing as democratic socialism. Liberty and planning were absolutely irreconcilable. An economic plan simply could not be decided upon and carried through by legislative referendum; it had to be imposed by administrative fiat, a planning board determining not only the goals of the collective effort but the means by which they were to be realized. And with this, economic freedom would disappear. What, after all, did the people know about market management, about production scheduling, about foreign exchange or rates of return? No, if economic activity was to be planned, it could only be planned by a "dictatorship of casual oligarchs . . . despots who tolerate no effective challenge to their authority." And such an authority, Lippmann concluded, was too costly a price for economic stabilization; if in fact the "oligarchs" could even guarantee this.[25]

But Lippmann's was not the typical response of American progressives. Most of those who had contributed regularly to *Common Sense* and the *New Republic* earlier in the decade remained strong for economic planning. The earlier enthusiasm, however, was balanced by a heightened appreciation of the dangers of over-centralization, a greater emphasis on democratizing the planning process, and a general shift, epitomized by Bingham, from the concept of total production planning to the more limited "strategic" regulation of Keynesian economics. Bingham, Loeb, Soule, and other former radical planners thus remained collectivists, shedding their socialist collectivism for a less encompassing capitalist collectivism.[26]

Bingham was one of the few of these repentant socialists to meet the criticism of anti-collectivists with a detailed program for democratic planning. In *Man's Estate* he proposed machinery for a democratically planned capitalism, while in *The Techniques of Democracy*, its political counterpart, he offered a plan to further democratize and make more socially efficient the emerging administrative state. Here was a complete agenda of liberal reconstruction, one of the decade's few speculatively ambitious and comprehensively rendered efforts to reconcile freedom and collective planning. It was Bingham's final attempt to balance the individualism he cherished with the institutional integration he believed to be the essence of social growth.

Man's Estate is a hugely ambitious work, part autobiography, part economic treatise, a book far too detailed and far too long. Bingham set for himself a staggering intellectual task; he went straight at what is still perhaps the commanding problem of modern political economy— how to devise "free institutions that will be both efficient and democratic, that will serve both our individual and our social welfare." Unfortunately, his conclusions and the general level of his analysis are not up to the complexity of the issue. The argument is certainly more learned than his first naive excursions into economic theory. The breadth of his economic understanding is often quite impressive. His recommendations for change, however, amount to scarcely more than an intelligent reformulation of economic ideas already gaining acceptance among advanced liberals; they hardly comprise a new departure. Yet for the historian this lends the book another dimension. For in documenting with rare and vivid detail one intellectual's transition from socialist to capitalist collectivism, it describes an odyssey of disillusionment characteristic of the last years of the decade. It is, in addition, one of the most insightful statements of the new liberal planning consensus.

Man's Estate opens with a description of Bingham's decade-long search for an economic system capable of guaranteeing both abundance and freedom, a search that commenced in the Soviet Union during the turbulent beginnings of the Five Year Plan. Then, continuing his quest for economic understanding, Bingham takes the reader on a global tour of the major economic systems of the world, as he weighs and judges each, finally deriving from them an economic strategy for his own country.

Bingham came to economics with little theoretical knowledge, convinced, however, that capitalism "was incapable of producing the abundance that was physically possible." Armed by the evidence of Russia and the findings of Technocracy, he had urged the replacement of the capitalist market by a system of comprehensive collective planning. Later in the decade, Bingham tells us, he detected the fallacy of this economic analysis. The market could not, as he had thought, be eliminated, for the simple reason that America was still "a long way from conditions of absolute abundance." "Because of the shortage of certain raw materials," he writes in *Man's Estate*, "all goods and services still tend to be relatively scarce." This discovery forced Bingham back to the belief that the market was essential as "a natural automatic device for rationing anything scarce."[27]

Ironically, it was a group of socialist economists who convinced Bingham of the indispensability of the market. In late 1937 he discovered a school of radical economists who argued that the market "could and should be used in a planned economy." This body of economic speculation, known as "market socialism," first emerged in Europe from the challenge of a brilliant Austrian conservative, Ludwig von Mises.

Von Mises was a staunch economic libertarian, suspicious of all government economic intervention. In 1922, shaken by the Bolshevik revolution, he published a slashing critique of collectivism, *Socialism: An Economic and Sociological Analysis*. Rational economic calculation, he insisted, was impossible in the absence of free markets. Socialism, lacking a market arrangement, was incapable of efficiently allocating resources. Even if operated by dictatorial mandate, it would be horribly wasteful, lacking as it did the correct market prices on which to base decisions on what to produce and how to produce it.

Provoked by von Mises' challenge, socialist economists in Europe and the United States, among them Oskar Lange, R. L. Hall, Abba Lerner, Eduard Heimann, Carl Landauer, and Fred M. Taylor, set out to reexamine the question of distribution in a planned system. The result was market socialism, a theory of planning based on simulated markets. Unwittingly von Mises had inaugurated a revolution in socialist economics, forcing socialists to a more adequate understanding of the problems of production planning. For his contribution to socialist economics, Oskar Lange declared, "in front of every Socialist ministry of planning there should be a statue to Ludwig von Mises."[28]

The market socialists argued that socialism could utilize the market as an automatic control of economic activity instead of relying on comprehensive production planning, which, as von Mises had demonstrated, would be inefficient and almost impossible to administer intelligently. By removing certain structural rigidities in the economy, a socialist system could thus make the market work "where capitalism could not." As Bingham explained it, managers of state-owned enterprises could be compelled to fix their prices in much the same way as capitalist businessmen, and, like capitalism, supply and demand could be balanced by "a trial and error method of price fixing." Of course, social considerations would "override certain consumer wants and stimulate others." Market socialism would not be a replica of the laissez-faire market. But on the whole, its advocates envisioned an economy where consumers buying freely in the marketplace and workers freely seeking employment determined in the aggregate which goods and services were produced. Industry, agriculture, and the services would be required to anticipate consumer wants, not dictate them.[29]

Although he could not accept their entire body of theory, the market socialists had demonstrated to Bingham the feasibility of democratic planning in a market arrangement. Yet still the question that had given rise to his economic search remained unanswered. Why was purchasing power under capitalism inadequate to release the nation's virtually limitless productive capacity? Finally, and ironically, in the capitalist economics of John Maynard Keynes he found the explanation and answer to the paradox of poverty in the midst of plenty; and upon the monetary and fiscal policies of Keynes he constructed his program of capitalist rehabilitation.

Keynes blamed the worldwide depression on the persistent tendency of savings to outstrip opportunities for profitable investment. Alvin Hansen, his most astute American disciple, argued the case cogently. Capitalism, Hansen claimed, had entered into a stage of long-term stagnation. The leveling off of population growth, government restrictions on immigration, the maturing of established industries on the spectacular scale of the past, together signaled the end of the breakneck economic expansion of the previous one hundred years. Under a "matured capitalism" savings did not find their way readily into new investment, causing the total demand for goods and services to fall far short of the capacity of the economy to produce. The result: "secular stagnation" and chronic unemployment.

Private enterprise itself, Keynes and his followers concluded, was incapable of restoring economic equilibrium at prosperity levels, with full employment. Only the state could guarantee this by becoming the nation's chief investor. Specifically, this meant government sponsorship, encouragement, and maintenance of new private investment. The federal government would have to use its controls over currency and its extensive taxing and borrowing powers to maintain full production. On the other hand, public expenditure would take up the remaining slack in new investment. In the past government spending was visualized by most liberal economists as an emergency economic instrument—pumppriming—to be utilized until private enterprise was able to go ahead on its own. Keynes suggested that such government spending become permanent policy.

In the main, Keynes's program was actually quite conservative. It abjured nationalization and production planning, urging instead a comprehensive socialization of investment. Limited or "strategic" planning of critical economic functions would, he insisted, be sufficient to achieve balanced economic growth.[30] This was a program that matched perfectly Bingham's more restrained mood, and by the end of 1938 he had scrapped socialist planning for the economic gospel of Lord Keynes. The present government would merely have to "coordinate existing controls at strategic points . . . in a coherent policy," he confidently announced, for the dream of full prosperity to be made real. "Perhaps now for the first time we know enough to make our capitalist system work. Perhaps, in making it work, we shall find we have accomplished the much-disputed transition to 'socialism.'"[31]

Where once he had drawn a sharp distinction between capitalism and socialism, Bingham now argued in *Man's Estate* that the differences between the two systems were largely "verbal and unreal." New economic processes were being pioneered that failed to fit either of these old labels. Impelled by war, revolution, and depression, the entire industrial West was moving irreversibly toward a new economic collectivism that was neither pure capitalism nor pure socialism. The economic aspects of this new synthesis were broadly similar everywhere "in spite of different attitudes towards private property and private enterprise." Everywhere economic depression had forced governments to institute new public controls, and everywhere there was a tendency to combine these controls with certain capitalist practices. In Hitler's Germany an added catalyst was a massive armaments drive; and the result, a warfare economy neither capitalist nor socialist. The Germans retained the market, but the state exercised considerable economic power, using deficit spending and public works programs to erase unemployment. Even Russia's economy retained a number of capitalist features. While originally aiming toward a totally planned economy, the Soviets had been forced back to a variation of the market system on the heels of the financial bungling of the second Five Year Plan. But of all the emerging collectivist systems Bingham found America's most appealing. The New Deal had moved America toward a planned capitalism capable of achieving economic abundance with no sacrifice of democratic freedom. Its already established economic strategy—of government planning and deficit spending—simply had to be pressed more vigorously and "integrated into a single comprehensive assault on capitalist failure."[32] In the concluding section of *Man's Estate* Bingham offered such a program.

Its centerpiece was Ezekiel's industrial reorganization plan, which accepted, even welcomed, the economic supremacy of the corporation, demanding merely that the corporate giants be brought under tighter public supervision. Since a return to the old free market competition was impossible, and since most prices in a monopolistic system would be administered anyway, Bingham urged that prices be openly administered by publicly supervised monopolies or trade associations. "The answer to the destruction of the laissez-faire market," he wrote, "is to set up an artifically managed market to approximate the ideal free market." This structuralist integration of industry was to be combined with a Keynesian program of permanent government investment. Finally, a central planning agency would oversee the entire economy. But unlike those in Bingham's earlier planning proposals, this economic general staff was to serve in a purely advisory capacity.

This was, Bingham admitted, a limited program. While providing for greater government economic direction and enlarged labor and consumer representation on the industrial councils, like the old NRA it left industry largely in charge of its own house. With a mild reprimand and closer restrictions on his future conduct, the prodigal capitalist was thus restored, in Bingham's plan, to full prominence in national economic decision making. He as much as anyone would be responsible for creating the abundance that would not only assure the triumph of the middle class and a new security for American democracy, but would provide an inspiration for free men everywhere. In so far as [these economic] measures proved workable and were initiated," Bingham confidently concluded, "the morale of the now harassed world would begin to mount. . . . Give the democracies a cure for unemployment and economic insecurity, and the fear of totalitarian ideologies, whether communist or fascist, will begin to fade like a bad dream."[33]

But economic abundance, the bulwark of democracy, was not in itself enough. If the democracies were to win out against fascism and communism, they would have to demonstrate their ability to apply the public controls essential to prosperity in a wholly democratic manner. Somehow political democracy would have to be made compatible with collectivism. In *The Techniques of Democracy* Bingham suggested a way.

The Techniques grew out of Bingham's decade-long search for a creative reconciliation between community and individuality, a search given new urgency by the menace of totalitarianism. Now as a liberal New Dealer he gave fresh consideration to an issue he had first addressed as an aggressive young radical. Yet however dissimilar his specific recommendations, his approach to the problem and the broad outlines of his response reveal deep continuities in his social analysis. The liberal synthesis of *The Techniques of Democracy* rests firmly on the structural foundations of an earlier radical collectivism.

American democracy, Bingham argued, had reached a crisis point. Many of our most sacrosanct political institutions—the ballot, the representative assembly, the political party, and others—were incapable of meeting the problems of the emergent age. Framed for a decentralized republic of farmers and independent merchants, they had shown their inability to respond efficiently and expertly to the concerns of a centralized industrial state. Their failure, in large, explained the expansion of the national bureaucracy, as the administrative arm of government moved to appropriate functions and responsibilities long considered the exclusive prerogative of the legislature. Here was the political counterpart of the economic collectivism Bingham had described in *Man's Estate;* and here also he urged an unblinking acceptance of the new organizational situation. The enlarged powers of the administrative branch were, he explained, the result of the press of urgent domestic and international problems such as war, depression, and class division, problems that the legislature alone could not cope with. It would, therefore, be both impossible and unwise to arrest this drift toward collectivism; rather, the administrative state would have to be made more democratic.[34]

Bingham attributed the spread of fascism to the failure of the traditional democratic techniques. Administrative management, he noted, was the "ruling principle of the totalitarian regimes"; these despotisms had gained the advantage in Europe by their ability to move swiftly and resolutely not only in military matters, but in the organization of domestic affairs as well. In Weimar, Germany, the cranky political machinery of democracy had failed utterly to solve the problems of depression and national discord. When Hitler took power, he did not destroy democracy; it had already rotted away, the victim of its own debility. There, as in Italy, "the inadequacies of the traditional techniques of democracy left a great vacuum . . . [and] into this vacuum rushed the total state." Autocratically managed, centrally coordinated, and focused in action, the fascist collective gave ominous illustration to the perils of democratic ineptitude.

Yet while Bingham assailed the inadequacies of traditional democratic techniques, he did not urge their replacement; he insisted instead that they be strengthened and supplemented by techniques geared specifically to modern administrative management. Even here there was no need for wholly new procedures. Scientific management experts had already fashioned administrative methods for private industry that could be applied to government.

The founder of scientific management was, of course, Frederick Winslow Taylor, whose theories had become a kind of bureaucratic bible to countless corporate managers seeking increased worker productivity. Implicit in Taylor's approach, however, was a cold disregard for the human attributes of the worker that Bingham found repellent. The industrial worker of Taylor's scheme, Bingham explained, was simply a means to a higher pecuniary end—enlarged output and higher profits—the idea being to make his job so rudimentary in execution that even the most mindless brute could execute it effectively. Yet Bingham found something democratically salvageable in Taylor's work. Taylor, he wrote, "realized that efficiency, particularly in the organized group, depends on consent and voluntary cooperation." Many of his disciples, men like Ordway Tead, Harlow Person, and Morris L. Cooke were, in fact, presently attempting to extend the democratic implications of his theories and to apply the science of efficient administration to the problems of democratic plant management. Inspired by their designs, enlightened business executives, often in cooperation with trade unions, were seeking ways to eliminate tedious, repetitive tasks and to restore to every worker "a sense of expressing himself in a vocation." Increasingly the modern manager was discovering that "good management is democratic management." Applied to public administration, these same techniques promised an invigorated democracy.

The growing hegemony of the expert in public administration made it all the more imperative that these techniques be extended to government. Decisions in modern industrial states were assuming a technical nature that defied popular understanding, giving expert bureaucrats dangerous powers for public control. If America was to avoid the example of Soviet Russia and Nazi Germany, institutional procedures would have to be devised to involve citizens more actively in decision making. Here also Bingham saw scientific management as the answer. "Modern scientific management is discovering new efficiencies in the small plant, in the distribution of authority, in reducing administrative tasks to the limitations of normal human beings." Just as the corporation had broken down administration into manageable units, so modern government, he argued, must diffuse its overwhelming powers and responsibilities. Centralization, coordination, and integration were imperatives of the new industrial state, but Bingham expressed the hope that the democracy of the future would provide for units of social action small enough to be manageable by ordinary citizens.[35]

In design, *The Techniques* was a bold and arresting book; it went straight at a problem of continuing concern to our age. Yet when Bingham moved from the general to the particular, from a discerning analysis of the need for democratic decentralization to the specifics of such a program, the results proved disappointing. Aware of the need to democratize administration without impairing its effectiveness as an agent of social betterment, he nevertheless recommended techniques that were hardly equal to the task. Most of the administrative methods proposed—the semi-autonomous corporation, the congressional investigating committee, interest group representation on government planning boards, strict personal guidelines for the issuance of administrative rulings in the courts—were already in operation at the state and federal level. Bingham simply urged their wider application.[36] Fearful of the dislocations that might result from massive institutional reconstruction, Bingham hesitated to prescribe the kind of imaginative administrative reorganization essential to the problem he had so compellingly described.

The capitalist corporativism Bingham suggested in *Man's Estate* and *The Techniques of Democracy*, based on an equilibrium of organized power and mediated by a neutral state, was designed to resolve conflict through official arbitration. It would be government's responsibility to insure an equitable distribution of its favors and to shore up the power of the weaker consumer groups, making them consequential countervailing forces to the more strongly established business, labor, and big farm lobbies. In this way all major interests would gain a fair hearing at the federal level; and just as importantly, the organized interest groups, with roots extending back to the local level, would become important agencies of citizen participation.[37] "The twentieth century problem," Bingham concluded, "is one of administration and management, rather than, as the Marxists thought, of ownership and political power. If every individual and group interest is given representation through responsible organization, society can learn to plan and still be free."[38] By 1940 Bingham had thus largely reduced the problems of social justice and economic democracy to the structural question of gaining the proper representation on an administrative board.

Bingham expressed surprisingly little fear that the corporation would achieve dominance under his plan. The corporation, he sanguinely argued, was already so hedged in by government and labor restrictions as to make it "almost a public agency." This plan would strengthen those restrictions. "There is no reason to fear monopoly, 'trusts,' cartels, trade associations, the 'self-government' of whole industries," he wrote, "so long as they are subject to constant public scrutiny and are strictly accountable for all they do."[39] Why nationalize the corporation when it is easier to monitor its policies in the public interest? In this way the benefits of socialism could be had without socialism. Bingham even went so far as to argue that his plan really amounted to socialism. Socialism had always meant, for him, the attainment of planned abundance, democracy, and a fuller individuality. And did not this pattern, Bingham asked, guarantee all of these?

Bingham was not alone in this outlook. By the end of the decade a number of former radical collectivists were urging a controlled capitalism similar to his. In an article proposing a new industrial design, Lewis Corey, the former Marxist, expressed what was fast becoming the disillusioned radicals' revised statement of socialism. "Socialism," Corey wrote, ". . . never meant more than the abolition of capitalist privilege and power, the planning of production for economic balance and plenty, and greater democracy and freedom. The economic pluralism I propose is socialism because it promotes greater democracy and freedom where absolute collectivism destroys them."[40] The programs of Bingham and Corey, so strikingly akin in argument and design, reveal as much about the limitations of 1930s collectivist thought as they do about the theoretical poverty that had spread across the entire American Left in these years. Earlier in the decade radical and liberal collectivists had enthusiastically accepted the emergent industrial order, urging that this collectivism be harnessed to generous ideals. By the end of the decade, however, most of these once fervent insurgents found the new collective order more difficult to master than they had anticipated. The result was not despair but diminished expectations; not acquiescence but accommodation. The general shape of the emergent economic order seemed fixed; they would merely seek to influence its immediate social priorities.

Ironically, by shifting his emphasis from socialism and third party politics to administrative management Bingham opened himself to precisely the kind of criticism he and other *Common Sense* radicals had directed at the early New Dealers. When in 1933 Rexford Tugwell proposed a publicly controlled economic integration much like the program of *The Techniques*, Paul Douglas, then a third party advocate, argued that the problem with such a program of legalized cartels lay in its assumption that there was "a sufficiently strong and independent force outside of capitalism which can control it. At the moment," Douglas continued, America had a "progressive" in the White House and a business community in the state of severe "despair." But if prosperity should return, capitalism would once again move to throw off any effective control, and the question would arise whether Roosevelt liberalism would be strong enough to check it. If America could not even regulate its public utilities in the consumer interest, he warned, how could it expect "to regulate industry as a whole?" Douglas proposed as the only effective answer to the existing might of the corporation the "organization of those who are at present weak and who need to acquire that which the world respects, namely, power." Trade unions and farmers' cooperatives were not enough. "The urban and rural workers of hand and brain need a strong party of their own." To rely on the good will of industry or the promises of New Dealers was the sheerest naiveté.[41]

There were other equally pronounced changes in Bingham's emphasis and approach. Where earlier he had excoriated organized labor for supporting corporate capitalism, now he waxed euphoric over the blossoming "partnership between management and labor," claiming that the exploitive "master-servant relation" in business was "being replaced by a concept of cooperation between specialists—specialists in management on the one hand and specialists in various technical and mechanical skills on the other."[42] Actually, this was not a complete reversal. Even as a radical Bingham had evinced a stubborn faith in the reforming tendencies of the middle class managers and technicians, anticipating that their concern for efficiency and productivity, for making goods rather than profits, would hasten the movement to a full production-for-use system. Now in *The Techniques* Bingham concluded that the functional hegemony of the managers made unnecessary the transition to socialism. Under their informed direction capitalism could be sufficiently humanized. The separation of ownership from control in the corporation and the rise of the managers thus symbolized to Bingham the approach of a new era in the conduct of business and public policy.

Not all critics shared Bingham's hopeful assessment of the managers. In a classic work, *The Managerial Revolution: What Is Happening in the World* (1941), James Burnham, the once zealous Trotskyite, assailed the root assumptions of the liberal collectivists and in the process laid down a stern challenge to the controlling thesis of *The Techniques.* Burnham did not deny the universal drift toward collectivism; but his was a dark prophecy of its authoritarian consequences. This irreversible institutional revolution he judged the principal threat to practicing democracy in the West.

Democracy, Burnham claimed, thrived best in a fragile institutional setting of competing autonomous interests; its survival hinged on a pattern of conflict in which no single interest or institutional force "so outdistanced the others that it could absorb, crush or neutralize them." Under the old individualistic capitalism big business was admittedly the preponderant social force. But its power was effectively checked or balanced by other institutional forces such as the church, labor, and the state. In the emerging "managerial society," however, a society characterized by "state control and . . . ownership of the principal means of production, and by a ruling or dominant class . . . of managerial and administrative groups, working together with politicians and military men," the state threatened to absorb, or in some cases already had absorbed, "all the organized social forces," leaving no effective rivals to its power. This tendency was most conspicuously evident in Germany and the Soviet Union; but America under the New Deal also appeared headed for the bloodless rule of the expert administrator, for the gray conformity and engineered efficiency of the total state. Given this implacable universal movement toward state collectivism, democracy, Burnham grimly concluded, appeared to be "on its way out, for the next historical period at least."[43]

Burnham's critique of collectivism would soon lead him to the extreme right, to a demand for an unfettered competitive capitalism. But in the *Managerial Revolution,* a book that offered no alternatives and little hope for the future, he brilliantly identified some of the more menacing implications of the coming collectivism.

Bingham and Burnham were thus in agreement on the emerging outlines of the collectivist revolution; both saw power in the modern state shifting from legislation to administration, from politicians to bureaucrats. But whereas Burnham saw the managers evolving into a self-serving administrative elite, and the state, under their direction, swallowing up all competing social forces, Bingham held that the administrative process involved the same adjustment of conflicting interests that was the health of parliamentary democracy and was subject to the same organized citizen pressures as the legislative process. The managerial revolution, in his view, was fully compatible with the extension of human freedoms. The need was simply for new methods of popular control, new methods of group planning, and new methods of functional representation. In a word, scientific management.

Bingham obviously miscalculated both the beneficence of the managers and the democratic possibilities of Taylorism. The separation of ownership from control in the corporation has not brought with it a markedly less acquisitive and more benign capitalism. The professional managers still identify with the corporation as their own, whether they hold stock in it or not. And the race for profits continues. "So complete is the identification of the managers with the interests of the owners," writes Loren Baritz in *The Servants of Power,* "that the profit motive operates as always. Because of their own loyalties the managers . . . cannot be distinguished from the earlier owner-managers."[44]

Nor has the widespread adoption of scientific management by corporate executives implied an aroused democratic consciousness on their part. Corporations, to be certain, began after World War 1 to utilize with increasing frequency behavioral techniques aimed at improving labor-management relations and enhancing job satisfaction. Bingham interpreted this as a harbinger of a more enlightened business order. But as Baritz and others have shown, management began to evince concern for worker satisfaction only when it became apparent "that such attention would pay"; only, in other words, when it became convinced that harmonious labor relations spelled higher productivity and higher profits. Democratic personnel techniques were thus grudgingly adopted by management, not out of heightened compassion for the workers' well-being, but out of a pecuniary concern for business efficiency. Scientific management techniques also placed in management's hands enormously sophisticated tools for employee control. The most frightening aspect of this new and in some ways more insidious discipline is that the worker is often blind to the very "fact of manipulation."[45]

But perhaps the commanding fallacy of Bingham's argument resides in its leading premise: that management is destined to be the next ruling class. As Bingham wrote in 1941, "The 'managerial revolution' as popularized by James Burnham represents the dominance of the function of management and a resultant shift in social and political dominance" away from the old big property capitalists to a new elite class of professional executives.[46] Yet while it is true that the managers have replaced the old captains of industry as the pivotal figures in modern capitalism, this has not amounted to a "managerial revolution," with big management replacing big capitalists as a new ruling class. Property, contrary to Bingham, remains the critical determinant of economic power. C. Wright Mills put the issue well:

> While owner and manager are no longer the same person, the manager has not expropriated the owner, nor has the power of propertied enterprise over workers and markets declined. Power has not been split from property; rather the power of property is more concentrated than is its ownership..... Under the owners of property a huge and complex bureaucracy of business and industry has come into existence. But . . . the legitimate access to the position of authority from which these bureaucracies are directed, is the right of property ownership.[47]

The argument for a "managerial revolution" also rests on the dubious assumption that political supremacy directly follows economic indispensability; that the class that is indispensably fulfilling the major function of society will become the next ruling class. But "if 'indispensability' were decisive," as Max Weber pointed out long ago, "then where slave labor prevailed and freemen usually abhor work as a dishonor, the 'indispensable' slaves ought to have held the positions of power, for they were at least as indispensable as [bureaucratic] officials and proletarians are today."

Yet while Bingham might have misgauged the beneficence and power of the new managers, he never condoned the use of scientific management as an instrument of worker discipline. His aims continued to be the workers' creative liberation and the achievement of a more responsive democracy. Unfortunately the collapse of his new party movement drove him to an administrative liberalism incapable of meeting the gathering challenges to individuality and freedom posed by the very collectivist revolution he proclaimed as the promise of democracy.

Not all independent radicals went the way of Bingham. John Dewey, for one, failed to see capitalist collectivism as the answer to the problem of industrial democracy. Appraising the New Deal in 1939, Dewey found its accomplishments at best "palliative." "The ultimate problem of production," he wrote, "is the production of human beings," the production of free and vividly alive citizens, the realization through social cooperation of a fuller and more creative individuality. "It is by this standard that the present system stands condemned."[49] Yet unfortunately Dewey's was more a plea than a clear program for human revitalization. And there were by this time precious few radicals prepared to give theoretical form and inspired political direction to the approach and social end he suggested.

Thus by the end of the decade the surging confidence with which insurgent intellectuals had confronted the issues of social democracy had given way to a new hesitancy and restraint. Few abandoned reform entirely. But the nature of the insurgent commitment had changed decisively. The genial certainty that science and the machine could usher in the good life remained a staple of the sobered social analysis of Bingham and other liberal collectivists. But having failed to alter significantly the emerging capitalist collectivism, most independent progressives settled down to an uneasy accommodation with it. The liberal intellectual's drift to pluralism (an ideology describing and sanctioning interest group capitalism) was underway, a movement powerfully catalyzed by the specter of totalitarianism. European totalitarianism, more than any other development, shaped the character of American social thought in these years, driving even the most resolute collectivists to a sharpened appreciation of the dangers of centralized authority. A pluralistic government of countervailing interest blocs seemed to many the only reasonable alternative to a bankrupt and impossible laissez-faire on the right and a rigidly authoritarian collectivism on the left.

9

WAR AND THE INTELLECTUALS
The Drift to the Vital Center

European totalitarianism influenced American progressive opinion in yet another significant way. The implacable territorial advance of fascism after 1935 provoked a furious foreign policy controversy among Leftist intellectuals, a dispute that broadened into a full-scale ideological debate over the historic meaning and future direction of American liberalism. Out of this clash of ideas would emerge a new style of liberalism—cautious, tough-minded, and resolutely anti-totalitarian—a reform posture and orientation that, when tied to the kind of interest-group pluralism Bingham recommended in *Man's Estate,* would become the reigning creed of the post–World War 2 democratic Left. The philosophic underpinnings of what some would later call "cold war liberalism" are clearly apparent in the foreign policy controversy that split the insurgent community in the last years of the 1930s.

When Mussolini stormed into Ethiopia in October, 1935, inaugurating a decade of fascist plunder, diplomatic crisis, and world war, most American progressives were proclaiming a policy of strict neutrality in foreign affairs. Memories of the blood and disillusionment of World War 1 haunted the Left, encouraging the view that America's interests were best served by remaining apart from Europe's troubles and directing our energies to the achievement of social justice at home. Disarmament, peace, and non-interventionism were the marching slogans of the American Left in the post-Versailles years. The economic depression only reinforced this determination to break clear of foreign entanglements. Democracy and peace, it was claimed, could best be secured by attacking the economic causes of war.

By 1938, however, this tight non-interventionist consensus had been blasted beyond repair, and the American Left stood divided into two hostile camps, irrevocably at odds over the question of a proper American response to fascist expansion. One group of independent progressives, among them Lewis Mumford, Reinhold Niebuhr, Waldo Frank, and Archibald MacLeish, along with the American Communist Party and its most steadfast fellow travelers, demanded strong collective security measures against Germany and Italy. World democracy, they insisted, could be preserved only by raising a diplomatic and military alliance that would include the United States. War itself, some collective security enthusiasts claimed, might be the sole effective deterent to fascist intransigence. Others on the American Left, including Bingham, Rodman, Thomas Amlie, John T. Flynn, Stuart Chase, Charles Beard, C. Hartley Grattan, and Oswald Garrison Villard vehemently disagreed. American participation in a coalition against fascism would, they maintained, bind the nation's vital interests to the immediate foreign policy aims of France, Great Britain, and the Soviet Union. The war that would result from the mobilization of such an alliance, moreover, would not be a morally clearcut struggle between freedom and totalitarianism, for the partners to that alliance shared in the sins of fascism. The Soviet Union, most of these unilateralists argued, was as harshly dictatorial a regime as Nazi Germany while both France and Great Britain boasted sprawling colonial empires maintained by racist exploitation. If there were a European war, it would be these imperial possessions, not the sacred principles of democracy, that they would be fighting to preserve. Nor, the non-interventionists insisted, did Hitler and Mussolini pose a direct military threat to the United States. The principal menace to American democracy, in their estimation, was war itself. A war to the death with fascism would bring in its wake a colossal home front mobilization, sweeping abridgments of democratic freedoms and a dangerous expansion of the national bureaucracy. War would also kill a promising but still unfulfilled movement for social justice at home; here the legacy of World War 1 remained strongly compelling. It was this vigilant opposition to war and its fearful consequences that united the Leftist critics of collective security. Up until 1941 *Common Sense* remained the most determined journalistic spokesman for their position.

These non-interventionists, however, were hardly a homogeneous group. They were not united by a common ideological commitment nor even by an identical foreign policy stance. While none among them advocated a total American disengagement from world affairs, most were "unilateralists," standing firm, as Manfred Jonas has shown, for a policy of independence in foreign affairs "which would leave the United States free at all times to act according to the dictates of national self-interest."[1] Their aim was to steer clear of all entangling diplomatic alliances. Yet several non-interventionists, Bingham most prominent among them, went beyond this unilateralism in urging a continuing American involvement in world problems. While committed to neutrality and military non-engagement, Bingham stressed America's responsibility to work actively for international peace and to aid in the creation of a new parliament of nations. His was a curious third position in the foreign policy controversy of the late 1930s, combining the internationalist concern of the collective security liberals with the neutralist sentiments of the unilateralists. Unalterably opposed to America's participation in a diplomatic alliance against fascism, he was nonetheless disturbed by the unilateralists' failure to frame a positive peace policy. His writings after 1935 join a determination to keep America neutral with an equal emphasis on this country's responsibility to wage a diplomatic campaign for peace and world government. A spirited proponent of neutrality, he remained also a determined internationalist.

The outbreak of the Spanish Civil War in the summer of 1936 set off the first major controversy on the Left over the issue of American neutrality. Mussolini's invasion of Ethiopia one year earlier had provoked outrage in the leftist press, but there had been no concerted effort by liberals and independent radicals to jettison the principles of American neutrality. The Spanish struggle invoked stronger emotions. Here in the debate on Spain the issues that would split the American Left for the next five years were first given full and heated expression.

In July, 1936, the armed forces of Spain, led by General Francisco Franco and backed by the Church and the more powerful landowners, rose up against the Popular Front government that had been elected in February, 1936. Official American reaction to the civil war was swift and uncompromisingly isolationist. President Roosevelt imposed a moral embargo on the sale of arms and munitions to Spain and asked Congress to tighten the neutrality statute of 1935 by embargoing shipments of military material to nations engaged in civil war. In January, 1937, Congress complied, placing a total embargo on the shipment of arms and munitions to Spanish ports.

No sooner had the embargo been imposed than it was denounced by the Left as a manifestly unneutral act, a measure that aided Franco, who was receiving considerable support from Germany and Italy, while leaving the Loyalists, who had only limited arms support from Russia, fearfully vulnerable. From the opening of the civil war there had been overwhelming Leftist support for American aid to the Loyalists. The announcement from Moscow in the summer of 1935 of an international Popular Front against fascism had already swung the Communist Party to a resolute policy of collective security. Yet while the Communists proclaimed the Spanish conflict as preeminently a struggle between fascism and socialism, independent Leftists like Mumford, MacLeish, Waldo Frank, and Van Wyck Brooks saw it as a struggle for civilization itself. Unless the fascist challenge were stopped in Spain, it would spread elsewhere, menacing the entire free world. We would do well to remember, Mumford wrote to his friend Brooks, "that Berlin is closer to New York than Boston was a century ago."[2]

Here, if ever, was a crusade for the right and the good. On the one side stood democracy, socialism, progress, and revolutionary heroism; on the other, fascism, repression, militarism, and clericalism. To men like Mumford the issue could not have been more clearcut. Seen this way, how could the cause of the beleaguered Loyalists be denied?

Not all American progressives, of course, saw the Spanish conflict this way. While morally and ideologically sympathetic to the Loyalists, Bingham and *Common Sense* strongly supported the embargo. In "War Mongering on the Left," a series of articles that appeared in the spring and early summer of 1937, at the height of the controversy over Spain, Bingham assembled a piercing indictment of the interventionist-Popular Front position, outlining a foreign policy platform his magazine would adhere to until the fall of France in June, 1940.

Bingham judged it essential that Americans gain an accurate understanding of the real issues involved in Spain; for this localized conflict could, he believed, become the bloody rehearsal for a world war that would eventually involve the United States. If America was to avoid involvement in another foreign war, it would have to coolly determine whether the national interest was in any vital way bound up with the courageous stand of the Spanish Republicans. Unfortunately, the passion-charged intensity of the debate on Spain made such rational calculation well-nigh impossible. Bingham compared the hysteria aroused by the Spanish issue with the fevered war atmosphere of 1917. Once more, he wrote, America was being prepared for a "slaughter" and "once more it will be a war to make the world safe for democracy." Only this time it was not profiteering bankers and munitions makers who were heading the drive for war, but the very same liberal and radical intellectuals who had condemned the earlier intervention as a monstrous mistake.

To see the Spanish struggle as they did—as an apocalyptic contest between freedom and fascism—was, however, to miss its larger significance and historic meaning. In its international aspects, the war, Bingham admitted, *was* a conflict between two powerful idea systems. But the contending factions were not democracy and fascism, as the interventionists insisted. Rather, they were communism and fascism; and no matter who the victor, democracy would suffer. Bingham depicted all three of the major powers involved in Spain—Russia, Germany, and Italy—as ruthlessly authoritarian dictatorships. While he did admit to certain important qualitative differences between Soviet Communism and fascism, principally Russia's commitment to international peace and economic equality, he insisted that these differences were not worth fighting for. Russia's progress toward a workers' commonwealth was "too halting, too compromised with the Fascist features of dictatorship . . . to give any assurance of a swift and certain arrival." Germany, on the other hand, had made enough progress toward achieving economic prosperity "to make one hesitant about condemning her to perdition." In addition, Bingham maintained that fascist territorial designs were limited rather than global, that they in no way threatened the major democracies—France, England, and the United States. Fascist aggression was fueled by economic urgency, by a driving need for natural resources essential for self-sufficiency. Once Italy and Germany had carved out spheres of economic influence in the Mediterranean and Central Europe, their appetite for conquest would be sated. Bingham even saw hope for the free world in all this. With an adequate flow of economic materials assured by conquest, the fascist powers could redouble their assault on poverty and unemployment, the sources of war and dictatorship. And with the achievement of full prosperity might come a softening of the repression. Just as economic scarcity had spawned fascism, so abundance might prove to be its most powerful antidote.

So the war in Spain, far from being a Manichean standoff between fascism and freedom, was actually a contest between totalitarian systems "too much alike . . . to make certain that a war between them will have bearing on the issues of democracy." Even if the conflict broadened into a European war involving England and France, democracy would not be the issue. Imperial powers, England and France would be fighting to protect their colonial empires and economic spheres of influence. "Are we interested," Bingham asked, "in getting killed so that the 'satisfied' imperial powers may keep their gains from the aggression of the unsatisfied powers?" In waging such an illusory war for democracy, moreover, America would be forced to arm to the teeth, disciplining its resources and its people in a home front mobilization of awesome magnitude. Germany and Italy, armed for conquest, are "prototypes," Bingham warned, "of what we shall all become in the next war."

Bingham concluded "War Mongering on the Left" with a plea for a complete and vigilant American neutrality. Yet while he steadfastly opposed war shipments to the Loyalists, he gave them his full moral support, even urging that American supporters of the Loyalists go to Spain and fight for the Republic if necessary. But he remained adamant against an official American involvement, a course of action he was certain would provoke a wider war.[3]

The foreign policy argument of "War Mongering on the Left" proceeded directly from Bingham's interpretation of the nature and internal dynamics of fascism, an interpretation sharply at variance with the Marxian analysis widely accepted on the Left. Most Marxists saw fascism as a futile effort to shore up a moribund profit system through state planning and collective discipline. Unable themselves to arrest economic decline, powerful capitalists turned in desperation to the fascists to save themselves from a workers' upheaval. Utilizing state planning and controls, the fascists and their capitalist cohorts hoped to stave off economic collapse. But no amount of government intervention, the Marxists claimed, could halt capitalism's inexorable downslide. Thus as the economy deteriorated and public dissatisfaction reached fever pitch, fascist governments would be impelled toward an aggressive imperial expansion that would eventuate in war. Finally, shaken by war abroad and economic depression at home, fascism would succumb to revolution, yielding eventually to a classless workers' state.[4] It is no wonder that the Marxists urged a resolute policy of collective security. By blocking fascism's furious outer advance such a diplomatic coalition would hasten the appearance of the internal economic preconditions requisite to its overthrow.

Bingham denounced this interpretation of fascism as both dangerous and distorted. By egregiously miscalculating the character and future direction of fascist development, it could, he argued, draw the United States into a war against an enemy that posed no immediate threat to its security or vital interests. Fascism was not simply a form of capitalism in decline. Neither pure capitalism nor pure socialism, it represented instead a possible "third way" to a full production-for-use economy. Anticipating the directing argument of *Man's Estate*, Bingham located certain constructive features in fascist economic development which gave promise of driving it in a more humane direction. Chief among these were its spending and planning policies, strategies admittedly concentrated for war, but which were nonetheless leaving the state, not private capital, the dominant repository of economic power.[5]

As early as 1935 Bingham had hinted that Germany might "develop into a true cooperative and classless society." By 1938 he was more strongly convinced of this. Fascism, he now wrote, had moved well beyond the "frozen" economics of state capitalism to a dynamic appreciation of the importance of collective planning as a way to maximize production. Yet while military preparedness might be moving fascism toward full socialism, Bingham refused to sanction this as an economic strategy. As with the Soviet Union, he distinguished between the methods employed and the end in sight. ". . . What a pitiful confession of the failure of intelligent statesmanship it is," he wrote in 1935, "when a nation must blunder by an accidental back-door path through near-barbarism into an intelligent and humane social order!"[6]

Throughout the late 1930s Bingham continued to underscore the positive features of fascist development. Even after Hitler forced the Anschluss with Austria and seized the Sudeten territory from Czechoslovakia in September, 1938, he continued to insist that the "main trend of fascism" was toward "self-contained nationalism or autarchy." Germany, Italy, and Japan were, he argued, "have-not" nations prevented from their fair share of the earth's resources by an unjust international status quo dominated by British and French imperialism and given official sanction at Versailles. Until this status quo were adjusted to the interests and pressing needs of the Axis powers, until, in other words, these nations were guaranteed access to the economic materials essential to autarchy, they would continue their territorial offensive.[7]

Bingham's interpretation of fascism thus led straight to a policy of diplomatic appeasement. Since the "have-not" nations would fight to gain economic advantages denied them by the treaty of Versailles, war could be avoided only by conceding these claims voluntarily. For Italy this meant a "new Roman Empire" in the Mediterranean; for Germany, hegemony in central and southeastern Europe, including the Balkans; and for Japan, economic dominance in southeast Asia and possibly the acquisition of all of China. While sober judgment would hardly call these "limited concessions," Bingham urged them as a reasonable ransom for peace.[8] Accordingly, after the Munich settlement (which he applauded as a courageous gesture for peace) Bingham called for a series of international peace conferences to begin to negotiate "a planned and equitable utilization of the world's scarce resources." At these conferences he proposed that the Axis nations be guaranteed access to the finished goods and raw materials essential to their economies and be given the go-ahead to expand into the "limited" spheres of influence they had already marked out for themselves.[9]

Bingham's peace program rested on the dubious proposition that Axis aggression would cease once an equitable balance of economic power was secured. Here, at least, he exhibited incredible naiveté. His analysis showed almost no appreciation of the imperial and psychopathic aspects of the fascist dynamic. To him, it was merely a rational calculation of economic survival that powered Axis aggression. Peace, from this sanguine perspective, turned on the willingness of the "have" nations to cede the territories coveted by the Fascists. Bingham insisted further that the United States take the initiative in promoting this new international design by calling a series of peace conferences to settle the claims of the Axis powers.[10]

There is no foundation, then, to the claim that Bingham was an "isolationist" before 1939.[11] Even when war finally broke over Europe in September, 1939, he continued to insist upon America's international responsibilities. Conceding now that some United States economic aid to France and England was inevitable, he urged that Roosevelt tie such aid to the Allies' acceptance of a positive American peace initiative.[12] In this way America would be able to use its considerable economic leverage to end the killing and clear the ground for a new international system. As the centerpiece of such a peace proposal, Bingham suggested a plan for the establishment immediately after the war of a federation of European nations, an organization that would hopefully serve as a harbinger for an eventual world federation of nations. In 1940 he gave concrete expression to his plan in *The United States of Europe*.

The war, Bingham argued, had underscored the need for a new international order, one firmly based upon "cooperation rather than clawing competition between sovereign states." The answer, however, was not a revivification of the League of Nations; for under the League nations retained their sovereignty intact, making the larger international authority powerless to enforce its will against the stronger member states. "Only a federation in which the constituent states surrender certain of their powers to a federal government can hope to achieve stability." Bingham realized that such a world government was impossible in the immediate future, but he recommended that a constructive beginning be made in Europe, where there was already active interest in a continental federation.[13]

Bingham proposed a federation embracing both the democracies and the dictatorships. The Allies, he was certain, would be unable to win a decisive military victory over Germany and Italy. To invite these states into the federation, therefore, would be merely a realistic concession to an unfortunate international reality. Initially then there could be no universal guarantee of democratic institutions in the member states. All Bingham asked was that Germany and Italy agree to the right of free migration for all minorities. The key to the entire proposal, however, was the willingness of the constituent states to surrender certain of their sovereignty to a European government organized along the lines of the American federal system. Member states would be permitted to keep their existing governmental institutions, but Europe's military forces, its foreign policy, and much of its economic life would come under the control of the new federal body. To guarantee its authority, the European government would require all member nations to disarm to an agreed-upon ratio, under the continuing supervision of a "European Arms Control Commission." Only small armies for local police action would be permitted.

To complement the political union, Bingham suggested a continental economic order akin to the plan he had framed for the United States in *Man's Estate.* Cartels had already come to dominate much of Europe's economic life; Bingham simply recommended that these cartels be consolidated on a pan-European basis (many of them already were) and placed under stricter public supervision. As a way of insuring industrial democracy, organized labor and a revitalized consumer movement would be made partners in the new corporativist order. Here was the Ezekiel plan applied to Europe; its aim—a continental collectivism programmed toward full abundance. But the solution to the economic problem, Bingham knew, demanded a set of institutions with a wider geographical base than regions or continents. Worldwide economic machinery and cooperation were essential. The beginnings of such machinery already existed, he explained, in organizations like the Bank of International Settlements, which could be developed into a true world central bank. The task was simply to expand these kinds of institutions and supplement them with new agencies to supervise and integrate international investment and trade and to assure the conservation and equitable distribution of the world's scarce resources. Eventually these economic bodies would develop political counterparts, and a world government would emerge. In the meantime Bingham was willing to accept much of the world as it was, including Hitler and Mussolini.[14]

Yet how would this new international order be built? What were the possibilities for ending the war and achieving European integration? Bingham was convinced that an overwhelming victory by either side, especially Germany, would kill all possibilities for international cooperation, as the victor would surely impose a harsh peace. It would be Versailles all over again. The most favorable basis for a new international order, he argued, would be a military stalemate and a negotiated "peace without victory." And the United States could contribute to such a settlement by remaining at least technically neutral and providing sufficient economic aid to the allies to prevent a fascist victory.[15]

This represented a subtle yet important shift in Bingham's foreign policy position. After the fall of France in June, 1940, he began to back American economic aid to the allies, persuaded now that without such aid England would fall. He even hinted in *The United States of Europe* that America *should* intervene militarily if the Allies were threatened with defeat. In the meantime he urged that Roosevelt continue to press for a negotiated peace, hoping that Hitler could be drawn to the negotiating table by the realization that America would never allow Germany a total victory.[16]

Applied to another adversary, these proposals might have seemed reasonable. But there was a demonic dynamic to Nazi aggression that Bingham never fully discerned. Hitler's fanatical unwillingness to stop short of all-out victory, his refusal to adhere to any of the established rules of international behavior, rendered Bingham's peace program hopelessly utopian. Its very rationality, its very insistence upon fascism's openness to reason and diplomatic compromise, was its outstanding fallacy.

Bingham's insistence upon fascism's economic foundations, its limited territorial designs, and its potentially constructive social direction set him off sharply from convinced internationalists like Lewis Mumford, Waldo Frank, and Archibald MacLeish. These "liberal traditionalists," as R. Alan Lawson has called them,[17] associated themselves with a universal moral heritage extending back to the classical cultures and transcending languages and continents. However they described this sustaining creed—Frank called it "the Great Tradition"; MacLeish, "the common culture of the West"; and Mumford, "ideal liberalism" —all saw it imperiled by fascism, and all assailed their fellow liberals for failing to defend it aggressively. The struggle in Europe, Waldo Frank wrote in 1940, is part of a world "revolution," a war to preserve humanity's shared ideals; and, like it or not, "we are in it," for our American culture and tradition were indissolubly part of this unified human "intuition."[18]

In May, 1940, with France about to fall to Hitler, Archibald MacLeish unleashed in the *Nation* what stands as perhaps the most famous attack on the non-interventionist intellectuals. This was the stinging essay "The Irresponsibles," in which he attacked his fellow liberal writers for advising a cowardly neutrality in the face of a monstrous threat to "the common culture of the West."[19] Mumford and Frank, however, took the argument of "The Irresponsibles" much further, marshaling a blistering indictment of pragmatic rationalism, a philosophic standard they believed responsible for the failure of the liberals to react decisively to fascism. Frank gave extended expression to his critique of pragmatism and liberal isolationism in two impassioned pieces, "Our Guilt in Fascism" and *Chart for Rough Water.*[20] But it was Mumford who penned the most encompassing challenge to the philosophy and foreign policy of Bingham and the liberal non-interventionists.

Earlier in the decade Mumford had written for *Common Sense* and had supported its program of production-for-use. Even then, however, there were important differences in the kind of future he and Bingham looked toward, as well as in the strategies they recommended for its attainment, differences in temperament and orientation which go far toward explaining their later and contrasting responses to fascism. And the sources of these differences, as we have seen, lay in their varying conceptions of the proper role and function of technology and material plenty as instruments of human renewal.

Bingham, of course, had a sublime faith in the regenerative powers of science and social engineering. An equitably distributed abundance and a new cooperative democracy would, he was certain, guarantee a radical spiritual revolution. Conversely, a pernicious and unjust social structure explained the malicious impulses of men and nations. Hence his interpretation of the origins of fascism, and his suggestion that fascism be given time to evolve a stable economic collectivism that might soften the dictatorship and sate its appetite for conquest.

Mumford, on the other hand, saw this faith in social engineering as the capital fallacy of both pragmatic liberalism and socialism. Structural change, while essential, would have to be preceded and informed by a transformation in the "psychological potentials" of men, otherwise, he argued, all that the reformers would have achieved by their institutional engineering was a system "uncomfortably like the system" they had "partly replaced."[21] The spread of European totalitarianism deepened Mumford's suspicions of economic planning as a social panacea. Planning divorced from an absorbing commitment to human values seemed to lead straight to the murderous coercions of Stalin and Hitler. It was this same failure to stand for clear values, this failure to enunciate a set of human ideals beyond the material and the rational, that explained, in his view, the pragmatic liberals' failure to stand up to fascism.

Mumford had been a critic of non-interventionism since the Loyalist embargo, urging American participation in an alliance against the fascists. By far his sharpest attack on the liberal non-interventionists, however, came in a 1940 *New Republic* piece, "The Corruption of Liberalism," which formed the basis of *Faith for Living,* a book he referred to as his "private Blitzkrieg."[22]

Once a proud and powerfully constructive reforming creed, liberalism, in the hands of torpid non-interventionists like Bingham, Chase, Dewey, and Beard, had become, Mumford charged, a doctrine "of shameful evasion and inept retreat." Certainly, he argued, all men of conscience favored peace. But the present liberal commitment to peace at any price represented a capitulation to an insurgent barbarism that menaced all of Western civilization. To urge peace under these circumstances was to engage actually in a "covert defense of Hitlerism."

Yet Mumford's was more than a harangue against non-interventionism. He carried his assault to the very philosophic basis of pragmatic liberalism, attributing the non-interventionism of the Binghams and the Beards to deficiencies embedded deep in the moral foundations of this philosophic creed. Here he paused to draw a distinction between what he described as the two principal variants of liberalism: "ideal liberalism," a body of universal values intimately associated with the Judeo-Christian and Western humanist tradition, and "pragmatic liberalism," a "transient doctrine" arising from the scientific and economic revolutions of the seventeenth and eighteenth centuries. Pragmatic liberalism, he conceded, shared certain of the directing values of "ideal liberalism," particularly its commitment to democracy, racial toleration, "justice," and "objective reason." But unfortunately it wedded them to an extravagant faith in scientific conquest and material growth. Reaching back to the dominating argument of *Technics and Civilization,* Mumford characterized pragmatic liberalism as a creed impervious to the inner and spiritual promptings of man. More than anything else, it was pragmatic liberalism's incessant concern for structural or material change, reform of "the machinery of life," along with its related belief in the essential goodness of man that he most brutally assailed. Children of Rousseau, the pragmatic utopians, he charged, proclaimed all men "naturally good." Crime, war, injustice, totalitarianism—all of the world's pressing evils—were attributed to strictly material factors, to malignancies in the socio-economic setting. This childishly simplistic emphasis caused the pragmatists to stand mute in the face of fascism, to fall back on the facile belief that fascism was developing a rational economic pattern that would ultimately curtail its most ruthless excesses. On this point Mumford surely had Bingham in mind.

Mumford insisted that there were obdurate obstacles to reform locked deep in the human psyche, stubborn traces of evil and irrationality that no amount of social engineering could subdue. Evil, then, was a permanent fact of the human condition. And certain men, Mumford charged, were so filled with evil, so pathologically malicious, as to be beyond reform. These were the fascists. Mere economic adjustment or a diplomacy of appeasement would not halt their destructive advance. Such policies rested on the erroneous conviction that fascism emerged from a flawed economic and international structure, from depression and revengeful memories of an unjust peace. The real sources of fascism, however, were not to be found in the Treaty of Versailles or in the economic blundering of Weimar. Rather, they were to be found in the recesses of the German character, in a perverse strain in the national psyche extending at least as far back as Martin Luther. "The raucous hatred that shouts on every page of 'Mein Kampf,'" Mumford declared, "received its first classic utterance in Luther's denunciation of the Peasants' Rebellion; and the direct line of connection between Luther and Hitler, through Fichte, Nietzsche, and Wagner, is familiar to all those who know the history of German culture." An economic or class analysis could not explain a movement whose springs were moral and psychological. ". . . It is not in Ricardo or Marx or Lenin but in Dante, Shakespeare, and Dostoevsky, that an understanding of the true sources of fascism are to be found."

Mumford's analysis of fascism thus led straight to an argument for war, just as surely as Bingham's led straight to a policy of appeasement. Since fascism was unresponsive to rational treatment, since its commanding dynamic was endemically irrational and perverse, only a war of extinction—forced "conversion," as Mumford put it—could save the democracies from its lawless fury. War, Mumford admitted, was a dangerous method of conversion; it "*does* brutalize the users of it." But "there are times when active resistance or coercion is the only safeguard against the conduct of men who mean ill against society; and without doubt," he concluded, "this is one of those times."[23]

Yet while the current crisis called for unhesitant action and unyielding force, the pragmatic liberals urged caution and compromise. Mumford attributed this paralytic tendency to two further defects in pragmatism: its pallid value relativity and its under-regard of the emotive or passional sources of behavior. Lacking a clear standard of values and countenancing an ex post facto logic, pragmatic liberals withheld judgment from repressive movements like Soviet Communism and National Socialism until these so-called experiments were given a chance to demonstrate their "success" or "failure." And too often the sole pragmatic criterion of success was economic progress. This dubious

standard of judgment explained their "tenderness" for fascism, a movement that had demonstrated some capacity for economic growth.

Not only did pragmatic liberalism's questionable standard of judgment lead to a "sneaking admiration for Nazi[sm] "; its slippery value
relativity, Mumford claimed, made it incapable even of distinguishing
between barbarism and civilization. Mumford dismissed entirely Bingham's argument that by aligning with England and France, America
would be siding with imperial powers as guilty of violating human rights
as the fascists. All men, he observed, were corrupted by evil; but not in
equal degrees. Those who were unable to discern the moral difference
between the atrocities of the fascists and the lesser evils of the
British and the French were color-blind to "moral values."

Yet Mumford professed to be unsurprised by the pragmatic
liberals' inability to make resolute ethical judgments, a deficiency
he linked to their "undervaluation of the emotional and affective sides
of life." Emotions and feelings, in pragmatic thinking, were callously
subordinated to rational calculation. This was the pragmatist's mark of
good judgment—a decision divorced from the heated claims of passion
and imagination. Yet this liberal effort to separate intellectual judgment from its emotional referent was not only impossible; in some
instances it was downright dangerous.

> If one meets a poisonous snake in one's path it is important, for a
> *rational* reaction, to have a prompt emotion of fear; for fear re-
> leases the flow of adrenin [sic] into the bloodstream, and that
> will not merely put the organism on the alert but will give it
> the extra strength either to run or to attack. Merely to look at
> the snake abstractedly . . . may lead to the highly irrational
> step of permitting the snake to draw near without being on guard
> against the reptile's bite.

This was the pragmatist's problem. Distrusting the emotions, lacking,
in truth, a developed "sense of danger," he was incapable of fathoming
the murderous potential of fascism.[24]

To meet the onrush of fascism Mumford urged in 1940 an immediate
program of national action that included the abrogation of all neutrality
legislation, the cessation of diplomatic and trade relations with the
fascists, a massive home front mobilization, and the erection of an
overpowering military force "ready, like the armies of Napoleon to
impose liberty and democracy if need be rather than to see them perish
utterly from the earth."[25] War, he insisted, was inevitable; and he urged

therefore that the United States enter the struggle at once. "One might as honorably keep out of Europe today," he wrote to Brooks, "as a doctor out of a stricken home."[26]

Nor did Mumford have any illusions about the savage human costs of such a struggle. War, he darkly predicted, would impose brutal sacrifices on the entire citizenry. America would not be able to afford both "guns and butter." To win out against Hitler all the nation's productive energies would have to be harnessed to war-related aims. A Herculean common effort, a total civilian dedication to the military effort, would be imperative. This would mean a sharp curtailment of luxuries and extravagances, a lessening of pecuniary reward, the transition, in sum, from an "economics of comfort to an economics of sacrifice." Wages and profits would be cut to the bone, grueling sacrifices would become commonplace and a relentless discipline universal. Those unwilling to "strip for action" and bend their all toward the defeat of the enemy would be coerced to do so. In this, as in any war, "the totalitarian element will be inescapable."[27]

Well before the United States joined the war, Mumford was calling for sweeping legal restrictions on those suspected of sympathizing with the fascists. At the very least, he demanded that these "poisonous" elements be denied the right of free speech and assemblage and the use of the federal mails; while for those *known* to be in league with the fascists, he recommended jail or exile under a new statute making their beliefs treasonous. "Neither our constitution nor our Bill of Rights nor our American traditions would survive," he argued in 1940, "if the nation itself went under: democracy must at least have the resolution to ensure its own survival."[28]

Sacrifices of this magnitude would be impossible to bear and the long war impossible to win, Mumford warned, unless the nation enlisted behind a common secular faith demanding total dedication and abdication in the interests of democratic survival; for only those committed to more than the aimless expansion of material culture would be able to stand up under the "fierce sacrifices and heroic efforts" the war would impose. To nurture and sustain this faith of sacrifice and patriotism (really a restatement of the neotechnic ideal he had advanced in *Technics and Civilization*), Mumford called for a return to the region and the land and for "a new joy" in family life and "fecundity." America, he announced, must become a "nation of villagers." Here in the village and the region, the emotional satisfaction of life close to the soil and enhanced by the warm pleasures of family and communal life would more than compensate for the spartan austerity of the national mobilization. Here also men could begin to

reestablish the intimate human contacts and reexperience the sensual
and spiritual stirrings that a sterile industrial civilization had coldly
discouraged. The region, the village, and the family would in this way
form the core and crux of a life-forwarding culture that would see the
nation through the immediate war crisis toward a spirited human
renaissance in the years beyond the democratic victory.[29]

Yet while Mumford called for an encompassing value reorientation,
he cautioned against excessive optimism. The rise of the totalitarians
had exposed the "Sunday School" naiveté of the pragmatic utopians.
For the foreseeable future he urged that the imperative of sacrifice be
coupled with an insight into the unavoidable tragedy of the human
condition. Man had demonstrated his inability to master all his social
problems; the world would never be swept clean of injustice. Still,
Mumford insisted that men make the effort. "Faith for Living" meant
seeking after perfection, knowing all the while that perfection was
impossible. "The real problem of evil—the problem that justifies
every attempt to sublimate war into legal conflict, to abolish economic
poverty, and to cure disease—is to reduce evil to amounts that can be
spiritually assimilated." In this Puritan spirit of clear-sighted realism
and stout sacrifice, buoyed by faith in the nation's sustaining ideals,
Mumford appealed to his countrymen to crush the fascists and "lay
the foundation of a world in which life—love, freedom, justice, truth—
will once more be sacred."[30]

It was in this same spirit of aggressive patriotism that Mumford
joined Herbert Agar, Hans Kohn, and other prominent interventionist
intellectuals in "A Declaration on World Democracy," denouncing pragmatism and fascism and calling for an American declaration of war on
Germany. Restating the central indictment of "The Irresponsibles," this
statement accused the pragmatic liberals of fostering an agreeable climate
for Hitler by spreading "a relativity that doubted all values, and a
degraded science that shirked the spiritual issues."[31] More a moral
promulgation than a considered philosophic statement, the declaration
has as one of its signatories the brilliant Protestant theologian Reinhold
Niebuhr. An interventionist by the time of the Munich crisis, Niebuhr
carried forward Mumford's two-pronged assault on pragmatism and non-
interventionism, erecting upon the blasted hopes of his generation a
sternly anti-utopian reformism as a counter to the hopeful credo of
Dewey and Bingham. In the ideological struggle against fascism he
armed liberals with a fighting faith for the coming crusade against
Communism. Mumford certainly contributed unwittingly to this new
democratic faith. But if cold war liberalism, the liberalism of "the
vital center," had a philosophic prophet and moral architect, surely
it was Reinhold Niebuhr.

In their attitudes toward pragmatic liberalism, Niebuhr and Mumford were in almost complete accord. Reviewing Mumford's *Faith for Living* in the *Nation,* Niebuhr hailed it as a book of surpassing importance for an understanding of the prevailing mood of "spiritual confusion and inertia" in the democratic West, a work "true and convincing in all . . . [its] specific indictments." "Mr. Mumford," Niebuhr wrote, "rightly recognizes isolationism as the political consequence" of a perfectionist rationalism devoid of a "tragic sense of life."[32] In an earlier article for the *Nation,* "Peace and the Liberal Illusion," Niebuhr had spelled out the specifics of his judgment against pragmatic liberalism, attributing the "capitulation of Munich" to the deluded "cultural foundation" of modern democracy. Anticipating the sovereign theme of his immensely influential book *The Children of Light and the Children of Darkness* (1944), Niebuhr drew a sharp distinction between democracy and liberalism, much like the distinction Mumford would make between "ideal" and "pragmatic" liberalism, arguing, like Mumford, that unless democracy severed its historic association with "idealistic" liberalism and acquired a more appropriately realistic philosophic foundation it would succumb eventually to the forces of cynicism and tyranny loose in the world. A fatuous and sentimental liberalism, in his view, lay at the heart of the crisis of the West.[33]

Western democracy, Niebuhr argued, had as its cultural foundation "eighteenth- and nineteenth-century liberalism," a creed informed by the facile notion "that it is comparatively easy to 'substitute reason for force,' and that mankind is embarked upon a progressive development which will substitute 'free cooperative inquiry' for political partnership and social conflict." Niebuhr denounced this faith as hopelessly ill equipped to meet the onrush of fascism, a demonic ideology incarnating war as the supreme ideal.

Is it possible [he asked] to meet the challenge of a civilization which glorifies force if the relation of force to reason in political action is understood no better than liberalism understands it? . . . Is it possible to resist a civilization organized for war if the forces which seek to guide mankind to a pacific way of life do not understand that political tension and friction between contending political wills are normal, or at least inevitable, characteristics of national and international life? Is liberalism, in short, not too simple a creed to suit the complexities of our tragic era?[34]

Niebuhr had long maintained the primacy of power in political conduct,[35] arguing that it was man's driving appetite for power, his ineradicably sinful and selfish nature, which made democracy imperative. Democracy "is a perennial necessity . . . ," he maintained, "precisely because liberalism as a culture is not based on truth, that is, because its interpretation of human nature is fallacious and too optimistic." The kinds of checks on unbounded power which democracy provided were necessary because men were prone to misuse power; democracy, seen this way, was our one sure bulwark against an ever-threatening tyranny. As Niebuhr put it, "A non-violent expression of the claims and counter-claims of politics is important precisely because political arguments are never rational arguments. The threat of force against recalcitrant minorities is always implied in them." This was the danger of the moment. By failing to appreciate the "coercive element" in all political relations, by naively advocating the rule of reason in dealing with the fascists, liberals jeopardized the very democratic freedoms they claimed to uphold.[36]

In an ironic departure, Niebuhr joined Mumford in condemning pragmatic liberals for embracing a dangerously puristic absolutism. The non-interventionist liberals, they charged, had made the "mere preservation of physical existence into an absolute good,"[37] failing to realize, as Mumford put it, "that a life sacrificed at the right moment is a life well spent." Related to this pacifistic absolutism they found in liberalism a "moral purism hesitant to preserve a culture or civilization because some absolute principle, absolute liberty or absolute rationality, must be sacrificed in the process of defense."[38] Niebuhr and Mumford would thus have it both ways, denouncing pragmatic liberalism for both its excessive relativism and its dogmatic absolutism, raising the suspicion that they were less interested in framing a sustained philosophic critique of pragmatic rationalism than in assailing certain non-interventionists who happened to be pragmatic liberals. For in the final analysis it was the failure of these liberals to countenance war that most incensed them. Neither Mumford nor Niebuhr disguised the fact that he was fashioning, in fact, an ideology for war, a war he saw as a massive struggle for democracy. "The major choice," they proclaimed in their "Declaration on World Democracy," "is no longer ours. War, declared or undeclared, actual or virtual, has chosen us."[39]

Niebuhr expressed his matured challenge to the pragmatic liberal sensibility and outlined an alternative democratic philosophy in *The Children of Light and the Children of Darkness*. While not published until 1944, this book is crucial to an understanding of the liberal controversy of the late 1930s in that it presents in full detail ideas Niebuhr pressed so intensely in the controversy over intervention. An arresting challenge to the leading presuppositions of reform pragmatists like Bingham and Dewey, it illuminates the issues that divided American progressives in the prewar years. It is a book, as well, that would powerfully influence the postwar liberal imagination. The pivotal ideas of *The Children of Light and the Children of Darkness* were not new to Niebuhr. They formed the ideological culmination of a career in dissent against the dominating optimism of both Social Gospel Christianity and pragmatic liberalism. Deeply influenced by the Christian orthodoxy of St. Paul and St. Augustine and by the "crisis theology" of Karl Barth, Niebuhr rejected early on in his career the hopeful reformism of Dewey and liberal Protestantism for a sobered Christian neo-orthodoxy humbly aware of man's indelibly sinful nature and of the impossibility of any final or perfect resolution of the social problem.[40] In *Moral Man and Immoral Society* (1932), a book written with John Dewey in mind, he had assailed liberalism for failing to acknowledge "the power of self-interest and collective egotism in all inter-group relations." The liberal remedies of rational planning and enlightened "social pedagogy" could never, he insisted, subdue these egotistic elements of collective behavior. These traits belonged to the "order of nature"; they were not socially or historically induced.

Such an analysis, attributing our social ills to the fact of original sin, could easily have lead to a philosophy of secular resignation. Yet Niebuhr shaped it into a challenging Christian radicalism. In man's selfish and contentious nature, at once a potent source of social disintegration, he found the catalyzing force for equal justice. Instead of attempting to tame conflict through rationality, Niebuhr urged a realistic acceptance of the primacy of conflict in social relations and an ever-going effort to harness this elemental force for higher human purposes. "Conflict," he maintained, "is inevitable, and in this conflict power must be challenged by power." Only by coalescing collectively to confront the owning classes, only by pitting organized power against organized power, could capitalism's exploited minorities gain their social ends.[41]

Emphasis upon force and contention as the ruling drives of collective behavior drove Niebuhr in the early 1930s to Marxism, an ideology that, while taking account of the predominance of self-interest in class relations, remained supremely confident that this force could be harnessed for social redemption. Niebuhr's unshakable Christian pessimism, however, prevented him from embracing Marxism unreservedly. In the end, despite his admiration for Marxism's profoundly realistic diagnosis of class relations, he judged it guilty of the same utopian optimism that infected pragmatic liberalism, a criticism he extended and amplified in *The Children of Light and the Children of Darkness.*[42]

Niebuhr could never accept the socialist idea that alienation and collective egotism were historically rooted in the prevailing forms of property relations. It was this "romantic" affirmation of the social basis of human nature, he argued, which led to the crowning error of Marxist thought—the "utopian hope" that communal ownership of property would bring an end to class contention.[43] The Marxist, Niebuhr observed in *The Children of Light,* "thinks that the inclination of men to take advantage of each other is a corruption which was introduced into history by the institutions of property," when in fact this impulse was anchored in man's immutably corrupt nature, making impossible the Marxist-Leninist millennium of "perfect mutuality." Ceaselessly vain and ruled by a passion for power, men were doomed to feud endlessly. In their social relations they were thus capable of only "proximate," not absolute justice.[44]

Not only was the Marxist understanding of human nature historically sentimental; it was downright dangerous. In naively assuming that man's drive for power had its source in the institution of private property, Marxism underestimated the possibility of tyranny of a non-economic kind. Economic equalitarianism was no guarantee against dictatorship. "An officious bureaucrat," Niebuhr noted earlier, "may cause intolerable injustices, even if he eats the same food and wears the same clothes as his victim." As early as 1932 Niebuhr had found in the Soviet Union disturbing indications of such injustices. In destroying concentrated capitalist power, the Soviets had wrought another potential source of tyranny—a centralized planning state manned by a zealous Communist officialdom. "The abuse of power by the communist bureaucrats," he wrote then, "is very considerable and is bound to grow. . . ."[45] Later in the decade Niebuhr saw these fears of congealed power given ugly confirmation not only in Russia but in Germany and Italy as well. At the same time the ascendancy of totalitarianism had a soberingly conservative influence on him, opening the way for a halting retreat from socialism. Although he continued to urge some kind of collectivization of industrial property, he frankly confessed in 1940 that "if socialization of economic power is purchased at the price of creating irresponsible and tyrannical power, our last estate may be worse than the first." Democratic social justice, he was more convinced than ever, prospered best in an atmosphere where contending social forces were free to exercise "pressures and counterpressures."[46] Niebuhr thus continued into the war years the search he had begun over a decade earlier for a social orientation and an institutional pattern capable of securing proximate justice within a framework of freedom. How to balance the contending claims of community and individuality?

This, the same crucial question Bingham had addressed in *The Techniques of Democracy,* Niebuhr approached comprehensively in *The Children of Light and the Children of Darkness.* And the answer he offered, a distillation of the matured insights of a disillusioned socialist, helped to shape a new philosophy of liberal reform.

Conceding the primacy of self-interest in human affairs, Niebuhr called for a democratic system that would "beguile, deflect, harness and restrain self-interest . . . for the sake of the community."[47] In outlining such a system in broad theoretical terms, he gave telling demonstration to the growing appreciation on the Left for a pluralistic government of checks and balances, and to the gathering distrust of ideology as an answer to public concerns. Finally, despite his polemics against liberal planners, Niebuhr, as much as any liberal planner prominent in these years of mounting social skepticism, expressed a clear preference for administrative approaches to social problems. By the early 1940s he was advocating not so much a program for progressive justice as a procedure for mediating class struggle and balancing social power. This shift from program to procedure, from ideology to technique, grew out of two related tendencies in his previous contribution: his consistent Christian pessimism and his guarded fear of concentrated power. Now, however, the spread of totalitarianism impelled him to shape these familiar presuppositions into a strenuous defense of liberal pluralism. In an error-torn world of sin and strife, perhaps the best any society could hope for was to arrive at a democratic procedure capable of equilibrating the unending struggle for proximate justice. And had not the New Deal liberals already begun to establish just such a framework for balancing power among competing organized groups?

While Niebuhr would not give clear endorsement to the New Deal's efforts to create a political economy of countervailing powers until after World War 2, his drift from Christian radicalism to a more minimal social reformism was subtly in evidence somewhat earlier. In *The Children of Light and the Children of Darkness* he continued to advocate democratic socialism as the system most likely to insure proximate economic justice, while curiously questioning the likelihood of ever achieving such a system. Even a socialism accomplished gradually through constitutional means, a socialism which "placed democratic checks upon the powers of the economic managers," could easily sink into tyranny, he warned, if the economic planners were to use their considerable powers "to establish control over the political institutions." Somehow the community would have to find a way to socialize property without creating an abusive oligarchy. Yet Niebuhr's argument hardly shouted with confidence about the possibilities. Instead, caution and restraint dominated; and apropos of the time, democratic freedoms took precedence over sweeping efforts to engineer economic equality. Socialized and centralized power might be essential for "unity and efficiency," but Niebuhr concluded that it might "be wise for the community to sacrifice something to efficiency for the sake of preserving a greater balance of forces and avoiding undue centralization of power."

Acknowledging, with Madison, the "inevitability of factions," Niebuhr urged a governing system that allowed these factions to express themselves "without destroying the unity and life of the community," a constitutional framework that distributed power in such a way as to allow "an uneasy equilibrium of social forces."[48] Such a system, more perhaps by accident than conscious design, America, he believed, had already significantly achieved.

Niebuhr found the strength of America's democratic culture in its rich diversity. America's multifarious class structure, in particular, with its "endless complexity and comparative fluidity," with no one class in clear hegemony, was a potent force of social stability. Like Bingham, however, Niebuhr realized that this very class diversity could deadlock democracy, producing "a confusion of forces which may immobilize the government which finds itself at the center of a vortex of class forces, no group having sufficient power to move in a positive direction and all of them having enough power to prevent positive action." To prevent such a democratic stalemate Niebuhr joined Bingham in urging a system of countervailing power in which the continuing class struggle issued not in impasse and irresolution but in a gradual shift in the political institutions "to conform to changing economic needs and unchanging demands for higher justice."

Niebuhr never rendered a detailed blueprint for the kind of political economy he envisioned. Yet the requirements he set for the attainment of democratic social justice were broadly consonant with the interest-group collectivism already advocated by Bingham, Corey, and other disillusioned radical collectivists. Instead of urging the nationalization of large corporations, Niebuhr joined Bingham in suggesting that they be closely regulated by a vigilant political government and that they be continually challenged by countervailing concentrations of economic power. In such balance lay the health of the democratic state.[49] By 1949 Niebuhr had ceased to argue seriously for socialism and was prepared to acknowledge what his argument already implied. The pressures of the Cold War and his redoubled skepticism about Marxism had pressed him to a defense of America as an "approximately just society," a society that had achieved an admirable measure of justice by equilibrating political and economic power. In recognizing yet balancing competition between organized social interests, the New Deal had pointed the nation toward a safe middle course between an outdated economic libertarianism on the right and a dangerous radical utopianism on the left, achieving, in the process, the efficiency and direction essential for social growth without jeopardizing the rich diversity of democratic life.[50]

Thus, despite their radical differences over foreign policy, Niebuhr and Bingham arrived eventually at remarkably similar political conclusions. And the common catalyst for this drift toward liberalism was the developing totalitarian state. Neither Niebuhr nor Bingham saw America confronted by a simple either/or choice between collectivism and freedom. Both sought, in Niebuhr's words, a "middle ground between a collectivism that would solve all problems by bringing economic life under political control and a laissez-faire theory which equates democracy with unregulated economic enterprise." By the early 1940s both agreed, moreover, that America's existing democratic pluralism offered the best possible framework for achieving social justice without "making power irresponsible." The only real remaining difference in their approach to domestic change lay in their dissimilar interpretations of human nature. Niebuhr as much as admitted this in his review of *The Techniques of Democracy*. Bingham, he wrote, "rightly regards the problem of leadership as the paramount problem of democracy" and has devised a "wise and prudent" program for lending democracy greater direction and decisiveness. But when he moved from an elaboration of democratic techniques to an analysis of the "underlying presuppositions of democracy," his argument was "not equally convincing." Democracy was not founded, as he supposed, upon a simple faith in man's capacity for reason and fair play; it grew up rather as a safeguard against his incessant contentiousness. Here Niebuhr cut to the heart of his disagreement with Bingham. Where Bingham founded his argument for liberal planning on the idealistic belief that such planning would release the constructive energies of an essentially

rational citizenry, Niebuhr based his case for a broadly similar democratic collectivism on a dour belief in man's utter corruptibility.
Where Bingham confronted the future with abounding optimism, confident that man could surmount his problems and literally create the
good life, Niebuhr urged a contrite Christian humility. Democracy, he
believed, demanded more than "moral idealism." It required as well
a humble acceptance of the impossibility of a perfect mutuality of
interest among men. "If human nature is as good as Mr. Bingham
thinks it is," Niebuhr observed, "he ought not to be so concerned
as he seems to be to make power responsible and to check it with
other forms of power."[51]

Writing during a critical transitional period in the history of democratic thought, Niebuhr accomplished almost singlehandedly a
revolution in the foundations of liberal political philosophy. The
brooding critic of liberal sentimentalism emerged ironically as liberalism's staunchest champion. His classic restatement of liberalism, rendered in the hard-boiled language of an earlier Marxism, became the
adopted creed of scores of disillusioned radicals like himself. Yet
Niebuhr's influence was not confined to repentant radicals stunned
by the Soviet betrayal. His writings were equally inspiring to young
non-Communist intellectuals who escaped completely the lure of
Russia. Here was a new company of insurgents with an altogether
new outlook. Where Bingham and his generation had been fired by
the depression and the promise of Russia to seek a new world, this
later generation, confronted in the glow of youth by the spread of
totalitarianism abroad and the collapse of radicalism in their own
country, had few illusions about the future. If anything, the shocking
events of their time deepened their allegiance to capitalism and country. In New Deal liberalism they found an agreeable democratic
alternative to the excesses of ideology. Yet the memory of Munich
convinced them that liberalism needed a more resolute philosophic
justification. This Niebuhr gave them. Armed with his faith, they set
out to combat Communism with a fervor equal to that with which
Bingham's generation had once assailed capitalism. Only, theirs was
less a vision of a reconstituted society than a spirited affirmation of
regnant values and practices. They would extend the boundaries of the
present rather than seek to fashion a new tomorrow. Perhaps no book
better evoked this new liberal spirit than Arthur M. Schlesinger, Jr.'s,
The Vital Center. Published in 1949 by a young historian born in 1917
and shaped by the politics of the 1930s, it stands as a striking testi-
monial to the pervading influence of Reinhold Niebuhr on the postwar liberal sensibility.

The Vital Center stated few original ideas. Its importance lies in its unexampled exposition of the unifying tenets of the new liberalism. The architects of this faith, Schlesinger admitted, were "the wiser men of an older generation," anti-communist intellectuals like Niebuhr, Orwell, Koestler, Hemingway, Silone, Gide, and Edmund Wilson, along with stalwart democratic activists like Roosevelt, Aneurin Bevan, and labor's Walter Reuther. Yet Schlesinger counted as its "chief beneficiaries" his own generation, young liberals aroused by the confident example of New Deal reform and repelled by the outrages of Stalin and Hitler. Voicing a sentiment as old as the history of insurgency, Schlesinger pronounced his generation possessed of a singularly realistic understanding of historic reality. Totalitarianism "reminded my generation rather forcibly that man was, indeed, imperfect, and that the corruptions of power could unleash great evil in the world." They would accordingly be wise and shrewdly realistic where a previous generation, deluded by the "Soviet mirage," had been foolishly utopian.[52]

Like Niebuhr, Schlesinger described the new liberalism as a reaction to the inadequacies of the old liberalism, attributing the advance of totalitarianism in large measure to these inadequacies. And just as Niebuhr had divorced democracy from a "sentimental liberalism," so Schlesinger drew a distinction between what he characterized as the two major strains of American liberalism: "utopian" or "doctrinaire progressivism," and the more realistic tradition of "radical democracy." Schlesinger gave as the defining characteristic of the radical democrat his tough-minded appreciation of the limits of political reform, distinguishing him from the "Doughface progressive," a dreamy utopian convinced "that the good in man will be liberated by a change in economic institutions." Lacking an understanding of the permanency of evil and of man's unsatiable craving for power, this innocent progressivism was ill-equipped to confront the challenges to freedom in the modern world. The new age demanded a faith less innocent, a politics and a diplomacy more coldly resolute.[53]

To a considerable extent the argument of *The Vital Center* is the argument of prewar interventionism applied to the realities of the Cold War. The "lessons" of Munich haunt every page. Throughout the book there is the same inflated rhetoric of freedom, the same fervid patriotism, the same hint of impending crisis, the same tendency to frame complex issues in terms of moral opposites, the same pose of realism and toughness, the same intolerance of ideological opposition, that marked the most heated polemics for intervention. The ruling characteristics of the argument are remarkably similar; only the political enemy has changed, Communism replacing fascism as the principal menace to the free West.[54] In language reminiscent of prewar interventionism, Schlesinger depicted the Soviet Union as a marauding colossus embarked upon a global course of ideological conquest. This "totalitarian imperialism," he warned, could be checked only by a vigilant diplomacy of containment.[55] But containment itself was not enough; for communism was a "deep and driving faith," emotionally appealing to millions seeking relief from the spiritual anxieties and material dislocations that accompanied full-scale industrialization; it could be effectively countered only by an equally compelling democratic faith, a faith and a social framework capable of guaranteeing the economic and psychic security communism promised without sacrificing essential freedoms. Schlesinger believed his own generation of tough-minded reformers were ideally suited to frame such a democratic faith. They were too young to have felt "the exultation of 1917." "Our memories of Russia," he explained, "are shaped, not by the glory of Revolution, but by the horror of Thermidor." This charged us with "a renewed sense of the meaning of freedom," an unqualified hatred of totalitarianism that was to form the moral center of what Schlesinger curiously called "the new radicalism."[56]

Schlesinger saw the "new radicals" united by certain distinguishing political principles, chief among them a "belief in the limited state"; not the laissez-faire state of an earlier century but a government that, while allowing conflict between organized groups, intervened regularly to redress the balance in favor of the weaker interests. Certainly some economic planning would be unavoidable, but democratic government, Schlesinger argued, must aim not at "pinpoint planning" and "direct physical controls," but at "establishing conditions for economic decisions." Not Marx, but Keynes, was to be the "prophet of the new radicalism."

Not surprisingly, Schlesinger found America's economic and political pluralism the one practicing system that most closely met this ideal of equitably balanced competition. Here government encouraged a balanced class competition that had resulted in a "systematic redistribution of wealth" without the horrors of totalitarian planning. Yet ours was not a perfect system; nor, Schlesinger warned, could it ever be. "Problems will always torment us," he paraphrased Niebuhr, "because all important problems are insoluble: that is why they are important. The good comes from the continuing struggle to try and solve them, not from the vain hope of their solution." Schlesinger warned, as well, against wholesale assaults upon social injustices. The new radicalism would operate in the short range, meeting problems as they arose; its overriding ideal was not the impossible classless millennium of Marx and Lenin but the restoration of "the center." "The center is vital: the center must hold. . . . The spirit of the new radicalism is the spirit of the center."[57] Even a cursory reading of *The Vital Center* reveals the far-reaching consequences of the prewar struggle over intervention. With Niebuhr in the vanguard, the intellectual interventionists raised in this dispute ideas and arguments that influenced the appearance of a new liberalism. Not all intellectual interventionists, certainly, endorsed the politics of the vital center. Mumford and Waldo Frank, for example, remained piercing critics of capitalist civilization; and both continued after the war to champion an encompassing value revolution as the prelude to a general cultural awakening. They found the liberalism of Schlesinger and Niebuhr even more narrowly uninspiring than the instrumentalism of John Dewey. Yet by joining their appeal for war to a concentrated assault upon pragmatic rationalism, they opened the way, unwittingly, for the advocates of tough-minded reform. Stormy critics of pragmatic liberalism, they won, at best, a Pyrrhic victory. For it was Niebuhr's gloomy neo-realism, not their challenging radical humanism, that formed the moral core of the emergent reform orientation.

This new liberalism was based, supposedly, upon a more realistic conception of human nature. Schlesinger presented it as a politics consistent with man's flawed nature, contrasting it with the deluded sentimentalism of "doctrinaire progressivism." Yet the facts fail to support this argument from human nature. Niebuhr's career alone challenges Schlesinger's claim. A consistent Augustinian pessimist, Niebuhr shaped this pessimism early in the 1930s into a spirited plea for socialism. A decade later, however, his view of human nature unchanged, growing fears of totalitarianism caused him to spurn Marxism for a more cautious reformism. His own writings tellingly demonstrate that a pessimistic theory of human nature can serve as easily as a moral rationale for socialism as it can for liberalism.

Thus, despite their pronounced foreign policy differences, liberals holding virtually opposite views of human nature were driven by fears of totalitarianism to remarkably similar political postures. Even these foreign policy differences would, as we shall see, eventually narrow to the point where the *Common Sense* liberals were urging a military preparedness program as ambitious as that advocated by the interventionists, a radical shift in policy also dictated by the murderous advance of fascism. In making this shift, moreover, they tied their program for economic democracy to the national defense effort, a dangerous precedent for the postwar years. And when after Pearl Harbor the *Common Sense* liberals joined the interventionists in support of the war effort, the crucial policy differences between these two wings of democratic reform narrowed even further. While they would remain at odds on a number of critical public issues, liberals like Bingham and Niebuhr moved into the immediate postwar years with a broadly consonant ideological orientation, the result of their confrontation with the forces of unfreedom.

10

GUNS AND BUTTER
Planning for War–and Peace

By the summer of 1940, with the Nazis occupying Paris and threatening a cross-channel invasion of England, the foreign policy dispute between the interventionist and the non-interventionist liberals had reduced itself to the ultimate question of war or peace. In the face of this threat the interventionists demanded an immediate American declaration of war, while Bingham and the *Common Sense* liberals continued to urge a policy of peace and diplomatic restraint.

The liberal non-interventionists, however, were hardly the tenderminded sentimentalists Niebuhr and Mumford made them out to be; nor was there anything in the pragmatic method that ruled against the resort to force. Dewey, after all, had used pragmatism to justify his support of an earlier world war, insisting in 1917 that "no ends are accomplished without the use of force."[1] There is, in fact, a considerable affinity between Dewey's criticism of the "moonstruck" non-interventionists of 1917 and Mumford's searing assaults upon Dewey and the 1930s non-interventionists. As Morton White reminds us, Dewey's World War 1 writings abound with "admiring references to the tough-mindedness of seventeenth- and eighteenth-century political theorists, to their frank recognition of the importance of force and power in politics."[2] Even in the heat of the 1930s interventionist controversy, moreover, he and Bingham had not proclaimed themselves unqualified pacifists. And as events were to prove, Bingham and his fellow liberal non-interventionists would eventually support a war they were powerless to stop, retreating to the very argument that Dewey had used in 1917–that war, properly directed, could be a powerful force for progressive democracy.

Actually, by 1940 it was more the kind of war Mumford and the extreme interventionists seemed to urge—a "holy war" for the single purpose of smashing the enemy—rather than war itself, that the *Common Sense* liberals aggressively opposed. They were given an ominous reminder of the damaging ferocity such a war could release in the polemics of the more militant interventionists. In answering these arguments for war Bingham and the liberal non-interventionists identified some of the more dangerous tendencies in the literature of interventionism, ideas and arguments that would set a fearful precedent for the postwar years. Where Mumford and Niebuhr would insist upon the superiority of force over reason as an instrument of international deterrence, so later neo-realists would use a similar argument in support of yet another campaign of ideological containment. And where understandable outrage against Hitler would provoke Mumford to demand a suspension of the Bill of Rights for those suspected of trafficking in fascism, so later democratic zealots (although happily not Mumford himself) would treat lightly of the Constitution in prosecuting an equally fervid campaign against communist sympathizers. The call for repression in the name of freedom was not unique to the era of communist containment.

As early as 1937 Bingham had warned against the developing war psychology on the Left. One year later, with passions further aroused by Hitler's advance, he met the liberal interventionists' fire with a bruising *Common Sense* editorial, "The Liberal and Anti-Fascism," accusing Mumford and company of allowing their hatred of fascism to develop into "a demonic cult of ignorance and crusading intolerance." It was a terrible symptom of liberalism's decline, Bingham wrote, that these erstwhile liberals could "find no way of meeting madness and hatred except with madness and hatred." In this sense, their anti-fascism had become "the reflection and duplicate of the monster it abhors." The real dispute between the interventionists and the non-interventionists, Bingham made it clear, was not over who hated fascism more, as Mumford implied. Rather it was a question of how best to contain and undermine it, a question of strategy rather than aim.

Bingham was especially disturbed by the interventionists' insistence that their position was more "realistic" than that of the non-interventionists. To the contrary, to oppose a policy of diplomatic concessions and to "propose to enforce international morality with more violence," he argued, was to take the "tough-guy" or fascist way of solving problems. It was hardly a sign of realism to imitate the methods of the enemy. In an editorial commenting on a speech by Mussolini, Bingham observed that "some of Il Duce's thrusts at British-French shilly-shallying and at liberalism's weakness in general strike the mark; much of the speech, curiously, sounds exactly like Lewis Mumford."[3]

Bingham, however, left the burden of rebutting Mumford's most controversial assault on the liberal non-interventionists, "The Corruption of Liberalism," to a fellow *Common Sense* writer, the young insurgent poet A. Fleming MacLiesh, who summarized perfectly the magazine's opposition to the Mumford-Frank position.

MacLiesh conceded Mumford's criticism that pragmatic liberalism undervalued "personality and the complex of psychic forces within the personality." Yet he insisted that there was "no basis for supposing" that liberalism's belief in reason, tolerance, and open inquiry would not lead it to embrace further "material" as well as "spiritual" truths." It was, in fact, liberalism's willingness "to open up, to investigate, and to weigh" the very ideals and moral imperatives Mumford put forward as the basis of an American intervention in Europe that was its strongest asset. Thus, while not discounting the importance of emotional and psychic considerations, MacLiesh, like Bingham, refused to accept arguments founded upon "the authority of feeling and dogmatic absolutes." Interventionists might claim that with bombs falling in Europe and fascism at England's door there was no time for a "nice examination" of the issues. Yet MacLiesh insisted that "there must be time . . . if we hope in any way for . . . a world which evolves in accordance with our present ideals."[4]

MacLiesh concluded by exposing what was perhaps the most telling flaw in Mumford's argument. In "The Corruption of Liberalism" Mumford had assailed the liberal non-interventionists for refusing earlier to speak out against the repressions in Stalin's Russia, citing this record of "passivism" and "inept retreat" as evidence of liberalism's moral bankruptcy.[5] This MacLiesh heatedly and convincingly denied. The majority of liberals opposed to intervention had not, he insisted, supported a pro-Stalinist line, "though Mr. Mumford himself, surprisingly did!"[6] Later, in a scalding letter to the *New Republic,* signed by Selden Rodman, Michael Bodkin, and Nathan Alexander, MacLiesh repeated his indictment, arguing that "it was not the 'liberals,' the Beards, the Chases, the Howes . . . who supported Foster for President in 1932 and the various 'United Fronts' in 1934–1939; it was the Lewis Mumfords." Perhaps, the authors concluded, if "the Führer of anti-fascism" was so eager for a war of extermination he ought to lead the charge to "the enlistment posts."[7]

MacLiesh was wrong to accuse Mumford of being a "pro-Marxist-Stalinist" fellow traveler.[8] Mumford had never openly endorsed Stalin's

Russia; nor had he dogmatically assailed critics of the regime. Yet he had kept silent about the fate of freedom in Russia at the very time that Bingham, Dewey, Beard, and other "pragmatic liberals" were inveighing against the dictatorship. This makes his indictment of these liberals unwarranted, and his distinction between "pragmatic" and "ideal" liberalism impossible to consider seriously. This distinction served, as MacLiesh indicated, as little more than a device for separating "the sheep, who agree" with him on intervention, "from the goats, who do not." This becomes abundantly clear when we set Mumford's charges against the record of Mumford's own private admission. "In the case of Soviet Russia," he had written in "The Corruption of Liberalism," pragmatic "liberals continued to preserve an embarrassed silence about the notorious plight of freedom and justice in that country because they had aesthetic scruples about appearing to align themselves with those forces in America that opposed Russia for purely reactionary reasons."[9] Mumford, however, admitted privately to Van Wyck Brooks what he refused to admit in print: that it was *he* who had refused to speak out against Stalin; and that the guilt and shame generated by that silence fueled the ferocity of his opposition to Hitler and all who refused to urge war on Germany. In February, 1940, he wrote Brooks:

> Maybe I am vehement on the subject [of intervention] now, all out of reason, because I feel deeply my own guilt during the past twenty years, when, despite my extreme skepticism of the totalitarian tyranny that was being built up in Russia, I said nothing and did nothing to counteract it, because Russia was Russia, and because the conservatives were against Russia. . . .

Like the loyal fellow traveler, "I made the mistake of thinking that Russia could work out its own salvation, and must therefore be protected from hostile criticism."[10]

Nor was this the first such admission. One year earlier, following the announcement of the Nazi-Soviet pact, Mumford had written to Brooks reproaching himself "for having remained so long silent about the villainies of its dictatorship: the period of suspended judgment lasted too long, and the suspense has now proved almost a noose around our own necks." As an "act of reparation" for these errors, Mumford declared his intention to break ties with the liberals he now believed were showing fascism the same tolerance he had once shown the Soviet Union.[11] The result, published shortly thereafter, was "The Corruption of Liberalism."

Along with Waldo Frank and other interventionists who had once sympathized with Soviet Russia, Mumford was thus determined to act with unqualified resolve against a similar threat to human freedom. Our aim, he told Brooks, must be to move at once to extinguish fascism and to erect a "universal society moved by a common set of human ideals."[12] There is no questioning Mumford's commitment to this more humane future. But "a man is a liberal," as MacLiesh wisely observed, "not only in what he thinks but in the way he thinks and the manner in which he applies his thinking to life."[13] And Mumford, in the heat of an undeniably just cause, indulged in a manner of thinking that radically contravened the liberal ideals he proposed to uphold and advance.

Common Sense was not the only journal to attack Mumford on this point. In a slashing editorial "Lewis Mumford's 'Mein Kampf,'" the *New Masses* denounced *Faith for Living* as "the most flagrant statement of the 'liberal' case for Fascism which the war has so far produced."[14] Not only were Mumford's rhetoric and program for victory dangerously extreme, the *New Republic* agreed, in an official reply to "The Corruption of Liberalism," but in pressing his case for war he had egregiously misrepresented the liberal position. Sensitive liberals had not discounted the contribution of Freud to an understanding of personality. Fully as much as Mumford they realized that emotions "must be recognized rather than repressed." Unfortunately, the editors added, Mumford "seems to have stopped there, rather than going on to understand that a main purpose of recognizing them is to coordinate them, by use of the reasoning faculties, and so to be capable of dealing effectively with reality." To insist, as Mumford came close to insisting, that "uninhibited . . . emotional reaction is the route to health and safety" was to engage in behavior characteristic of Nazism. Was it not, after all, the mark of the fascist to set "primitive emotional impulses against reason . . . glorifying the former by contrast"?[15]

While the liberal and radical press responded with vehemence to Mumford's charges, it was, however, in the sedate *Southern Review* that the most detailed and fiercely accusatory critique of his position appeared. The war in Europe, the novelist and critic James T. Farrell argued, "has produced a new generation of American war intellectuals," whose efforts "to express a faith which will justify a new war in defense of democracy" have damaged "what is best in the democratic tradition." Chief among these new philosophers of war was Lewis Mumford, once an outstanding spokesman for peace and democratic toleration. When asked in a 1935 *Modern Quarterly* symposium what he would do if America went to war, Mumford, Farrell noted, had replied that in the event of war he would consider it his "duty as a writer . . . to remain sane, to think clearly, to correct emotional distortions and patriotic biases. . . ." Now this same Lewis Mumford was urging "holy crusades," selective censorship, jail and exile for fascist sympathizers, labor camps for American youth, compulsory national service for the entire citizenry, and the temporary abrogation of constitutional freedoms, while randomly accusing those who opposed war of indulging in a dangerously one-sided rationalism. Mumford's "case against empiricism" was, however, "stated on the worst possible level, that of mere name-calling and abuse." In fact, Mumford was not even capable of describing the essentials of his own faith. His "ideal liberalism," Farrell concluded, was nothing more than a philosophic catch basin for all he considered valuable in the human tradition. Incapable of framing an intellectually defensible argument for war, Mumford, like the other war intellectuals, offered "no real ideas to refute. He has only muddled assertions and abuse left in his arsenal."[16]

The debate over intervention raged in the liberal and radical press well into 1941. But the increasing likelihood of American intervention after the fall of France in June, 1940, changed its character somewhat, forcing even decidedly non-interventionist journals like *Common Sense* and the *New Republic* to declare for American aid to England "short of war."[17] The non-interventionists had previously insisted that England and France could defeat Germany without American aid, and that, in any event, the Western Hemisphere was invulnerable to military attack. Germany's furious territorial expansion soon, however, undercut both these assumptions. The frightening sweep and success of the Nazi blitzkrieg of 1939–40, with the Reich armies overwhelming in lightning succession Poland, Denmark, Holland, Belgium, Luxembourg, and France, killed once and for all the illusion of a fortress America, while Hitler's redoubled persecution of the Jews made it impossible to argue that there were no pressing moral issues at stake in Europe. By June, 1940, Germany and Italy commanded virtually the entire European coast, and England stood fearfully exposed to a poised German invasion force. Nazi Germany had shown herself to be considerably more than a "have not" nation struggling for the economic materials essential to autarchy. Her ambitions, to a horrified democratic world, appeared limitless, her military might awesome and increasing. Americans now began to fear that if England fell they would be Hitler's next target. Thus, while a *Fortune* poll of October, 1937, had found 62 percent of Americans neutral toward Germany and unprepared to risk war for England's sake, by January, 1941, a Gallup poll indicated 68 percent of Americans supporting all-out aid to England, even at the risk of war. This revolution in national opinion was reflected in the Congress. In November, 1939, Congress repealed the arms embargo, allowing the Allies to purchase munitions in the United States on a cash-and-carry basis; in September, 1940, it passed the first peacetime selective service act in the nation's history; and in March, 1941, it approved the lend-lease agreement, tying our interests ever more firmly to England's. Within less than two years following Hitler's strike into Poland, Congress and the majority of the American people had made plain their commitment to the security and survival of Great Britain. While not yet prepared to declare war, America would become, in Roosevelt's words, "the great arsenal of democracy."[18]

Now, with the Nazis in Paris, Bingham was finally prepared to admit that Hitler aimed quite possibly at "world domination," and that without massive American aid England would fall, making a decent peace impossible.[19] His own peace program threatened by a German victory, Bingham ceased from this point on to urge a diplomacy of territorial appeasement. Hitler, he was convinced, had to be stopped militarily. Yet while conceding the preponderant argument of the interventionists—that this was in fact a struggle for democratic civilization—Bingham remained opposed to our immediate entrance into the war, giving as his principal reason Britain's resolve to press for the "all-out defeat of Germany." If the United States joined England in war, we too, he argued in a May, 1941, editorial, would be sworn to "total victory" through a "counter-invasion of the continent," a military aim that would be humanly ruinous and probably unrealizable. "If Germany, with 6 million of the best fighting men the world has ever seen, has been unable to conquer Britain, what chance," Bingham asked, "has Britain even with the manpower of the United States, to conquer Germany?" Even if such a total victory were possible, Bingham did not consider it worth the "cost in human lives blasted and blighted. . . ." The most he believed it "reasonable to hope for" was "a successful [English] defense against German aggression, making possible a negotiated peace. That," he observed, "is not only the most reasonable hope but it is probably also the best outcome." Bingham thus remained convinced into 1941 that a military deadlock would establish the most favorable basis for a negotiated peace involving a fair distribution of the world's economic resources. This conviction of the unlikelihood and undesirability of total victory over Germany kept him officially opposed to American belligerency to the very eve of Pearl Harbor.[20]

Yet while he continued to urge a negotiated peace with Germany, Bingham privately doubted that America would be able to remain out of the war for long. Events appeared to be pulling the nation irresistibly toward war. Even several of Bingham's published writings of 1940–41 betray a gathering resignation to the inevitability of war.[21] Bingham, nonetheless, insisted that this was all the more reason for the United States to proclaim an agenda of peace aims, so that if we went to war our participation would be directed toward ends and ideals beyond the utter devastation of people and nations. Accordingly, he continued to press for the peace program he had earlier enunciated in *The United States of Europe* and *The Techniques of Democracy*. Only, where before Bingham had presented this plan for international union abroad and full economic democracy at home as the program for a nation he had expected to remain at peace, now in late 1940 and into 1941 he pressed it as the foundation of our war effort.[22] Powerless to stop the drift toward war, Bingham trimmed his ideas to fit the likelihood of America's imminent participation, arguing that war could be an instrument for human betterment.[23] This dramatic turnabout in Bingham's attitude toward war, as important in some ways as his transformation from radicalism to liberalism, was preceded and given impetus by his changing attitude toward military preparedness.

Common Sense had before 1939 been an outspoken critic of American military expenditures.[24] Yet by early 1939 its editors were combining pleas for non-interventionism with support for an enlarged American arms program. Like countless other non-interventionists, both in and outside the Congress, they saw no contradiction in arguing for both neutrality and military preparedness. Aside from sheer defensive purposes, Bingham discerned an additional social feature in an expanded arms program: it was a way to full production and full employment. Germany had verified this.

Bingham was not blind to the moral dilemma that America's arms buildup posed for anti-war liberals like himself. We are, he remarked in 1939, being confronted with the insane situation where the way to abundance is being paved through preparedness for "mutual slaughter." Yet while conceding that military spending was "a stupid and dangerous way of achieving" prosperity, Bingham refused to oppose unalterably such spending. Nor did he seem altogether sensitive to the fact that military mobilization would drive the nation ever closer to the war he opposed. "It is not that a great arms program is necessarily wicked or dangerous," he wrote in 1939. "It is that it is so stupid." Prosperity could be had through more constructive social spending.[25]

By the summer of 1940 Bingham had shed whatever ambivalence he had had about defense spending and emerged as an eager proponent of the arms buildup, seeing in the unfolding mobilization effort immense possibilities for the enlargement of social democracy.[26] Bingham, however, was uneasy about the prominent positions businessmen had marked out for themselves in the defense effort. Along with the editors of the *Nation* and the *New Republic,* he denounced businessmen for stalling the mobilization by refusing to expand plant and production until they had been insured against all risks. Here was the ironic circumstance of previously pacifistic intellectuals, including the young I. F. Stone, assailing the nation's military contractors in Veblenesque fashion for sabotaging the defense drive. These industrialists, Bingham charged, had shown a monumental unwillingness to plan together, to accept price controls or production priorities, or to curtail the excessive profits they reaped from defense work. Unwilling to accept wholesale nationalization of industrial concerns, Bingham, however, suggested a mere administrative remedy, urging that, wherever possible, businessmen be replaced in defense service by New Deal planners sensitive to the social opportunities of the arms program. With them at the economic helm, the preparedness program could result in the "fulfillment of the New Deal."[27]

Unlike Mumford, then, who saw mobilization as a grueling experience in scarcity and sacrifice, with the nation forced to forgo social and economic benefits for the sake of the war industries, Bingham believed America rich enough to have both "guns and butter." Once again we see his faith in the nation's inexhaustible plenty influencing his program for human justice. Armed with this faith, he urged that preparedness be a period of "opportunity" and "confident advance." Thus, in a fashion reminiscent of 1917, Bingham and other liberals saw in the war an opportunity to enact their social designs. In the case of Bingham, in particular, war replaced revolution as the principal instrument of social transformation. That is undoubtedly why he repeatedly described the war in the language of revolution.[28]

The Japanese attack on Pearl Harbor finally ended the debate over intervention, elevating the preparedness issue to ever more acute importance. Only now the preparedness question became preeminently a question of war strategy. What would be the aims of the nation's war effort? More than the isolationists, whose concerns had been narrowly national, Bingham entered easily into this debate, joining the liberal interventionists in an effort to secure a generous peace. Throughout the first years of our military participation, Bingham urged that, even as we fought the Axis, we pursue a "grand political strategy" along the lines *Common Sense* had already recommended. Bingham considered these constant proddings absolutely essential, for while he greatly admired Roosevelt as a democratic leader, he was disturbed by his preoccupation with military considerations almost to the exclusion of the pressing political concerns which would affect the shape of the postwar world. Even in 1944, with the Allies within reach of victory, the President, Bingham protested, had given the nation no clear indication of the kind of peace he favored. Unconditional surrender seemed his sole concern. In *The Practice of Idealism* (1944), a book written just before he entered military service, and a book drawing its purpose from his understanding of the war as a revolutionary upheaval, a struggle between "competing principles of human organization," Bingham made one last effort to influence America's war strategy.[29]

Bingham considered a deeper understanding of the war essential to the achievement of a lasting peace. The war, he argued, was being fought against the background of five interrelated revolutions which had been gathering momentum for years. The first of these, "The Revolt of the Common Man," or what Ortega y Gasset called "The Revolt of the Masses," was the global struggle of the exploited and the disprivileged for enlarged freedom, dignity, and material security, a revolution that had broadened out to include the embittered lower middle classes of the industrial nations. Merged with and virtually indistinguishable from this social upheaval was the "Technical Revolution," the permanent revolution of science and industry. This revolution held out the promise of a universally abundant life, yet thus far it had meant only chronic unemployment, spreading misery, and aggravated despair for millions of the world's poor. By widening the chasm between the haves and the have-nots, it had contributed to the revolt of the common man. It was, moreover, the inability of traditional governing institutions to master this material revolution that had touched off the "revolution in forms of government" that Bingham had described in fuller detail in *The Techniques of Democracy*. That same technical revolution was rendering obsolete the old nation-state system, as an increasingly interrelated technology demanded new methods of control spanning traditional political boundaries, giving rise to the possibility of a global commonwealth of nations.

The final and in some ways the most crucial world transformation was spiritual at base: this was "the crisis in belief" inspired by the failure of the previously dominant ideologies to explain and address the new agenda of world problems. Bingham saw this failure as responsible for the ascendancy of false secular religions like communism, nationalism, and fascism; and his aim in writing *The Practice of Idealism* was to offer a faith powerful enough to counter these emergent belief systems. The faith he urged had as its moral center the idea that all men "have an unalienable right to freedom and to institutions through which they can advance their own welfare." Supremely confident that science, supplied with an energizing human vision, could achieve this dream in the immediate future, Bingham closed with a program to master the five world revolutions, a program that amounted to little more than a restatement of the peace strategy he had already proposed in *Common Sense*.[30]

The keynote of Bingham's plan and of his global faith was its repudiation of the realpolitik approach to world affairs best exemplified by Walter Lippmann's then influential book *United States Foreign Policy: Shield of the Republic,* an approach emphasizing national interest, balance of power, and power politics as the basis of a realistic foreign policy. Lippmann's "geopolitics," Bingham observed, "would be immediately understandable by the theorists of present-day Germany. The ordering of the world by preponderant force, in accordance with 'vital national interests,' is what many people have thought we were fighting against." This Machiavellian "checkerboard" diplomacy, in ignoring the twentieth-century world of social revolution, anti-imperialism, and aroused racial consciousness, was as "reactionary" as the established order these forces had set themselves against. In its place Bingham called for a foreign policy animated by democratic idealism. We are, he wrote, on the verge of making the world "one neighborhood." Yet if we continue to think in terms of power and national interest to the exclusion of all else, we will create for ourselves nothing but "an impossible state of perpetual latent war."[31]

Bingham, however, proposed that his idealism be balanced by an attention to the practical and the possible. The peace settlement would necessarily be "an imperfect adjustment to stubborn realities." The most that could be hoped for was a conversion of the United Nations war alliance to peacetime purposes and its extension to all nations. Such an imperfect organization would not be able to impose democracy on the Soviet Union or China, nor would it result in the immediate abandonment of the nation-state system. But combined with a European federation and the expansion of existing forms of world cooperation, it would stand as a stirring prelude to an eventual world government.[32]

Although in some ways the most enthusiastically received of Bingham's books,[33] *The Practice of Idealism* was not an original or particularly insightful work. The five revolutions it described were the human concerns Bingham had been addressing since his entrance into public life, while the program it proposed for mastering them restated ideas already familiar to his readers. The book is important, nonetheless, as an expression of the powerful social optimism liberals like Bingham brought to the war effort. By interpreting the war as a great force for democracy, Bingham and those like him unwittingly prepared the way for their own political and spiritual disenchantment in the postwar years. It would have been well for them to have recalled Randolph Bourne's prophetic insight, that war, once released, was impossible to bend to decent purposes. "If war is too strong for you to prevent," Bourne had asked an earlier generation of liberals, "how is it going to be weak enough for you to control and mould to your liberal purposes?"[34]

While hopeful that the war would unleash a democratic social revolution, Bingham was afflicted by mounting doubts about his own role in encouraging this transformation, doubts akin to those he had felt as a young man witnessing in Russia another kind of revolution. As in 1932, he wanted now to influence the anticipated upheaval; and as before, he searched anxiously for a role consonant with his talents and intentions. Yet while his dilemma remained much the same, by this time Bingham had lost confidence in his ability to inspire sweeping change. After over a decade of urgent effort as an editor and political theorist he found little indication of his public influence or impact. These accumulating anxieties arising from his political ineffectiveness eventually culminated in a paralyzing personal crisis that cut short Bingham's career as an editor and activist intellectual.

Bingham's crisis in confidence had been building since at least 1937 when he abandoned third party politics to support and influence the New Deal. Even as a New Dealer, however, his ideas went unheeded, his influence remained minimal, and the immediate result was a deepening loss of confidence in *Common Sense*. It would perhaps always remain, he began to believe, a small voice of uncertain effect. Finally, in 1940 Bingham left the daily editorial responsibilities of *Common Sense* to Rodman and returned to Connecticut to run for the state senate. Perhaps in politics he could be a more formidable force for change?[35]

Bingham did not consider this decision an abandonment of the intellectual life. He continued to write the feature editorials of *Common Sense* and to work on his books. But if successful at the state level, he indicated to those closest to him that he would make politics his career. The United States Congress, he wrote in his diary at the time, "is a forum for ideas and a place of decision . . . for which all my training and experience fit me for greatest effectiveness."[36]

Unfortunately, Bingham never had the opportunity to join theory to action as an intellectual in politics. He was elected in November, 1940, to the state senate, the first Democrat to carry the staunchly Republican twentieth district since 1912. However, after serving only one frustrating term, during which time he confessed to seeing most of his "pet ideas" relegated "to the waste basket," he lost his bid for reelection in 1942. "Connecticut," he conceded to his father, who had urged him to run a more conservative campaign, "is still 'the land of steady habits.'"[37]

Affairs at *Common Sense* had, meanwhile, reached a crisis point. Rodman had actually managed to raise the magazine's circulation from 6,000 in 1940 to 10,000 in 1942. But just as Bingham was losing the Connecticut senate race, Rodman received word that his appeal for a draft deferral had been denied. With Rodman about to enter the service, *Common Sense* would either have to cease publication or be turned over to the new editors; unless, of course, Bingham agreed to return as full-time editor.[38] For a time in 1942 Bingham seemed prepared to do just that, for he dreaded losing what had been his public sounding board for over a decade. His faith in the transforming power of ideas, moreover, remained undiminished. Since 1932 he had considered it his chief life aim "to help direct" the "world-wide upheaval which now has exploded into war"; and this could best be accomplished, he told his father, who was pressing him to volunteer for active military service, "in the field of ideas rather than military action. A magazine like *Common Sense* can . . . be as important as a whole army. This is as much a war of ideas as it is a military struggle."[39]

Bingham, however, was convinced that *Common Sense* could not be fully effective in its present form. Its readership was too small, confined to a few thousand like-minded liberals. He would return to *Common Sense,* he told Rodman, only if he could secure the financial backing to boost its circulation tenfold, to near 100,000. Bingham realized that such an effort to encourage a mass readership would entail some dilution of *Common Sense's* intellectual content, and quite possibly a complete revision of its format. He even considered making it a popular weekly of news and commentary along the lines of *Time* magazine. Anything to raise it to greater effectiveness.[40]

With the war on, however, Bingham was unable to gather the financial backing for an enlarged *Common Sense.* Unwilling to return as active

editor to the magazine in what he deemed its "present state of ineffectiveness," and with no other promising career prospects in
sight, Bingham frantically searched for a position that would give him
a shaping role in the war effort.[41] Like innumerable other liberal intellectuals,
he was stimulated by the war to a passion for active service. Not content to remain on the periphery as an editor and publicist, he yearned
to be at the center of things, preferably overseas, helping to ease the
transition to peace. He had served briefly in the summer of 1942 in the
Connecticut Office of Price Administration under his old friend
Chester Bowles. But he found his bureaucratic duties tediously oppressive.[42] Finally, after failing to land a position with the American
Friends Service Committee or any of the government civilian agencies
operating overseas, he applied for and was commissioned a captain in
the Army's military government, eventually serving two years abroad,
mostly in Germany. "Vanity—a sense of pride to be secured in uniform,"
along with his father's promptings, had, he confessed, influenced his
decision.[43] In the end, however, it was the decision of a man who had
exhausted his alternatives; and Bingham entered military service humbly
aware of that fact, acknowledging in a letter to his father, before leaving
for Germany, that the most he could hope to accomplish in his new
position was to have some "slight effect on how people in other countries look on Americans and on the atmosphere in which peace begins."[44]

With Bingham and Rodman in military service, editorial direction of
Common Sense passed to a group of young social democrats, Sidney
Hertzberg, Richard H. Rovere, Maurice J. Goldbloom, and Daniel Bell,
with Hertzberg serving as editor-in-chief. Katrina McCormick Barnes,
the renegade niece of Colonel Robert Rutherford McCormick, editor
and publisher of the *Chicago Tribune,* became acting publisher. Bingham
and Rodman retained some editorial control and remained as the
majority owners, but after June, 1943, the magazine—in both tone and
policy—ceased to be theirs.[45]

"Trini" McCormick had joined *Common Sense* as a financial partner
in 1941. An exuberant and delightfully irrepressible rebel, she, like
Bingham, had broken from a family of wealth and influence to attempt
a career in insurgent journalism. And she shared Bingham's dream of
making *Common Sense* a broadly influential mass magazine. Yet she
wanted to be the publisher of her own, not of someone else's, magazine. With Hertzberg as her ally, she attempted to wrench full financial
and editorial control from the other partners, something Bingham and
Rodman were unwilling to allow. They wanted, it seems, to keep open
the possibility of returning to *Common Sense* after the war.[46]

The Hertzberg-McCormick challenge eventually forced the other partners to fire Hertzberg and bring in as the new editor Varian Fry, formerly of the *New Republic*. Fry, however, inherited an enterprise burdened by sinking morale and a crushing financial deficit. Despite a steady gain in circulation, *Common Sense* was running at an estimated annual loss of $25,000. Only Bingham's and Rodman's massive dedication had kept it going this long. Finally, when McCormick pulled out of the partnership and efforts to gain new backing failed, the remaining partners decided to cease publication. The January, 1946, issue was the magazine's last. With Bingham overseas, his wife signed the documents closing down the journal that had announced his entrance into radical politics in the grave winter of 1932.[47]

For Bingham this was the end of a career as well. He would never return to journalism and to the intensely active intellectual life he had pursued into the war years. He came back from the war in a spirit of high uncertainty, without anything he could call an occupation. In this he was not unlike countless other veterans. Only, he was over forty; and the war, rather than interrupting a going career, had brought his to an end. Reserved and quietly intellectual, not much of a "hand-shaker or backslapper," he began to doubt whether he was even cut out to be a politician. Nor did he have a strong political base from which to become effective. "I had," he later recalled, "no real roots in any community, despite my ancestors in the family cemetery." Nor did he possess the desire or the driving confidence to start afresh as an editor of some other publication. He might have resumed political writing as an independently based critic, but the memories of his previous ineffectiveness crippled his creative urge. Adrift without clear purpose or direction, Bingham was afflicted by a massive psychological depression. "The creative artist," as he wrote some years later, "may, perhaps, carry on without appreciation, but only exceptionally and at great cost. So, when my creative work ceased for lack of anyone who would pay me, or even listen to me, I began to shrivel, like any unemployed man."[48]

Finally, after several years of psychoanalysis, which he claims saved him from "complete disaster,"[49] Bingham resumed a career in law and politics, although not nearly on the scale he had once intended. In 1949 he opened a local Connecticut law practice, and over the years he has held a number of minor local and state offices, forced to content himself with activity on the fringes of public life while friends like Chester Bowles went on to national service. Only another personal crisis, his son's active involvement in the radical dissent of the 1960s, drove him back to the writing desk. In 1970 he collaborated with his brother Congressman Jonathan B. Bingham of New York on *Violence and Democracy,* an update and reiteration of the ideas of *The Techniques of Democracy,* and a book that concluded with the same abounding social confidence that echoed through *The Practice of Idealism.* "With the help of a saving sense of proportion" and an appreciation of the vitality of existing democratic institutions, the outrage and despair of the young, Bingham was confident, could be transformed into a secular faith capable of leading America into an era of permanent peace and unexampled social democracy. This time, however, Bingham expressed no inclination to head the struggle, while privately he advised his son to abandon radical activism for a career in law and politics.[50] Although others might disagree, he would continue to consider his *Common Sense* experience a "mistake," a waste of creative energies that would have been better spent in the career he had originally set out upon at Yale. For his aim had always been service—to promote "a new integration of humankind."[51] And as a publicist he had carried on for over a decade without the audience or the public impact he considered essential for sustained intellectual effort. How could he possibly lead when so few were willing to follow?

11

EPILOGUE

Bingham's efforts to fashion a New American Radicalism grew out of his belief that the depression exposed a crisis in American political ideology. Capitalism had reached its breaking point, yet neither radicals nor reformers were prepared with a realistic program for its replacement. Convinced that the core moral ideals of liberalism and socialism were still fresh and humanly relevant, he insisted, nonetheless, that both these creeds had been rendered inappropriate to the concerns of a new socio-political reality. Marxism, in the hands of Soviet interpreters and their slavish American disciples, had been transformed into a sterile orthodoxy impervious to criticism or revision while liberalism, once a spirited insurgent creed, was now a cautious reformism without clear social purpose or intellectual content. John Dewey's *Liberalism and Social Action,* cut to the heart of what Bingham saw as the modern liberal dilemma: liberalism's inability to join its original aims to a comprehensive program for their attainment in the emerging collectivist-industrial situation.

Yet Dewey and Bingham did more than assail the deficiencies of the dominant orientations. They suggested a radical program and philosophy of high specificity and deep moral purpose, one that avoided the dogmatism of official Marxism and the programless relativism of American liberalism. Their intellectual aim was the fusion of the best of these two proud traditions, liberalism and democratic socialism—employing socialist collectivism for the attainment of the classic liberal ideals of democracy, equal justice, full individuality, and a widely available abundance. Without abandoning the common moral ideals of liberalism and socialism, the ideals really of the Western humanist tradition, they advanced a compelling response to the crisis of twentieth-century ideology.

Obviously, they failed to win political power or even a good measure of public influence; and, eventually, the spread of totalitarianism drove independent radicals like Bingham to an accommodation with the very liberalism they had once assailed. In some ways, in fact, their own statement of radicalism smoothed the way for this political retreat. For Bingham and most of his fellow *Common Sense* radicals, socialism had been more a means than an end, more a structural technique for the furtherance of liberal ends than a wholly new conception of culture and society. This interpretation of socialism placed them closer to the New Deal reformers than they realized at the time.

Yet while many of their social proposals were deeply flawed, and although they never gained the public impact they sought, in a truly important sense the "new radicals" did not fail. They raised profoundly searching questions concerning the nature and direction of industrial society and set forth a number of social proposals that still demand attention. The pressing public concerns they addressed are still our own; the relationship between collectivist planning and freedom in the modern administrative state, the role of the managers and the experts in our immediate future, the problem of providing prosperity without inflation, the place and function of labor and the middle classes in social change, the relevance of Marxism to modern industrial society, the question of violent versus democratic change, the proper interplay between radical criticism and radical action, and countless others. Finally, they entered into a dialogue on the history and future prospects of radicalism in this country that is of inestimable importance to all engaged in the continuing search for the community of man. And while their specific programs and proposals might strike us as extravagantly utopian, the unflagging confidence with which they approached the problems of their time can be instructive to this age of increasing public skepticism.

In their effort to free American radicalism from its reliance upon foreign revolutionary models, the *Common Sense* intellectuals confronted a problem of particular relevance to present-day radicalism. A growing number of modern critics and historians, including Christopher Lasch and James Weinstein, attribute American radicalism's record of repeated failure after 1919 to its refusal to tailor its program and strategy to uniquely American conditions. We still lack in this country a challenging democratic radicalism attractive to labor and the aggrieved middle classes, a radicalism capable of pursuing power without sacrificing principle. Yet the answer does not lie in a revivification of the New American Radicalism; for while there is much that remains fresh and relevant in its analysis and content, this radicalism is inappropriate to the problems and challenges of our own age. And the locus of that inadequacy is in its allegiance to the material aims and values of liberalism and socialism, creeds of a human epoch that is passing irretrievably into history.

Human society in the industrial West has already entered an age where liberalism and socialism have proved their inability to meet and master our social problems, an age, ironically, where some of the very ideals and aims of the older creeds have become part of the current problem. Liberalism and socialism, as C. Wright Mills argued, "arose as guidelines to reflection about types of society which do not now exist. John Stuart Mill never examined the kinds of political economy now arising in the capitalist world. Karl Marx never analyzed the kinds of society now arising in the Communist bloc." We now confront "new kinds of social structure which . . . resist analysis in the liberal and in the socialist terms we have inherited."[1]

Yet this does not signal the end of ideology. To the contrary, the crisis cries out for a fresh and convincingly modern image and orientation, one that retains the inviolate moral ideals of liberalism and socialism but redefines them in terms of the ascendant threats to their social fulfillment.[2] In the depression decade Bingham and Dewey attempted just such a restatement. But they were too closely wedded to the sanguinely rationalistic values and thrust of the standard orientations to effect the kind of sweeping philosophic revision the dawning age demands.

This becomes apparent when we put their pragmatic rationalist approach to a criticism that goes beyond the analysis of C. Wright Mills. Liberalism and socialism are, as Mills tells us, orientations of secular humanism; their crisis is part of a crisis in the humanist tradition itself. But liberalism and socialism are also ideologies of industrialization; and their crisis reflects a deeper crisis in Western industrial society.

Liberalism and socialism grew to influence in an age of breakneck material expansion and full-throated faith in science and its applications. As creeds, they echoed the age's exuberant confidence in the inevitability of progress through scientific and industrial growth. Both saw and continue to see the release of economic plenty through the intelligent use of the machine as their outstanding material aim. Both judge abundance as the ground and basis of the good life. Neither directly challenges nor threatens the structure of integrated industrial society. In twentieth-century practice both have shown a common respect, even reverence, for technology, efficiency, mass production, expertise, and social engineering. This is one of the reasons Bingham and other early 1930s radicals could turn with remarkable ease to an advanced form of corporate liberalism toward the close of the decade: it was so very much like the socialist collectivism they had earlier embraced.

Liberalism, released from the cautions of John Stuart Mill, especially cultivates the mythology of limitless material expansion, along with the related tendency to see material growth as the sine qua non of human progress. But the example of American independent radicalism testifies to the contagious power of this view. The magnificent productivity of the machine will make all men comfortable, and with universal plentitude will come the end of social strife and the beginning of a new age of human solidarity and cooperation: such was the faith of Bingham and Dewey, a faith commensurate with the liberal belief in the bottomless possibilities of abundance, and a faith that firmly equated community and social justice with proper public administration.

But this faith—which burned bright in the planning designs of the 1930s collectivists—is flawed by the fact that realities will no longer support it. We now confront a cruel paradox. Accelerated economic growth, the announced material aim of both liberalism and socialism, has brought us to a state of development in the industrial West where man's survival as a species is endangered. Our fragile planet, biologists tell us, cannot sustain further expansion of the sort witnessed in the past. So a new age beckons; and if man is to survive and socially prosper in this new age, he must move beyond the creed of limitless growth to a standard of individual and collective behavior congruent with emergent environmental circumstances.[3]

Bingham, it is clear, never defined abundance as an end in itself; nor did he believe that the brotherhood of man could be engineered by technology and its agents. Yet the thrust of his social argument led dangerously in this direction. It was not his commitment to science and rational planning that was the problem; rather, it was his almost uncritical celebration of the uplifting possibilities of these admittedly essential human instruments. Even planned abundance, equitably distributed, seems incapable of inaugurating social harmony, peace between nations, or a rising level of human happiness. Despite claims to the contrary, there appears to be no positive relationship between economic progress and the advancement of the human spirit. Nor can social engineering create the cooperative community. ". . . Communities," as Peter Clecak wisely reminds us, "cannot be legislated into existence. Nor can they be permanently institutionalized once they appear, since they have lives of their own: they come into existence, live, and die out mysteriously. Both in historical and personal terms, the experience of community is momentary. . . ." No one, Clecak cautions, can adequately explain or hope to arrange "the complex emotional and intellectual sinews of a group pursuing common objectives." When this does occur, it invariably occurs at the local level, among small groups, the product of forces mysteriously human. "Such phenomena lie beyond the direct control of social planners."[4]

The vision of utopia remains a necessity for socialism. Without it there is no directing moral norm for socialist politics. Bingham realized this. But he stressed too heavily planning as the way to this ideal. Much like the Technocrats he failed to discern the limitations of social organization as an instrument of human happiness. This was the capital fallacy of collectivist planning.

Admittedly, it might seem unfair to put Bingham to this kind of criticism. In a time of scarcity, with one out of every four Americans out of work, only the most astute critic could have been expected to perceive the dangers of unchecked economic growth. Yet another of his contemporaries, a man equally committed to social justice, saw beyond the immediate economic crisis to the emerging crisis in machine civilization and to the dilemma this crisis posed for the standard radical and liberal approaches. Of all the decade's insurgent intellectuals, Lewis Mumford had the shrewdest insight into the approaching problems of post-modern society.

We are already familiar with Mumford's indictment of machine civilization and its insensate ideology of limitless growth. But this much at least bears deeper emphasis, for it reaches to the heart of Bingham's unguarded faith in the possibilities of science, social organization, and material prosperity. Many of the problems assumed by radicals to lie in the competitive ethic and in the private ownership of wealth were, Mumford maintained, rooted in the fact of mass industrialization itself. And these problems could be effectively confronted only when the reigning ideologies of industrial man—liberalism and socialism—gave way to a philosophy of community renewal stressing balance and measure rather than the Lockean idea of plunder and growth as its supreme imperative. The aim of socialism, Mumford insisted, must be a society of organic balance and economic sufficiency, not an engineered utopia of unbounded plenty.

The economy of sufficiency Mumford suggested in *Technics and Civilization* differed in yet another important way from the abundance radicalism of Alfred Bingham. In Mumford's ideal social arrangement the community squarely confronted the issue of economic distribution. As we have seen, America's traditional way of meeting the demands of the lower and middle classes for a higher material standard has been to increase the overall output, thereby increasing the income of all classes, while leaving the income of the upper strata virtually untouched. But Mumford's more stationary economy sharply challenged this standard national approach to wealth distribution. In the economy of "basic communism" the claims of the lower and the middle classes for a decent income could be met only by diminishing the income of the upper groups. All would be forced to accept a "normalized standard of consumption." The constraints on growth would in this way, Mumford hoped, encourage a new cooperative ethic and a more disciplined consumption pattern among all segments of the population.[5]

"The problem of how to function *in* the world and yet not become *of* that world," is, as Warren Susman suggests, the preeminent challenge of American radicalism. There is a proud measure of decency and much that is still immediately relevant in the radicalism of Alfred Bingham. Yet in his efforts to overcome socialism's alienation from the life of the nation, he developed programs and tactics that were in important ways supportive of the very order he went up against. Not only did Bingham's radicalism mirror the excessively mechanistic and utilitarian ideals of the political economy he assailed, but the tactics he advanced to reach socialism rested on the very acquisitive values he proposed to transform. In his quest for a socialist America, he failed like most of us to abide by that difficult Puritan injunction to be "in but not of" the society we are committed to change.[6]

NOTES

INTRODUCTION

1. See especially R. Alan Lawson, *The Failure of Independent Liberalism, 1930-1941* (New York, 1971); and Frank A. Warren, *Liberals and Communism: The "Red Decade" Revisited,* (Bloomington, Ind., 1966).

2. The most astute studies of the independent Left in these years are Richard H. Pells, *Radical Visions and American Dreams: Culture and Social Thought in the Depression Years* (New York, 1973); Lawson; Warren, *Liberals and Communism;* Warren, "Alfred M. Bingham and the Paradox of Liberalism," *The Historian* 28 (Feb., 1966): 252-67; and Robert Crunden, *From Self to Society, 1919-1941.* Donald R. McCoy's *Angry Voices: Left-of-Center Politics in the New Deal Era* (Lawrence, Kans., 1958) briefly describes the *Common Sense* third party effort, but focuses almost entirely on organizational work to the virtual exclusion of the movement's intellectual contribution. For a discussion of the economic thought of various political leaders, see Theodore Rosenoff, *Dogma, Depression, and the New Deal: The Debate of Political Leaders over Economic Recovery* (Port Washington, N.Y., 1975).

3. Peter Gay, *The Dilemma of Democratic Socialism: Eduard Bernstein's Challenge to Marx* (New York, 1952), p. 73.

4. See especially Kenneth Keniston, *Young Radicals: Notes on Committed Youth* (New York, 1968).

5. Pells, p. xii.

6. Christopher Lasch, *The New Radicalism in America, 1889-1963: The Intellectual as a Social Type* (New York, 1965), pp. xiii-xvi.

7. Gay, pp. ix-xi.

CHAPTER 1

1. [Alfred M. Bingham], "1776-1932," *Common Sense* Collection, Yale University, New Haven, Conn. (hereafter cited as *CS* collection), 1 (December 5, 1932): 2; *New York American,* November 14, 1932, p. 6; Bingham, "Original Prospectus," MS, October, 1932, p. 10, *CS* collection.

2. *New York American,* November 14, 1932, p. 6; *New York Times,* November 14, 1932, p. 38; Robert Cantwell, "Second Generation," *Modern Youth* (winter,

1932): 8–12; interview with Bingham, September 7, 1970 at Salem, Conn.

3. Hiram Bingham, "Freedom under the Constitution with Calvin Coolidge" (New Haven, 1924). Most of my information on Hiram Bingham and the Bingham family history was obtained from the Bingham Family Papers, Yale University, New Haven, Connecticut. Alfred Bingham also made available to me extensive family papers and records from his Salem, Connecticut files (hereafter cited as Bingham Personal Papers).

4. Alfred M. Bingham, "Law and Politics," MS, n.d., pp. 2–4, Bingham Personal Papers.

5. Hiram Bingham to Alfred M. Bingham, February 3, 1941, Bingham Personal Papers.

6. Hiram Bingham, *A Residence of Twenty-One Years in the Sandwich Islands* (Hartford, 1843), p. 125; "Hiram Bingham I," *Dictionary of American Biography*, 21 vols. (New York, 1928–36), 2: 276; "Hiram Bingham II," ibid., 276–77; "Hiram Bingham," *Current Biography* (1951), pp. 41–43; Harold Bradley, *The American Frontier in Hawaii: The Pioneers, 1789–1893* (Stanford, 1942), pp. 124–29; J. C. Furnas, *Anatomy of Paradise: Hawaii and the Islands of the South Seas* (New York, 1948), pp. 129–47, 180. There is a good deal of information on the Hawaiian mission in the Bingham Family Papers.

7. "Hiram Bingham II File," Bingham Family Papers; "Hiram Bingham II," *DAB* 2: 276–77.

8. "Hiram Bingham III File," Bingham Family Papers; "Hiram Bingham," *National Cyclopaedia of American Biography* (1926): 28–29; "Hiram Bingham," *Current Biography*, pp. 41–43.

9. Hiram Bingham, *The Journal of an Expedition across Venezuela and Colombia, 1906–1907* (New Haven, 1909); *Across South America: An Account of a Journey from Buenos Aires to Lima* (Boston, 1911); *The Discovery of Machu Picchu* (New York, 1913); *The Ascent of Coropuna* (New York, 1912). "Obituary: Hiram Bingham," *Proceedings of the American Antiquarian Society* 66 (October 17, 1956): 60–62; Jerry Patterson, "Obituary Notes: Hiram Bingham, 1875–1956," *Hispanic American Historical Review* 37 (February, 1957): 131–37.

10. Alfred M. Bingham, *Man's Estate: Adventures in Economic Discovery* (New York, 1939), pp. 17–19, 21; interview with Bingham, September 7, 1970.

11. Bingham, *Man's Estate*, pp. 19, 23–24; interview with Bingham, September 7, 1970.

12. Quoted in Richard Hofstadter, *The American Political Tradition* (New York, 1948), p. 319.

13. Quoted in James MacGregor Burns, *Roosevelt: The Lion and the Fox* (New York, 1956), p. 15; interview with Bingham, September 7, 1970; Bingham to Endicott Peabody, March 6, 1937, Alfred M. Bingham Papers, Yale University, New Haven, Conn. (hereafter cited Bingham MSS).

14. Bingham, *Man's Estate*, pp. 22–23.

15. Bingham, "ASA: A Young Man's Creed," MS, n.d., p. 81, Bingham Personal Papers; "Law and Politics," p. 3.

16. Bingham to Annie Olivia Mitchell, February 17, 1926, Bingham Personal Papers; *Man's Estate*, p. 24.

17. Bingham, *Man's Estate*, pp. 25–35; interview with Bingham, January 8, 1970 at Salem, Conn.

18. Bingham, *Man's Estate*, p. 35.

19. Bingham, "ASA," pp. 2–11, 16–21, 24–34, 36–94.

20. Ibid., p. 34.

21. Bingham, "Youth," undated poem, Bingham Personal Papers.

22. Bingham, "Law and Politics," pp. 1–2; interview with Bingham, September 7, 1970; "Hiram Bingham III File," Bingham Family Papers; Hiram Bingham obituary, *New York Times*, June 7, 1956, p. 31.

23. Bingham, "ASA," p. 94.
24. Bingham, "The Sword," undated poem, Bingham Personal Papers.
25. Interview with Bingham, January 8, 1970.

CHAPTER 2

1. Alfred M. Bingham, *Man's Estate: Adventures in Economic Discovery* (New York, 1939), pp. 29-31.
2. Ibid.
3. Bingham, "A Bourgeois Meets Bolshevism," MS, n.d., p. 1, Bingham Personal Papers.
4. Ibid., pp. 1-4, 11-12, 16.
5. Bingham, "A Study of Communist Russia in 1931," MS, 1931, pp. 19-20, Bingham Personal Papers.
6. Bingham, "Bourgeois Meets Bolshevism," p. 15. This exhilarating idealism was observed by countless other Russian observers in these years. See especially Louis Fischer, "Russia's New Revolution," *Nation* 130 (March 19, 1930): 322-23; see also Lewis Feuer, "American Travelers to the Soviet Union, 1917-32: The Formation of a Component of New Deal Ideology," *American Quarterly* 14 (summer, 1962): 122, 124-25; and Peter Filene, *Americans and the Soviet Experiment, 1917-1933* (Cambridge, Mass., 1967).
7. Bingham, "Bourgeois Meets Bolshevism," p. 10.
8. Ibid., p. 15; Bingham, "A Study," pp. 39-40; Bingham, "Why I Am Not a Communist," MS, 1933, Bingham MSS.
9. Bingham, *Man's Estate,* pp. 236-37.
10. Ibid.; Bingham, "Bourgeois Meets Bolshevism," pp. 26, 42.
11. Bingham, *Man's Estate,* pp. 31-33; "A Study," pp. 3, 12.
12. Bingham, "The Five Year Plan on the Farms," MS, 1931, Bingham Personal Papers, pp. 5, 19; "A Study," pp. ii, 2, 6, 15.
13. Bingham, "A Study," pp. viii, 34-37. For an example of the relativist attitude of these Soviet sympathizers, see Roger Baldwin, *Liberty under the Soviets* (New York, 1928), p. 4; see also Frank A. Warren, *Liberals and Communism: The "Red Decade" Revisited* (Bloomington, Ind., 1966).
14. Bingham, "Bourgeois Meets Bolshevism," pp. 10, 26, 37-39.
15. Ibid., pp. 27, 39, 45; "A Study," p. 44.
16. Bingham, "Bourgeois Meets Bolshevism," p. 38.
17. Ibid., pp. 15-17, 40, 49-50; "A Study," p. 23.
18. Bingham, "Bourgeois Meets Bolshevism," pp. 16, 33, 40-41, 52-53.
19. Ibid., pp. 20-21, 26, 41.
20. Ibid., pp. 56-57; *Man's Estate,* p. 33.
21. Bingham, "A Study," pp. v, 21; "Common Sense and the Community," MS, June-July, 1932, p. 27, Bingham Personal Papers.
22. Bingham, "Common Sense and the Community," pp. 26-29.
23. Bingham, "Bourgeois Meets Bolshevism," pp. 21, 43; private diary, n.d., Bingham Personal Papers; interview with Bingham, January 8, 1970 at Salem, Conn.
24. Bingham, private diary, n.p.
25. Bingham, "Common Sense and the Community," pp. 1-3, 35, 42, 45; see also "Collectivism vs. Individualism," MS, May 1, 1933, Bingham MSS.
26. Bingham to Annie Olivia Mitchell, May 30, 1933, Bingham Personal Papers.
27. Bingham, "Common Sense and the Community," pp. 44-51; "Original Prospectus," MS, October, 1932, pp. 2, 11-12, 16, 19-20, CS collection; Bingham to Hiram Bingham, May 27, 1933, Bingham Personal Papers.
28. Bingham to Annie Olivia Mitchell, May 30, 1933, Bingham Personal Papers.

29. Bingham, "Original Prospectus," pp. 8-10; "Common Sense and the Community," pp. 51, 54-56; "Notes for 'The Community: A Revolutionary Weekly,'" MS, n.d., *CS* collection.

30. Bingham, private diary, n.p.

CHAPTER 3

1. Quoted in Selden Rodman, "Two Cities of Fortune: Pittsburgh and Detroit," in Alfred M. Bingham and Selden Rodman, eds., *Challenge to the New Deal* (New York, 1934), p. 27; William E. Leuchtenburg, *Franklin D. Roosevelt and the New Deal, 1932-1940* (New York, 1963), pp. 1-3.

2. Quoted in William Manchester, *The Glory and the Dream* (Boston, 1974), p. 31.

3. Alfred M. Bingham, "Prospectus for a New Magazine," MS, n.d., *CS* collection; *Man's Estate: Adventures in Economic Discovery* (New York, 1939), p. 36.

4. William Saroyan, *Inhale & Exhale* (New York, 1936), p. 81; Studs Terkel, *Hard Times: An Oral History of the Great Depression* (New York, 1970), p. 5.

5. Bingham, "Original Prospectus," MS, October, 1932, p. 2, *CS* collection.

6. Bingham, "Common Sense: Prospectus of a New Magazine," MS, n.d., *CS* collection; "Original Prospectus," pp. 2-6; quoted in Selden Rodman, review of Sidney Hook's *Toward the Understanding of Karl Marx*, "Books," *CS* 2 (May 11, 1933): 18; see also Rodman, "Prophets and Disciples," review of Bertram Wolfe's *Marx and America, CS* 3 (February, 1934): 29.

7. Bingham, introduction to reprint series of *Common Sense*, 15 volumes (New York, Greenwood Press Reprint Corporation, 1968), vol. 1 (1932): Stanley Kunitz and Howard Haycroft, eds., *Twentieth Century Authors* (New York, 1942), pp. 836-37; interview with Selden Rodman, June 28, 1977, Oakland, N.J.

8. Bingham, "Law and Politics," MS, n.d., p. 4, Bingham Personal Papers.

9. Bingham, "Original Prospectus," pp. 9, 13-14.

10. John Dewey, "A Great American Prophet," *CS* 3 (April, 1934): 6-7; Selden Rodman, review of Thorstein Veblen's *The Engineers and the Price System*, in "Books," *CS* 2 (February 2, 1933): 33.

11. See, for example, Walter W. Liggett, "Mr. Mellon's Pittsburgh: Symbol of Corruption," *CS* 1 (December 5, 1932): 4-6, 28-31; James Rorty, "Advertising: America's Narcotic," *CS* 1 (December 5, 1932): 17; Dwight MacDonald, "The Real Rulers: Myron C. Taylor," *CS* 2 (March 16, 1933): 12-14; John T. Flynn, "Government by Millionaires," *CS* 2 (March 2, 1933): 10-11.

12. Bingham, "Common Sense and the Community," MS, June-July, 1932, pp. 3-4, 9-10, 13, 21-22, Bingham Personal Papers; editorial, *CS* 2 (February 16, 1933): 2-3; "Draft Program and Statement of Aims for a New Party," MS, winter, 1932-33; Bingham MSS; Stuart Chase, "The Economy of Abundance," *CS* 1 (December 5, 1932): 16, 26.

13. Wayne W. Parrish, "What Is Technocracy?" *New Outlook* 161 (December, 1932): 13-17; for a full scale study of the Technocracy movement, see Harry Elsner, Jr., *The Technocrats: Prophets of Automation* (Syracuse, 1967); and William E. Akin, *Technocracy and the American Dream: The Technocrat Movement, 1900-1941* (Berkeley, Calif., 1977).

14. Thorstein Veblen, *The Engineers and the Price System* (New York, 1921); see also his *Absentee Ownership and Business Enterprise in Recent Times* (New York, 1923).

15. Veblen, "The Technicians and Revolution," in Max Lerner, *The Portable Veblen* (New York, 1948), pp. 438–65; Edwin T. Layton, "Veblen and the Engineers," *American Quarterly* 16 (Spring, 1962): 64–72.
16. Leon Ardzrooni, "Veblen and Technocracy," *Living Age* 344 (March, 1933): 39–42; Elsner, pp. 23–26; Akin, pp. 27–45; Howard Scott, "Technocracy: 1933," *CS* 2 (December, 1933): 6–7; Parrish, pp. 13–18.
17. Harold Loeb, "The Stupidity of Poverty," *CS* 3 (February, 1934): 6; Harold Loeb, *Life in a Technocracy: What It Might Be Like* (New York, 1933), pp. 3, 6–10, 20–32, 36–41; Howard Scott, "Technocracy Speaks," *Living Age* 343 (December, 1932): 298–302; Scott, "Technology Smashes the Price System: An Inquiry into the Nature of Our Present Crisis," *Harper's Magazine* 166 (January, 1933): 131, 142–48.
18. Wayne W. Parrish, *An Outline of Technocracy* (New York, 1933), pp. 5–6, 31–32; Scott, "Technocracy Speaks," p. 302.
19. See "Twenty-Five on Technocracy: A Symposium," *CS* 2 (February 2, 1933): 8–9.
20. [Bingham], "Technocracy: A Hope and a Warning," *CS* 2 (January 19, 1933): 3–4; Selden Rodman, review of Veblen's *Engineers*, p. 33.
21. Bingham, "Looking Forward: 1. Introduction," *CS* 2 (March 30, 1933): 3–5; *Man's Estate*, p. 297; Dewey, pp. 6–7.
22. Bingham, "Looking Forward." The other articles in the series are, Bingham, "The New Society: II: The Democracy of Industry," *CS* 2 (April 13, 1933): 3–5; C. Hartley Grattan, "The New Society: III: Money and Banking," *CS* 2 (April 27, 1933): 3–5; Bingham, "The New Society: IV: Wages and Income," *CS* 2 (May 11, 1933): 8–9; Bingham, "The New Society: V: Political Organization," *CS* 2 (May 25, 1933): 14–15; Bingham, "The New Society: VI: Life, Liberty and the Pursuit of Happiness," *CS* 2 (June 8, 1933): 13–15.
23. Quoted in John A. Garraty, *The New Commonwealth: 1877–1890* (New York, 1968), p. 319.
24. Bingham, "Common Sense and the Community," pp. 21, 29, 32; diary, n.d., Bingham Personal Papers; interview with Bingham, September 7, 1970.
25. Bingham, "Common Sense and the Community," pp. 21–23, 29, 32–33; *Man's Estate*, p. 307.
26. Bingham, "New Society: II," pp. 3–5; Bingham, "New Society: V," pp. 14–15; Bingham, "Looking Forward," pp. 3–5.
27. Bingham, "New Society: V," pp. 14–15.
28. Sidney Hook, *Toward the Understanding of Karl Marx* (New York, 1933), p. 101.
29. George Kateb, ed., *Utopia* (New York, 1971), p. 8.
30. Lewis Mumford, *The Myth of the Machine: The Pentagon of Power* (New York, 1970), p. 210.
31. Kateb, p. 8.

CHAPTER 4

1. Lewis Mumford, *Technics and Civilization* (New York, 1934), passim. The most coherent expression of the views of the Southern Agrarians is contained in *I'll Take My Stand* by twelve southerners (New York, 1930), and its sequel Herbert Agar and Allen Tate, eds., *Who Owns America?* (Boston, 1936).
2. George Soule, "An American Policy toward Russia," *Annals of the American Academy of Political and Social Science* (July 31, 1931): 87; Peter Filene, *Americans and the Soviet Experiment, 1917–1933* (Cambridge, Mass., 1967), p. 198.
3. Frank A. Warren, *Liberals and Communism: The "Red Decade" Revisited* (Bloomington, Ind., 1966), pp. 66–70, 76–77.

4.   Alfred M. Bingham, *Insurgent America: The Revolt of the Middle Classes* (New York, 1935), p. 5; Bingham, "Liberty, Democracy and Hokum," *CS* 3 (October, 1934): 3.

5.   Bingham, *Man's Estate: Adventures in Economic Discovery* (New York, 1939), pp. 296-97.

6.   George Soule, *The Coming American Revolution* (New York, 1934). See also Stuart Chase, "A Ten Year Plan for America," *Harper's* 163 (June, 1931): 1-10; Chase, *The Economy of Abundance* (New York, 1934), pp. 309-10; Paul H. Douglas, *The Coming of a New Party* (New York, 1932), pp. 93-94, 96-102.

7.   Bingham, "Common Sense and the Community," MS, June-July, 1932, pp. 14, 47-51, Bingham Personal Papers; W. W. Brickman, ed., *John Dewey's Impressions of Soviet Russia* (New York, 1964); Filene, pp. 152-54.

8.   These themes run through the entire literature of Technocracy; see especially Harold Loeb, *Life in a Technocracy: What It Might Be Like* (New York, 1933). For an insightful analysis of modern collectivist thought, see James B. Gilbert, *Designing the Industrial State* (New York, 1972); for a discussion of this theme of collectivism as social control, see Samuel Haber, *Efficiency and Uplift: Scientific Management in the Progressive Era, 1890-1920* (Chicago, 1964); and Loren Baritz, *Servants of Power: A History of the Use of Social Science in American Industry* (Middletown, Conn., 1960); for an excellent critique of Technocracy from Bingham's perspective see Paul H. Douglas, "Technocracy," *World Tomorrow* 16 (January 18, 1933): 59.

9.   Stuart Chase, *The Nemesis of American Business* (New York, 1931), p. 107; *Economy of Abundance*, p. 313. Chase, like Veblen, also suggested the idea of a bloodless revolution of the engineers and their allies in the professions and white collar ranks. See "Declaration of Independence," *Harper's* 164 (December, 1931): 35.

10.   Loeb, pp. v, 75-80, 84, 93, 103, 115-17; Loeb, *The Way It Was* (New York, 1959); for a more sympathetic analysis of Loeb's thought see William E. Akin, *Technocracy and the American Dream: The Technocrat Movement, 1900-1941* (Berkeley, Calif., 1977), pp. 116-130. Akin stresses Loeb's democratic intentions, distinguishing him from the more undemocratic Howard Scott; Loeb's papers are at Princeton University Library, Princeton, N. J.

11.   For a penetrating critique of Croly, Lippmann, Brandeis, and other progressive collectivists, see Haber. See also Charles Forcey, *The Crossroads of Liberalism: Croly, Weyl, Lippmann, and the Progressive Era, 1900-1925* (New York, 1961); Milton Derber, *The American Idea of Industrial Democracy, 1865-1965* (Urbana, Ill., 1970); W. H. G. Armytage, *The Rise of the Technocrats: A Social History* (Toronto, 1965).

12.   Howard Scott, "The Scourge of Politics in a Land of Manna," *One Big Union Monthly* 2 (September, 1920): 14-16; Wayne W. Parrish, "Technocracy or Politics?" *Churchman* 146 (October 29, 1932): 8-9; Technocracy, Inc., *Technocracy Study Course* (New York, 1934), pp. 105-27, 143-50.

13.   Lewis Mumford, *The Golden Day: A Study In American Experience and Culture* (New York, 1926), pp. 243-46.

14.   John Dewey, *Individualism Old and New* (New York, 1930), pp. 36-52, 56, 65, 68, 70.

15.   Ibid., 30-52, 65-70, 71-77, 81-85, 119, 131-33, 144-45.

16.   Ibid., pp. 99, 146, 148, 166-70.

17.   Mumford, *Technics and Civilization* (New York, 1934), pp. 3-5, 107-12, 139, 142-50.

18.   Ibid., pp. 23-28, 151-211.

19.   Ibid., pp. 212-215, 265-67.

20.   Ibid., pp. 280-83, 364-435.

21.   Ibid., pp. 390, 410-27.

22. Mumford, "The Need for Concrete Goals," *CS* 2 (October, 1933): 10–11; "The Corruption of Liberalism," *New Republic* 102 (April 29, 1940): 568–73; interview with Lewis Mumford, June 28, 1977, Amenia, New York.
23. Mumford, "Concrete Goals"; *Technics,* pp. 433–35.
24. James T. Farrell, "The Faith of Lewis Mumford," *Southern Review* 6 (winter, 1941): 417–38.
25. Interview with Bingham, September 7, 1970, at Salem, Conn.; *Common Sense*'s subscription and financial records are in the *CS* collection at Yale.
26. [Bingham], "The League for Independent Political Action," *CS* 2 (April 13, 1933): 2; League for Independent Political Action (hereafter cited LIPA), News Bulletin, in *CS* 2 (April 13, 1933): 17; John Dewey to members of the LIPA, March 31, 1933, *CS* collection.

CHAPTER 5

1. *New York Times,* September 9, 1929, p. 1; September 17, 1929, p. 30; Donald R. McCoy, *Angry Voices: Left-of-Center Politics in the New Deal Era* (Lawrence, Kans., 1958), pp. 3–6; LIPA, *Wanted: A New Political Alignment* (New York, 1930), pp. 1–2.
2. Paul Douglas, *The Coming of a New Party* (New York, 1932), pp. 3–5, 7–8, 11, 18–23; see also Douglas, *Why a Political Realignment?* (New York, 1930).
3. Douglas advocated a gradual program of socialization focusing first on those industries, such as railroads and bituminous coal, most in need of government assistance. When these mini-experiments in collectivism had proved successful, the way would be clear for a "wider extension of social control." See *Coming of a New Party,* pp. 93–94, 96–102, 117.
4. Ibid., pp. 116–17, 121–40, 174–78, 183–84.
5. Ibid., pp. 192, 199–202, 208–09.
6. Ibid., pp. 202–7, 215–16.
7. Dewey wrote a series of articles in 1931 on the aims and strategy of the LIPA: "The Need for a New Party," *New Republic* 65 (January 7, 1931): 203–5; "The Present Crisis," *New Republic* 66 (March 18, 1931): 115–17; "The Breakdown of the Old Order," *New Republic* 66 (March 25, 1931): 150–52; "Policies for a New Party" *New Republic* 66 (April 8, 1931): 202–5.
8. James Weinstein, *The Decline of Socialism in America* (New York, 1967), pp. 272–326.
9. For a record of LIPA's organizational drive in Minnesota and the Midwest, see Howard Y. Williams Papers, Minnesota Historical Society, St. Paul, Minn., boxes 2 and 3.
10. *New York Times,* December 26, 1930, p. 1; for Dewey's reply see ibid., December 31, 1930, p. 3; see also Richard L. Neuberger and Stephen B. Kahn, *Integrity: The Life of George W. Norris* (New York, 1937), pp. 182–86.
11. Thomas, with the ill-fated La Follette candidacy of 1924 clearly in mind, also opposed organizing a hastily assembled progressive front in 1932. Norman Thomas, "The Future of the Socialist Party," *Nation* 135 (December 14, 1932): 584–86. For Thomas's disagreements with the LIPA see Norman Thomas to Hilda Busick, February 28, 1933; and Thomas to Henry Weihofen, December 7, 1933, in the Norman Thomas Papers, New York Public Library. For a sensitive examination of the Socialist Party in the 1930s, see Frank A. Warren, *An Alternative Vision: The Socialist Party in the 1930s* (Bloomington, Ind., 1974).
12. The league concentrated in the election campaign on publicizing its "Four Year Presidential Plan," a sweeping blueprint for economic revival prepared by a panel of league economists and labor experts; see LIPA, "A Four Year Presidential Plan," LIPA *News Bulletin* (February-March, 1932), pp. 1–9; John Dewey, "Can the People Take Power?" LIPA *News Bulletin* April-May, 1932), p. 1.

13. LIPA, *News Bulletin* (November-December, 1932), p. 2; Howard Y. Williams to editor, *Nation* 136 (February 1, 1933): 122.
14. Quoted in William E. Leuchtenburg, *Franklin D. Roosevelt and the New Deal, 1932-1940* (New York, 1963), p. 24.
15. Alfred M. Bingham, "Progressivism vs. Radicalism," MS, n.d., pp. 1-2, 4-5, 10, Bingham MSS; Bingham to Cutting, December 1, 1933, Bingham MSS.
16. Bingham to George T. Schneider, August 19, 1938, Bingham MSS; Robert Whitcomb and Selden Rodman, "Amlie: New Party Builder," *CS* 5 (May, 1936): 17-20. For a full description of Amlie's political career, see Robert Long, "Thomas Amlie: A Political Biography" (Ph.D. dissertation, University of Wisconsin, 1969); see also Amlie, "Thorstein Veblen Today," *CS* 4 (April, 1935): 14-16; "The Collapse of Capitalism," *CS* 2 (October, 1933): 6-9.
17. Bingham to Schneider, August 19, 1938, Bingham MSS; Amlie to Howard Y. Williams, August 17, 1933, Bingham MSS.
18. LIPA *News Bulletin,* in *CS* 2 (May 11, 1933): 17.
19. [Bingham], "The Continental Congress," *CS* 2 (May 25, 1933): 2; LIPA *News Bulletin,* in *CS* 2 (May 25, 1933): 3.
20. [Bingham], "Continental Congress"; LIPA to National Committee of the Socialist Party, n.d., Bingham MSS.
21. LIPA *News Bulletin,* in *CS* 2 (May 25, 1933): 17; and 2 (July, 1933): 26-27.
22. LIPA *News Bulletin,* in *CS* 2 (July, 1933): 27; and 2 (August, 1933): 28-29; LIPA, *Audacity! Audacity! Always Audacity!* (New York, 1933). This pamphlet was issued especially for the United Action Campaign.
23. Quotations from James MacGregor Burns, *Roosevelt: The Lion and the Fox* (New York, 1956), pp. 145, 168.
24. *New York Herald-Tribune,* March 15, 1933.
25. For a comprehensive analysis of the intellectual position of the *New Republic* and the *Nation* in the 1930s, see Frank A. Warren, *Liberals and Communism: The "Red Decade" Revisited* (Bloomington, Ind., 1966).
26. Oswald Garrison Villard, "The Roosevelt Revolution," *Nation* 137 (July 26, 1933): 91.
27. [Bingham], "Not Enough, Mr. Roosevelt," *CS* 2 (May 11, 1933): 2; "An Open Letter to President Roosevelt," *CS* 3 (March, 1934): 2-3; "Franklin Delano Roosevelt," *CS* 3 (September, 1934): 2-3.
28. [Bingham], "Panic and Panaceas," *CS* 2 (April 27, 1933): 2; "One Enemy and One Goal," *CS* 3 (January, 1934): 3; Bingham, "Original Prospectus," MS, October, 1932, pp. 3-4, *CS* collection; LIPA, *Audacity!* pp. 17-18; [Bingham], "For a Farmer-Labor Party," *CS* 2 (August, 1933): 2-3.
29. [Bingham], "Not Enough"; "A Real New Deal," *CS* 2 (March 16, 1933): 2. "News behind the News," *CS* 2 (August, 1933): 5; 2 (September, 1933): 4; 2 (April 27, 1933): 6. [Bingham], "Farmer-Labor Party"; LIPA, *Audacity!*
30. [Bingham], "FDR," p. 2.
31. For a careful history of the National Industrial Recovery Act, see Ellis W. Hawley, *The New Deal and the Problem of Monopoly* (Princeton, N.J., 1966). Others in the administration advanced bolder designs for national planning; see especially Rexford G. Tugwell, *The Industrial Discipline and the Government Arts* (New York, 1933), pp. 129-30, 193-96, 203-19.
32. John T. Flynn, "NRA:1934,"*CS* 3 (May, 1934): 11; "The New Partnership," *CS* 2 (August, 1933): 14-16; "News behind the News," *CS* 3 (January, 1934): 4.
33. "News behind the News," *CS* 2 (August, 1933): 5; LIPA, *Audacity!* pp. 20-22.
34. John T. Flynn, "The Collapse of the New Deal," *CS* 3 (November, 1934): 6-7; "Partnership," pp. 14-16. Bingham and Rodman regularly covered the New Deal in their column "News behind the News." Contemporary historians generally agree with Bingham's assessment of Roosevelt as a president responsive, especially in the

first years of his term, to the major interest groups of American capitalism. See especially Burns, pp. 183, 192, 197-98; even William E. Leuchtenburg, an historian generously sympathetic to Roosevelt, argues that under the early New Deal government benefits were usually distributed in proportion to the strength of the pressure groups pushing for them, and that causes not promoted by influential lobbies generally went unheeded (pp. 87-88).

35. Bingham to Senator Bronson Cutting, December 11, 1933, Bingham MSS; Bingham, "Progressivism vs. Radicalism," MS, n.d., p. 1, Bingham MSS; "For a Farmer-Labor Party." There were also some within the administration who felt Roosevelt could have gone further; see especially Rexford G. Tugwell, *The Brains Trust* (New York, 1969), p. xxi.

36. John Dewey, *Liberalism and Social Action* (New York, 1935); [Bingham], "The Liberal and Anti-Fascism," *CS* 7 (October, 1938): 3-5; [Bingham], "Liberty, Democracy and Hokum," *CS* 3 (October, 1934): 3.

37. Dewey, *Liberalism*, pp. 20, 32; "The Future of Liberalism," *School and Society* 41 (January 19, 1935): 73-74; "The Meaning of Liberalism," *Social Frontier* 2 (December, 1935): 74.

38. Dewey, *Liberalism*, pp. 21, 32-34, 54; "Future of Liberalism," pp. 74-77; "Meaning of Liberalism," pp. 74-75.

39. Dewey, *Liberalism*, pp. 21, 28-34, 47-52, 54, 62, 88-91; "Future of Liberalism," pp. 74-78; "Meaning of Liberalism," pp. 74-75.

40. Dewey, *Liberalism*, pp. 58-61, 75-81, 91.

41. Ibid., pp. 58, 61-62, 91.

42. Well before the 1930s Randolph Bourne had assailed instrumentalism for its moral and pragmatic obscurity, its elevation of method over content. As Bourne saw it, the problem of instrumentalism was that it was at heart a philosophy of technique; it instructed men how to accomplish an end once that end had been made clear. See especially Bourne, "Twilight of Idols," *The Seven Arts* 11 (October, 1917): 688-702. Bourne gave early expression to what has become a familiar criticism of instrumentalism. Morton White, for example, argues that pragmatism supplies us with "no hard and fast principles . . . no particular or specific political position that can be acted on, only a plea for intelligence." White, *Social Thought in America: The Revolt Against Formalism* (New York, pp. 200-201, 240-46.

43. Letter to Jim Cork, undated and quoted in part in Cork's "John Dewey and Karl Marx," *John Dewey: Philosopher of Science and Freedom*, ed. Sidney Hook (New York, 1950), pp. 348-49.

44. The "radical progressivism" of the *New Republic* was, as George Soule described it, primarily a "mental attitude . . . experimental and scientific. It pins its faith to no exclusive dogma, orthodoxy, or group of absolutes." Soule, "Hard-Boiled Radicalism," *New Republic* 65 (January 21, 1931): 261-265. Yet Soule and his fellow editors carried this reform relativism to the point where they refused to identify their magazine with any one social program or any one movement for change. Aside from a general advocacy of economic planning and third party politics, the *New Republic* never developed or supported a well-wrought program of political and economic change, choosing instead to "mediate among the many schools of radical thought" and to urge a left coalition which would include the Communists. "Liberalism Twenty Years After," *New Republic* 81 (January 23, 1935): 290-92.

45. Some historians still persist in using the term "pragmatism" to describe Roosevelt's experimental approach to reform. Perhaps the most prominent is Arthur Schlesinger, Jr., who employs the term both to describe the New Deal's experimental temper and to set off Roosevelt's "centrist" government from its "ideological" opponents on the right and the left. Schlesinger labels all leftist opponents of the New Deal, including Dewey and Bingham, as "ideologists," "platonists preferring essence to existence and considering abstractions the only reality." He sees the New Deal, on the other hand, as unfailingly practical and vigorously anti-ideological. See especially Schlesinger, *The Age of Roosevelt* (Boston, 1957-60);

Schlesinger, "Sources of the New Deal: Reflections on the Temper of a Time," in Otis L. Graham, Jr., *The New Deal: The Critical Issues* (Boston, 1971), pp. 108–21. Schlesinger also claims that Roosevelt took America as far left as it was willing to go in these years. Perhaps he is right. But he errs when he connects the politics of the "vital center" with philosophic pragmatism.

46. John Dewey, "The Imperative Need for a New Radical Party," *CS* 2 (September 1933): 6–7; [Bingham], "An Opportunity for Action," *CS* 2 (September, 1933): 2–3.

47. Selden Rodman, "A New Radical Party," *New Republic* 76 (September 20, 1933): 151–53; "The Farmer-Labor Political Federation," *CS* 2 (October, 1933): 17–20.

48. Thomas Amlie, "Speech to the United Conference for Progressive Political Action," n.d., Bingham MSS; Rodman, "New Radical Party."

49. Bingham, "Farmer-Labor Political Federation," pp. 19–20; Rodman, "New Radical Party."

50. "Report of Committee on Organization and Political Action," n.d., Oswald Garrison Villard Papers, Houghton Library, Harvard University, Cambridge, Mass.; Rodman, "New Radical Party."

51. Bingham, "Farmer-Labor Political Federation," p. 19; LIPA News Bulletin, in *CS* 2 (October, 1933): 27.

52. LIPA News Bulletin, in *CS* 2 (October 1933).

53. Bingham, "Farmer-Labor Political Federation," p. 18; [Bingham], "The Chicago Conference," *CS* 2 (October, 1933): 2–3; Amlie, "Speech."

CHAPTER 6

1. Thomas Amlie to Alfred M. Bingham, September 28, 1933, Bingham MSS.

2. Alfred M. Bingham, *Insurgent America: The Revolt of the Middle Classes* (New York, 1935).

3. Werner Sombart, "American Capitalism's Economic Rewards," in John H. M. Laslett and Seymour Martin Lipset, eds., *Failure of a Dream? Essays in the History of American Socialism* (Garden City, N.Y., 1974), p. 599, translated by Howard A. Fleming, Jr. Selected, edited, and revised by John H. M. Laslett. Sombart was professor of political science at the University of Berlin.

4. Selig Perlman, *Theory of the Labor Movement* (New York, 1949 [originally 1928]), pp. 168–69.

5. Leon Sampson, *Toward a United Front: A Philosophy for American Workers* (New York, 1934); for a perceptive review of Sampson's thesis, see Frank A. Warren, *An Alternative Vision: The Socialist Party in the 1930s* (Bloomington, Ind., 1974), pp. 49–68.

6. Leon Sampson, "Americanism: A Substitute for Socialism," *Modern Monthly* 7 (July, 1933): 367; see also *The American Mind* (New York, 1932).

7. These were the very arguments Paul Douglas attempted to deflate in *The Coming of a New Party* (New York, 1932).

8. I have obviously not attempted here a complete bibliography on the failure of socialism. One of the more common arguments advanced since the 1930s is that in the absence of a feudal tradition America produced a liberal consensus that effectively deterred socialism. See Louis Hartz, *The Liberal Tradition in America: An Interpretation of American Political Thought since the Revolution* (New York, 1955); for a persuasive critique of the Hartz thesis, see Kenneth McNaught, "American Progressives and the Great Society," *Journal of American History* 52 (December, 1966): 504–20. Building from the Sampson argument, Michael Harrington has recently argued that America's irrepressible utopianism, its very receptivity to egalitarian ideals and secular panaceas of all sorts, delayed the appearance of a radical labor movement. He also argues that abundance, contrary to Sombart, often acted

as a spur to discontent, inciting workers to strike or riot for a larger share of the nation's grossly maldistributed wealth. For bibliographies on American labor and socialism, see Maurice Neufeld, *A Bibliography of American Labor Union History* (Ithaca, N.Y., 1958); Gene S. Stroud and Gilbert E. Donahue, *Labor History in the United States* (Champaign, Ill., 1961); Fred D. Rose, *American Labor in Journals of History* (Champaign, Ill., 1962).

9. Bingham, "Common Sense: Prospectus for a New Magazine," MS, n.d., *CS* collection; *Insurgent America,* pp. 65-99; "Communism in America," MS, 1932, Bingham Personal Papers.

10. Bingham, *Insurgent America,* pp. 30-43, 63.

11. Ibid., pp. 47-64.

12. Ibid., pp. 2, 23-24, 43, 47; "Communism in America," p. 2. See also Rodman, review of Sidney Hook's *Toward the Understanding of Karl Marx,* "Books," *CS* 2 (May 11, 1933): 18; and "Prophets vs. Disciples," *CS* 3 (February, 1934): 34.

13. Bingham, *Insurgent America,* pp. 2, 23-47. Other scholars since Bingham have stressed "internal" considerations as the key to socialism's failure, citing the movement's tendency toward ideological absolutism and its fractious record of intra-organizational feuding and intrigue. Daniel Bell, for example, argues that socialism failed because of its inability "to relate itself to the specific problems of social action in the here-and-now, give-and-take political world." In his recent biography of Norman Thomas, Bernard Johnpoll also attributes socialism's surprisingly limited influence in the 1930s to problems of ideology and internal schism. See Bell, *Marxian Socialism in the United States* (Princeton, 1967), p. 5; Johnpoll, *Pacifist's Progress: Norman Thomas and the Decline of American Socialism* (Chicago, 1970). While disagreeing with much of Bell's analysis, radical historians Christopher Lasch and James Weinstein, along with the sociologist T. B. Bottomore, also cite internal problems as critical to socialism's failure, attributing American radicalism's difficulties after 1919 in large part to its excessive allegiance to the Soviet Union and to its slavish reliance on classic Marxism. Lasch and Bottomore, in particular, point to the failure of American intellectuals to fashion a radical theory uniquely tailored to national conditions and attractive to the middle classes as well as labor. They fail to mention, however, Bingham's efforts to do just this. James Weinstein, *The Decline of Socialism in America, 1912-1925* (New York, 1967); Christopher Lasch, *The Agony of the American Left* (New York, 1969), pp. 31, 43-47, 161-62, 201, 211-12; T. B. Bottomore, *Critics of Society: Radical Thought in North America* (New York, 1968). See also Gabriel Kolko, "The Decline of American Radicalism in the Twentieth Century," *Studies on the Left* (September-October, 1966), pp. 10-26; and Ira Kipnis, *The American Socialist Movement, 1897-1912* (New York, 1952).

14. Bingham, *Insurgent America,* pp. 23-24, 56-63; "Does the Middle Class Want a New Social Order?" MS, n.d., pp. 2-3, Bingham MSS.

15. Bingham, *Insurgent America,* pp. 48-65; Bingham to Lewis Mumford, August 8, 1934, Bingham MSS.

16. Bingham, *Insurgent America,* pp. 27, 65, 74-76, 79-99.

17. Ibid., pp. 104-5, 125-26, 177-79, 194-201; review of Harold Loeb's *Chart of Plenty,* in "Books," *CS* 4 (April, 1935): 27.

18. Bingham, *Insurgent America,* pp. 76-89, 189-97.

19. Bingham to Amlie, January 11, 1934; Amlie to Aubrey Williams, January 25, 1934; Amlie to Harold Loeb, January 25, 1934; Amlie to Philip La Follette, February 8, 1934; all in Thomas Amlie Papers, State Historical Society of Wisconsin at Madison.

20. Loeb, *The Chart of Plenty* (New York, 1935); "The Stupidity of Poverty," *CS* 3 (February, 1934): 6-10; "Non-Production of Wealth," *CS* 4 (October, 1935): 14-17.

21. Bingham, review of *Chart of Plenty,* p. 27.

22. Bingham, "Does the Middle Class Want a New Social Order?" pp. 3-4; *Insurgent America,* pp. 189-92.

23. Bingham, *Insurgent America*, pp. 206–13; "A Plan of Transition," *CS* 4 (May, 1935): 6–10; [Bingham], "For a Commonwealth Party," *CS* 4 (May, 1935): 2–3; Upton Sinclair, "The EPIC Plan," *CS* 3 (May, 1934): 6–8; "National EPIC," *CS* 4 (August, 1935): 9–10.
24. Bingham, "Further Light on Transition," *CS* 4 (June, 1935): 13–16.
25. Bingham, *Insurgent America*, pp. 211–15; "A Plan of Transition," pp. 8–10; [Bingham], "For a Commonwealth Party," p. 3; Bingham, "Further Light," pp. 13–16.
26. Bingham, *Insurgent America*, pp. 27, 76.
27. R. Palme Dutt, *Fascism and the Social Revolution* (New York, 1934), pp. 77–88; John Strachey, *The Menace of Fascism* (New York, 1933), pp. 125–27.
28. Bingham, *Insurgent America*, pp. 104–9, 132–35, 156–57.
29. Ibid., pp. 120–32.
30. Bingham, "The Enigma of Fascism," *CS* 4 (February, 1935): 12–14; [Bingham], "Will It Happen Here?" *CS* 5 (July, 1936): 3–4; "What Dictatorship Is Like: Impressions of Fascist Germany," MS, n.d., Bingham MSS.
31. Bingham, *Insurgent America*, p. 117.
32. Ibid., pp. 171–79, 185–94; "Progressivism vs. Radicalism," MS, n.d., p. 1, Bingham MSS.
33. John Dewey, review of Bingham, *Insurgent America*, "Books," *CS* 4 (December, 1935): 23; Harry Elmer Barnes, "Critical Trends in United States," review of Bingham's *Insurgent America* in *New York World Telegram*, November 16, 1935, p. 16; Ernest Sutherland Bates, "The American Middle Class," review of Bingham's *Insurgent America* in *New York Herald Tribune*, November 24, 1935, p. 6; John Chamberlain, "The New Middle Classes," review of Bingham's *Insurgent America* in *Saturday Review of Literature* 13 (December 28, 1935): 6–7; Louis M. Hacker, "Address to the Middle Class," review of Bingham's *Insurgent America* in *Nation* 141 (November 27, 1935): 625–26.
34. Lewis Corey, *The Crisis of the Middle Class* (New York, 1935).
35. Esther Corey, "Lewis Corey (Louis Fraina), 1892–1953: A Bibliography with Autobiographical Notes," *Labor History* 4 (spring, 1963): 113. I am indebted to Paul Buhle for allowing me to examine portions of his unpublished manuscript on Lewis Corey.
36. Lewis Corey, *Crisis*, pp. 112–365.
37. Ibid., pp. 194–243.
38. A. J. Muste, "Middle Class or Working Class," *CS* 3 (March, 1934): 23–25; "An American Revolutionary Party," *Modern Monthly* 7 (January, 1934): 713–19.
39. V. F. Calverton, "Will Fascism Come to America?" *Modern Monthly* 8 (September, 1934): 469–78. See also "What Is Fascism," *Modern Monthly* 7 (July, 1933): 325–332.
40. Lewis Mumford to Bingham, August 6, 1934, Bingham MSS.
41. Mumford to Bingham, August 6, September 2, 1934, Bingham MSS.
42. Bingham to Mumford, August 8, September 5, 1934, Bingham MSS.
43. Thomas Amlie to Bingham, August 4, 1937, Bingham MSS.
44. Bingham to Amlie, August 6, 1937, Bingham MSS.
45. Ibid.
46. Bingham to Mumford, September 2, 1934, Bingham MSS.
47. Bingham to Amlie, August 6, 1937, Bingham MSS.
48. Mumford to Bingham, September 2, 1934, Bingham MSS.
49. Bingham, *Insurgent America*, pp. 186–89.

CHAPTER 7

1. Thomas Amlie to Alfred M. Bingham, September 28, 1933, February 28, 1934, Bingham MSS.

2. Amlie to Bingham, February 28, 1934, Bingham MSS; Bingham, "Reform and Revolt in the West," *CS* 3 (January, 1934): 27.
3. Bingham to National Committee of Action, n.d.; Amlie to Bingham, February 24, 1934, Bingham MSS; Bingham, "Reform in the West," pp. 26–27; Bingham, "Plans of the F.L.P.F. for Third Party Action," MS, n.d., Bingham MSS.
4. Amlie to Bingham, September 28, 1933, Bingham MSS.
5. Bingham to Amlie, October 3, 1933, Bingham MSS.
6. Bingham to D. B. McCalalmont, Jr., September 24, 1934, Bingham MSS.
7. [Bingham], "On Obtaining Power," *CS* 4 (January, 1935): 2.
8. [Bingham], "Planned Revolution," *CS* 2 (December, 1933): 2–3; Amlie to Bingham, February 28, 1934, Bingham MSS.
9. Amlie to Bingham, September 28, 1933; Bingham to Amlie, October 3, 1933, Bingham MSS.
10. Selden Rodman, "Young America," *CS* 2 (December, 1933): 24–25; "Youth and New America," *CS* 3 (July, 1934): 17–18.
11. [Bingham], "Ballots or Bullets," *CS* 3 (November, 1934): 3.
12. Edward N. Doan, *The La Follettes and the Wisconsin Idea* (New York, 1947), pp. 177–78, 181–82; Donald R. McCoy, *Angry Voices: Left-of-Center Politics in the New Deal Era* (Lawrence, Kans., 1958), pp. 44–60; Arthur M. Schlesinger, Jr., *The Age of Roosevelt*, 3 vols. (Boston, 1957–60), vol. 3, *The Politics of Upheaval* (1960), pp. 105–6.
13. Wallace S. Sayre, "Left Turn in Wisconsin," *New Republic* 80 (October 24, 1934): 300.
14. Amlie to Bingham, February 28, May 21, 1934, Bingham MSS.
15. Amlie to Bingham, February 19, 1934, Bingham MSS; Doan, pp. 182–83; Francis Scott, "Making History in Wisconsin," *CS* 3 (April, 1934): 16–17; Bingham, "Western Pioneers," *CS* 3 (June, 1934): 20–21.
16. Amlie to Bingham, May 21, 1934, Bingham MSS.
17. Amlie to Bingham, May 21, 1934; Bingham to Amlie, June 18, 1934, Bingham MSS; Bingham, "Recent Moves on the Farmer-Labor Front," *CS* 3 (August, 1934): 23; Howard Y. Williams, "The Odds in Midwest Politics," *CS* 3 (September, 1934): 26–27.
18. Doan, pp. 186–87.
19. Bingham to Amlie, May 24, 1934; Amlie to Bingham, November 7, 1933, Bingham MSS; Amlie to Philip La Follette, July 16, 1934, Amlie MSS.
20. Bingham, "Notes on the Fall Campaign," *CS* 3 (October, 1934): 19.
21. Anne Ross, "Radical Parties: The Farmer-Labor Party of Minnesota," *CS* 4 (March, 1935), 14–15; George H. Mayer, *The Political Career of Floyd B. Olson* (Minneapolis, 1951), pp. 18–24. The Farmer-Labor Association was originally called the Farmer-Labor Federation. The association's papers are housed in the Minnesota Historical Society, St. Paul, Minnesota.
22. Mayer, pp. 7–16, 95–96, 119, 148–58; Floyd B. Olson, "A National Third Party," *CS* 2 (November, 1933): 10–11; "My Political Creed," *CS* 4 (April, 1935): 6–7; Olson's papers are housed in the Minnesota Historical Society, St. Paul, Minn.
23. Bingham to Amlie, December 4, 1935, Bingham MSS.
24. Quoted in Mayer, p. 171.
25. Bingham, "Western Pioneers," p. 20; *Farmer-Labor Leader*, March 39, 1934, p. 5.
26. Mayer, pp. 173–80.
27. Quoted in ibid., pp. 10–11, 251–55.
28. Bingham, "Notes on Fall Campaign"; interview with Bingham, January 8, 1970, Salem, Conn.
29. Howard Y. Williams, "The LIPA," *CS* 2 (November, 1933): 28. "Notes from the LIPA Field," *CS* 2 (December, 1933): 27; "Iowa Takes the Lead," *CS* 3 (February, 1934): 27; FLPF Bulletin, June, 1934, p. 3; September, 1934, p. 2, Bingham MSS; Bingham to National Committee of Action, n.d., Bingham MSS.

30.   FLPF *Bulletin,* June, 1934, p. 2, Bingham MSS; Bingham, "Progress on the Farmer-Labor Front," *CS* 2 (December, 1933): 26.
31.   Bingham to National Committee of Action, n.d.; Bingham to Howard Y. Williams, February 13, 1934, Bingham MSS.
32.   Bingham to Oswald Garrison Villard, April 20, 1934, Oswald Garrison Villard Papers, Houghton Library, Harvard University, Cambridge, Mass.
33.   C. L. Moore, "Production for Use Marches On," *CS* 5 (August, 1936): 19; Charles Larsen, "The EPIC Campaign of 1934," *Pacific Historical Review* 27 (May, 1958): 134.
34.   Bingham to Amlie, December 4, 27, 1935; Amlie to Bingham, December 18, 1935; Bingham to National Committee of Action, n.d., Bingham MSS.
35.   Eunice Clark, "After the Elections," *CS* 3 (December, 1934): 11–14.
36.   Bingham to L. E. Hurton, n.d., Bingham MSS.
37.   [Bingham], "Toward a New Party," *CS* 3 (December, 1934): 2.
38.   "Political Paragraphs," *CS* 4 (June, 1935): 25; Schlesinger, pp. 1–2, 8–11, 15–68; McCoy, pp. 61–67.
39.   "Minutes of the Conference of Progressive Leaders," May 4, 1935, Bingham MSS.
40.   Olson, "My Political Creed," p. 6.
41.   Bingham to Amlie, November 6, 1934, Bingham MSS.
42.   Selden Rodman, "A Third Party by March?" *CS* 4 (January, 1935): 17–18; *New York Times,* December 10, 1934, p. 5.
43.   "Minutes of the Conference of Progressive Leaders," May 4, 1935; "Call for the Chicago Conference," June 11, 1935, Bingham MSS. "Political Paragraphs," *CS* 4 (June, 1935): 24–25.
44.   *New York Times,* July 6, 1935, p. 12.
45.   "Minutes of the Chicago Conference," July 5–6, 1935, Bingham MSS.
46.   Ibid.
47.   Ibid.; Robert Morss Lovett, "A Party in Embryo," *New Republic* 83 (July 24, 1935): 295–96; *New York Times,* July 7, 1935, p. 21; Bingham, "Notes on the Chicago Conference," *CS* 4 (August, 1935): 8.
48.   Lovett, p. 295.
49.   *New York Times,* July 6, 1935, p. 1.
50.   Lovett, p. 296.
51.   Bingham, "Notes on Chicago Conference"; Bingham to Members of the National Committee of Action, July 25, 1935, Oswald Garrison Villard Papers, Houghton Library, Harvard University, Cambridge, Mass; Bingham to Howard Y. Williams, March 13, 1936, Bingham MSS; Thomas Amlie, "The American Commonwealth Federation," *CS* 4 (August, 1935): 6–7.
52.   "Minutes of Chicago Conference," Bingham MSS; Bingham, "Notes on Chicago Conference"; Lovett, p. 296.
53.   "Platform of the American Commonwealth Federation," Bingham MSS; Bingham to Members of the National Committee of Action, July 25, 1935, Villard MSS.
54.   *New York Times,* July 7, 1935, p. 1. Marcantonio also objected to the exclusion of the Communists from the ACF. Ernest Lundeen also declined to join the ACF on the grounds that it excluded the Communists. Lundeen favored a "United Front" Farmer-Labor party of all progressive and radical organizations. See Amlie to Bingham, August 7, 1935, Bingham MSS.
55.   Amlie to Bingham, April 3, 1936, Bingham MSS; Mayer, pp. 296–97.
56.   Thomas R. Amlie, *The Forgotten Man's Handbook: 500 Questions Answered* (Elkhorn, Wis., 1936); Harold Loeb, *Production for Use* (New York, 1936); Floyd Olson, *Why a New National Party,* ACF pamphlet, 1935, Bingham MSS; Ernest Lundeen, *A Farmer Labor Party for the Nation,* ACF pamphlet, 1935, Bingham MSS; *Toward a New Party,* ACF pamphlet, 1935, Bingham MSS.

57. Bingham, *"Common Sense:* Purposes and Accomplishments," MS, October, 1934, Bingham MSS. "Circulation Statistics of *Common Sense,"* n.d., *CS* collection; Bingham, "Original Prospectus," MS, October, 1932, *CS* collection; interview with Bingham, January 8, 1970.

58. Amlie to Bingham, September 28, 1933; January 9, 1934, Bingham MSS.

59. Bingham to Nathan Fine, October 24, November 23, 30, 1935; Fine to Bingham, November 11, 1935; Amlie to Bingham, December 2, 1935, Bingham MSS. "The American Commonwealth Plan," 1935. "Builders' Manual," 1935, Bingham MSS.

60. Moore, p. 19. "New Party News," *CS* 4 (July, 1935): 24; Amlie to Bingham, December 18, 1935; Amlie to End Poverty League, February 10, 1936, Bingham MSS.

61. Amlie to Bingham, March 15, 1934, December 2, 1936; Bingham to the *Nation,* April 3, 1935, vol. 140, p. 387.

62. Bingham to Floyd Olson, February 18, 1936, Bingham MSS.

63. Mayer, p. 297; interview with Bingham, Jan. 8, 1970; *New York Times,* November 17, 1935, p. 29. Schlesinger, pp. 104, 509.

64. *New York Times,* March 29, 1936, p. 11; "Political Paragraphs," *CS* 5 (May, 1936): 25.

65. Amlie to Bingham, April 3, 1936; Fine to Bingham, April 1, 3, 1936, Bingham MSS.

66. Quoted in Schlesinger, p. 593. "Political Paragraphs," *CS* 5 (May, 1936); "Letter to Contributing Subscribers," May 18, 1936, *CS* collection.

67. [Bingham], "Roosevelt: Radicals' Nemesis," *CS* 5 (June, 1936): 3; Bingham to Howard Y. Williams, May 19, 1936; Amlie to Bingham, April 16, 1936; Fine to Bingham, April 17, 1936, Bingham MSS.

68. Howard Y. Williams to Bingham, April 21, 1936, Bingham MSS. "Political Paragraphs," *CS* 5 (June, 1936): 24.

69. Amlie to Bingham, June 2, 1936; Bingham and Amlie to State Committee of Farmer-Labor Association, May 16, 1936, Bingham MSS.

70. "Press Release from the ACF," May 26, 1936, Bingham MSS.

71. Howard Y. Williams to Bingham, March 18, 1936; Williams to Paul Douglas, June 18, 1936; Williams to Bingham, May 20, 1936; Fine to Bingham, April 3, 1936, Bingham MSS.

72. Howard Y. Williams to Amlie, May 20, 1936; Williams to Bingham, May 20, 1936, Bingham MSS.

73. *New York Times,* May 31, 1936, p. 20; June 1, 1936, p. 2; "Political Paragraphs," *CS* 5 (July, 1936): 24; Howard Y. Williams to Amlie, June 4, 1936, Bingham MSS. Olson died on August 22, 1936.

74. Bingham to Fine, March 11, 1936; Fine to Bingham, April 3, June 12, 1936, Bingham MSS.

75. Schlesinger, pp. 555-59; David H. Bennett, *Demagogues in the Depression: American Radicals and the Union Party, 1932-36* (New Brunswick, N.J., 1969).

76. Bingham to Howard Y. Williams, June 22, 1936, Bingham MSS.

77. Bingham to Amlie, June 25, 1936, Bingham MSS; [Bingham], "Perilous Days," *CS* 5 (August, 1936): 3.

78. Bingham to Fine, July 23, 1936; Bingham to Williams, June 26, 1936; Bingham to Amlie, n.d., Bingham MSS; "ACF Bulletin to Union Party," n.d., Bingham MSS.

79. Bingham to Amlie, August 3, 1936, Bingham MSS.

80. [Bingham], "How Shall I Vote?" *CS* 5 (October, 1936); 2-3. Amlie also supported Roosevelt in 1936.

CHAPTER 8

1. "Third Party Items," *CS* 5 (December, 1936): 23; J. K. Kyle, "Progressives Sweep Wisconsin," *CS* 5 (December, 1936): 23; Howard Y. Williams, "Minnesota

Farmer-Laborites Triumph," *CS* 5 (December, 1936): 24. In the 1936 elections the third parties received approximately 3% of the total vote. In Wisconsin Governor Philip La Follette was reelected, and seven Progressives were returned to the House of Representatives. In Minnesota five Farmer-Laborites were elected to Congress, and Elmer Benson won the governorship.

2. Bingham to Amlie, November 19, 1936; Fine to Bingham, December 19, 1936, Bingham MSS; [Bingham], "Not a Labor Party," *CS* 5 (December, 1936): 3–4; Bingham, "ACF and N.Y. Commonwealth Federation Program," MS, 1936, Bingham MSS. "Political Paragraphs," *CS* 6 (January, 1937): 24; [Bingham], "A Positive Program for Progressives," *CS* 6 (February, 1937): 3–5.

3. Stuart L. Weiss, "Maury Maverick and the Liberal Bloc," *Journal of American History* 57 (March, 1971): 880–95; Arthur M. Schlesinger, Jr., *The Age of Roosevelt*, 3 vols. (Boston, 1957–60), vol. 3, *The Politics of Upheaval* (1960), pp. 143–44; Bingham, "Unbranded: Maury Maverick, Spokesman for New America," *CS* 6 (February, 1937): 21–24; Richard B. Henderson, *Maury Maverick: A Political Biography* (Austin, Tex., 1970).

4. Bingham to Amlie, January 20, 1937, Bingham MSS. "Commonwealth Congress for Progressive Social Legislation: Agenda," April, 1937, Bingham MSS; Thomas Amlie, "The Human Rights Amendment," *CS* 6 (May, 1937): 19–21.

5. Mordecai Ezekiel, *$2,500 a Year: From Scarcity to Abundance* (New York, 1936), pp. 30, 38, 83; *Jobs for All through Industrial Expansion* (New York, 1939), pp. 12, 20, 186; "AAA in Reverse," *CS* 6 (June, 1937): 10–12; Harold Loeb, "Economic Planning through 'Industrial Adjustment,'" *CS* 6 (June, 1937): 12; Thomas Amlie, "The Answer to Fascism," *CS* 6 (August, 1937): 8–10; Herbert Harris, "This Bill Bears Watching," *Survey Graphic* 27 (April, 1938): 227–32, 246–48; Schlesinger, pp. 215–18.

6. Quoted in Harris, p. 227.

7. Bingham to Amlie, March 8, June 29, 1937; Bingham to Stuart Chase, January 5, 1938, Bingham MSS; [Bingham], "Economic Planning Gets to Congress," *CS* 6 (June, 1937): 3–4.

8. Bingham, "A Campaign to Push Legislative Proposals," MS, n.d., Bingham MSS. *Planning for Abundance*, ACF pamphlet, 1937, Bingham MSS.

9. U. S. Congressional Record, 75th Congress, 1st Session, 1937, vol. 81, part 5, pp. 2429–34; Harris, "This Bill Bears Watching"; pp, 227–46; Bingham to Kate R. O'Hare, June 8, 1937; Bingham to Amlie, May 10, 18, September 10, 1937; Amlie to Bingham, May 12, 20, September 14, 1937, Bingham MSS.

10. Weiss, p. 886; William E. Leuchtenburg, *Franklin D. Roosevelt and the New Deal: 1932–1940* (New York, 1963), p. 250.

11. Amlie to Howard Y. Williams, August 30, 1937, Amlie MSS; see also Amlie to Bingham, August 4, 20, 1937, Bingham MSS. Howard Y. Williams also supported the New Deal after 1938. See Bingham to U.S. Civil Service Commission, July 14, 1941, *CS* collection.

12. [Bingham], "New Deal or New Party?" *CS* 6 (September, 1937): 3–5. Bingham had reached his decision to support the New Deal earlier in the summer of 1937. See Bingham to Amlie, July 28, 1937, Bingham MSS.

13. Interview with Bingham, January 8, 1970, at Salem Conn.; Bingham, "Law and Politics," MS, n.d., p. 5, Bingham Personal Papers; Bingham to Earl Webster, November 12, 1941, *CS* collection.

14. Bingham, "New Deal or New Party?" pp. 3–5. "ACF Statement to Members," August 23, 1937, Bingham MSS. "Political Paragraphs," *CS* 6 (October, 1937): 23.

15. Bingham, *Insurgent America: The Revolt of the Middle Classes*, 2nd ed. (New York, 1938), p. xvi; [Bingham], "Temptation to Patriotism," *CS* 6 (July, 1937): 3–4; [Bingham], "An Editorial View," *CS* 6 (March, 1937): 20; Bingham, *Man's Estate: Adventures in Economic Discovery* (New York, 1939), pp. 295–96.

16. Bingham to Amlie, April 5, 1939, Bingham MSS; [Bingham], "USSR and U.S.A.," *CS* 6 (October, 1937): 3–5.

17. Bingham, "Forces for and against Democracy in the United States," speech to the New School for Social Research, March, 1940, Bingham MSS; Bingham to Frank Underhill, n.d., *CS* collection; [Bingham], "New Deal or New Party?" pp. 3-5.

18. Bingham, "Why I Am a Radical," MS, 1934, Bingham MSS.

19. Bingham, "Law and Politics," pp. 2-13; interview with Bingham, January 8, 1970.

20. Bingham, *Man's Estate*, p. 375.

21. Bingham, address to League for Industrial Democracy, June 19, 1939, Bingham MSS; [Bingham], "The New Deal and the 'Recession,'" *CS* 7 (January, 1938): 3-5; Bingham to C. Ware, October 30, November 17, 1941, *CS* collection; Bingham to Amlie, April 5, 1939, Bingham MSS.

22. [Bingham], "Economic Planning: 1938," *CS* 7 (July, 1938): 3-5. Bingham, for example, laid the blame for the economic decline of 1937 squarely on Roosevelt's decision to cut back federal spending; [Bingham], "Monopoly Will Get You . . . ," *CS* 7 (April, 1938): 3-5; "New Deal and the Recession."

23. Bingham, address to LID, pp. 2-7.

24. James Burnham, *The Managerial Revolution: What Is Happening in the World* (New York, 1941); John Chamberlain, "It's *Your* State," *CS* 7 (October, 1938): 8-10; Chamberlain, *The American Stakes* (New York, 1940).

25. Walter Lippmann, *An Inquiry into the Principles of the Good Society* (Boston, 1937); Lippmann, "Planning in an Economy of Abundance," *Atlantic Monthly* 159 (January, 1937): 39-46.

26. For a brief discussion of the declining interest in socialist planning among independent progressives, see Frank A. Warren, *Liberals and Communism: The "Red Decade" Revisited* (Bloomington, Ind., 1966), pp. 61-62. Alan Lawson has an interesting section on Chase and Soule in *The Failure of Independent Liberalism: 1930-1941* (New York, 1971), pp. 225-51. For a stimulating analysis of the "Rediscovery of America," see Richard H. Pells, *Radical Visions and American Dreams: Culture and Social Thought in the Depression Years* (New York, 1973), pp. 310-319; Robert Skotheim offers an intelligent analysis of the impact of totalitarianism on American thought in *Totalitarianism and American Social Thought* (New York, 1971).

27. Bingham, *Man's Estate*, pp. 17-116, 316-25; Bingham, "What Is Production for Use?" *CS* (May, 1936): 21-24.

28. Ludwig von Mises, *Socialism: An Economic and Sociological Analysis* (New York, 1936) (English translation). For a somewhat dated but still competent bibliography of "market socialism," see Eduard Heimann, "Literature on the Theory of a Socialist Economy," *Social Research* (February, 1939). See also Oskar Lange and Fred Taylor, *The Economic Theory of Socialism* (New York, 1938); Lange quotation in *New York Times*, October 11, 1973, p. 48.

29. Bingham, *Man's Estate*, pp. 324, 365-67; review of Oskar Lange and Fred Taylor's *The Economic Theory of Socialism*, "Books," *CS* 7 (July, 1938): 27-28. The October, 1937, issue of *Plan Age* has several excellent articles on "market socialism."

30. Alvin Hansen, *Full Recovery or Stagnation?* (New York: 1938); John Maynard Keynes, *The General Theory of Employment, Interest, and Money* (New York, 1936), pp. 20-98, 105-174; Seymour E. Harris, *John Maynard Keynes* (New York, 1955), pp. 190-96.

31. Bingham, *Man's Estate*, pp. 332-68.

32. Ibid., pp. 71-72, 89, 116-44, 162, 173-86, 221, 291-92, 365-68, 399; Bingham, "The Outlook for Capitalism, 1938," MS, n.d., Bingham MSS; Bingham, *The United States of Europe* (New York, 1940), pp. 169-73.

33. Bingham, *Man's Estate*, pp. 354-62, 380-89, 402, 420-25; *The Techniques of Democracy* (New York, 1942), pp. 215-20.

34.   Bingham, *Techniques of Democracy,* pp. 17, 62–65, 142–52; Bingham, "The Technology of Democracy," in *Whose Revolution? A Study of the Future Course of Liberalism in the United States,* ed. Irving DeWitt Talmadge (New York, 1941), pp. 44–56.
35.   Bingham, *Techniques of Democracy,* pp. 16, 64–65, 73, 82–84, 94–101, 107–8.
36.   Ibid., pp. 61–62, 156–80, 198–200; Bingham, "Technology of Democracy," p. 58.
37.   Bingham, *Man's Estate,* pp, 371–444; *Techniques of Democracy,* pp. 153–54, 182–95, 219–32; "Technology of Democracy," pp. 71–72; *United States of Europe,* pp. 175–80.
38.   Bingham, "Books," *CS* 9 (May, 1940): 27–28.
39.   Bingham, *Techniques of Democracy,* pp. 231–32.
40.   Lewis Corey, "The Need Still Is: A New Social Order," in Talmadge, p. 279.
41.   Paul Douglas, "Roosevelt Liberalism," review of Rexford Tugwell's *The Industrial Discipline* in *Nation* 136 (June 21, 1933): 702–3.
42.   Bingham, *Insurgent America,* pp. 11–12; *Techniques of Democracy,* pp. 233–40.
43.   Burnham, "Is Democracy Possible?" in Talmadge, pp. 187–215.
44.   Loren Baritz, *Servants of Power: A History of the Use of Social Science in American Industry* (Middletown, Conn., 1960), pp. 8–9.
45.   Ibid., pp. 15–17, 119–38, 196–210; see also, C. Wright Mills, *White Collar: The American Middle Classes* (New York, 1951), p. 110.
46.   Bingham, "Technology of Democracy," p. 45; see also *Insurgent America,* pp. 47–64.
47.   Mills, pp. 100–101.
48.   Quoted in Mills, p. 298. Mills attempted to develop a "more open and flexible model of the relations of political power and stratification"; his argument raises serious questions about Bingham's notion that economic democracy can be realized without socializing the major concentrations of economic power, that private property is, in fact, irrelevant to the achievement of economic justice. For an excellent discussion of this issue of property ownership under socialism and a searing critique of the "capitalist-socialist" argument that ownership is no longer the critical economic issue, see Michael Harrington, *Socialism* (New York, 1972), pp. 200–14, 270–302.
49.   John Dewey, "The Economic Basis of the New Society," in *Intelligence in the Modern World* (New York, 1939), pp. 416–33.

CHAPTER 9

1.   Manfred Jonas, *Isolationism in America, 1935-1941* (Ithaca, N.Y., 1966), pp. 5–6.
2.   Lewis Mumford to Van Wyck Brooks, February 1, 1940, *The Van Wyck Brooks-Lewis Mumford Letters: The Record of a Literary Friendship, 1921-1963,* Robert Spiller, ed., (New York, 1970), p. 177; for a full study of the Popular Front, see Frank A. Warren, *Liberals and Communism: The "Red Decade" Revisited* (Bloomington, Ind., 1966), ch. 7.
3.   Alfred M. Bingham, "War Mongering on the Left (I)," *CS* 6 (May, 1937): 8–10; "War Mongering on the Left (II)," *CS* 6 (June, 1937): 15–18; "War Mongering on the Left (III)," *CS* 6 (July, 1937): 11–14; [Bingham], "Why Commit Suicide?" *CS* 7 (May, 1938): 3–5; "Freedom for Whom?" *CS* 8 (December, 1939): 16–17; Bingham, "We Shall Have Peace," MS, n.d., Bingham MSS; "'Isolation' vs. 'Collective Security,'" *CS* 7 (February, 1938): 3–5.
4.   R. Palme Dutt, *Fascism and the Social Revolution* (New York, 1934), pp. 77–88; John Strachey, *The Menace of Fascism* (New York, 1933).

5. [Bingham], "The Liberal and the Anti-Fascist," *CS* 7 (October, 1938): 3–5; Bingham, *Insurgent America: The Revolt of the Middle Classes* (New York, 1935), pp. 138–41.
6. Bingham, *Insurgent America,* p. 171; *Insurgent America* (1938 edition), p. xiv; [Bingham], "The Liberal and the Anti-Fascist."
7. [Bingham], "Why Commit Suicide?" Bingham, *Insurgent America,* pp. 138–42; "We Shall Have Peace," p. 7, Bingham MSS.
8. Bingham, "Why Commit Suicide?" p. 4; *Man's Estate: Adventures in Economic Discovery* (New York, 1939), p. 428.
9. [Bingham], "Footnote to Anti-Fascism," *CS* 7 (November, 1938): 4. As part of these concessions Bingham proposed the dissolution of the French and British empires and the end of the United States' exclusionary economic hegemony in Latin America; Bingham, "Waging Peace," *CS* 8 (March, 1939): 3–5; [Bingham], "A Positive Program for Peace," *CS* 7 (August, 1938): 3–5.
10. [Bingham], "Peace Preparedness," *CS* 8 (August, 1939): 16–17.
11. Jonas, for example, describes Bingham as an isolationist, pp. 79–80; but as early as 1932 Bingham had assailed the United States for refusing to enter the League of Nations. He also urged that the League be transformed "into a true federation of nations" with wide-reaching enforcement powers. Bingham, "Common Sense and the Community," MS, June-July, 1932, pp. 38–39, Bingham Personal Papers.
12. [Bingham], "Peace Terms Now," *CS* 8 (October, 1939): 16–17.
13. Bingham, *The United States of Europe* (New York, 1940), pp. 8, 32, 47–50, 319. Bingham proposed that the League of Nations continue to exist until a world federation was established. The European federation was to be represented in the League. For another influential plan for European federation, see Clarence K. Streit's *Union Now* (New York, 1939).
14. Bingham, *U.S. of Europe,* pp. 91–121, 131–66, 195–233, 235–38, 241–75, 284.
15. Ibid., pp. 285, 296, 300–308, 319–20.
16. "Review of the Month," *CS* 9 (July, 1940): 18; Bingham, *U.S. of Europe,* pp. 314, 320–21, 323.
17. R. Alan Lawson, *The Failure of Independent Liberalism, 1930–1941* (New York, 1971), pp. 155–79.
18. Waldo Frank, "Our Guilt in Fascism," *New Republic* 102 (May 6, 1940): 603; Archibald MacLeish, "The Irresponsibles," *Nation* 150 (May 18, 1940): 618–23; Lewis Mumford, "The Corruption of Liberalism," *New Republic* 102 (April 29, 1940): 568–73.
19. MacLeish.
20. Waldo Frank, *Chart for Rough Water* (New York, 1940).
21. Lewis Mumford, *The Conduct of Life* (New York, 1951), p. 22; Mumford to Brooks, November, 1925, April 10, 1932, *Brooks-Mumford Letters,* p. 35.
22. Mumford, *Faith for Living* (New York, 1940); Mumford to Brooks, July 14, 1940, Van Wyck Brooks Papers, Charles Patterson Van Pelt Library, University of Pennsylvania. By 1940 Mumford had joined several of the prominent interventionist organizations, including William Allen White's Committee to Defend America by Aiding the Allies. When White's committee refused to urge an American declaration of war in early 1941, Mumford joined the militantly interventionist Fight for Freedom Committee. Mumford to Brooks, May 2, 1941, Brooks-Mumford letters, pp. 202–3.
23. Mumford, "Corruption," pp. 568–73; *Faith for Living,* pp. 90–93.
24. Mumford, *Faith For Living,* pp. 88–89, 104–5, 116–17; "Corruption," pp. 568–72.
25. Mumford, *Faith for Living,* p. 194; see also "The Passive Barbarians," *Atlantic* 166 (September, 1940): 274–76.
26. Mumford to Brooks, February 1, 1940, *Brooks-Mumford Letters,* pp. 178–79.

27. Mumford, *Faith for Living*, pp. 194, 310–21.
28. Ibid., pp. 106–7.
29. Ibid., pp. 185–98, 212–17, 233–79; "Corruption," p. 573.
30. Mumford, *Faith for Living*, pp. 220–25, 331. For an interesting analysis, from another perspective than my own, of the intellectual debate over intervention, see Edward A. Purcell, Jr., *The Crisis of Democratic Theory: Scientific Naturalism and the Problem of Value* (Lexington, Ky., 1973), pp. 218–31.
31. Herbert Agar et al., *The City of Man: A Declaration on World Democracy* (New York, 1940), pp. 14–19.
32. Reinhold Niebuhr, "Challenge to Liberals," review of Mumford's *Faith for Living*, in *Nation* 151 (September 14, 1940): 221–22.
33. Niebuhr, "Must Democracy Use Force? Peace and the Liberal Illusion," *Nation* 148 (January 28, 1939): 117–19; *The Children of Light and the Children of Darkness* (New York: Charles Scribner's Sons, 1960 ed.).
34. Niebuhr, "Must Democracy Use Force?"; *Children of Light*, p. 9.
35. For an excellent discussion of this theme in Niebuhr's thought, see Donald B. Meyer, *The Protestant Search for Political Realism, 1919–1941;* see also Arthur M. Schlesinger, Jr., "Reinhold Niebuhr's Role in American Political Thought and Life," *The Politics of Hope* (Boston, 1962), pp. 97–125.
36. Niebuhr, "Must Democracy Use Force?", pp. 117–18; Niebuhr to Gilbert Cox, February 27, 1935, Reinhold Niebuhr Papers, Library of Congress, Washington, D.C.
37. Niebuhr, "Challenge to Liberals," p. 221.
38. Quoted in ibid.
39. Agar, pp. 14–19.
40. Niebuhr, "Religious Limitations," *World Tomorrow* 3 (March, 1920): 77–78. Niebuhr had felt the pull of the Social Gospel movement at Yale Theological Seminary, but the disillusionment of World War 1 and his later experience as a pastor in a desperately poor working class district of Detroit shattered his youthful liberal optimism. See Niebuhr, "Mechanical Man in a Mechanical Age," *World Tomorrow* 13 (December, 1930): 493; *Leaves from the Notebook of a Tamed Critic* (New York, 1929), pp. xii–xiv, 14, 42.
41. Niebuhr, *Moral Man and Immoral Society: A Study in Ethics and Politics* (New York, Charles Scribner's Sons, 1960 ed.), pp. xi–xv, xxii–xxiii, 143–68.
42. Ibid., pp. 155–56, 169–99, 276–77. While Niebuhr argued that he was willing to accept the Marxist ideal of absolute justice as a myth indispensable for catalyzing mass action, he seemed more determined in *Moral Man and Immoral Society* to dispel this "religio-political dream" than to persuade the reader of its essentiality.
43. Ibid., pp. 163–68, 192–99; *Children of Light*, pp. 30–33.
44. Niebuhr, *Children of Light*, pp. 31–33, 110–18; *Moral Man*, pp. xxiv–xxv, 195–96.
45. Niebuhr, *Moral Man*, pp. 163–64, 192–93, 232.
46. All quotations from Schlesinger, "Niebuhr's Role," pp. 97–125.
47. Niebuhr, *Children of Light*, pp. xii–xiii, xiv–xv, 40–41.
48. Ibid., pp. 112–20, 124–52. Niebuhr resigned from the Socialist Party over its refusal to take a more militantly interventionist stand.
49. Ibid., pp. 119–20, 147–48, 151–52; see also Niebuhr, *The Irony of American History* (New York, 1952), p. 103.
50. Niebuhr, *Irony*, pp. 89, 101, 128–30.
51. Niebuhr, "The Middle Ground," review of Bingham's *The Techniques of Democracy*, in *Nation* 155 (December 5, 1942): 627–28.
52. Arthur M. Schlesinger, Jr., *The Vital Center: The Politics of Freedom* (Boston, Houghton Mifflin, 1962 ed.; original ed. 1949), pp. xxi–xxiii, 147–48.
53. Schlesinger's definition of the "Progressive" left no doubt that he had the supporters of Henry Wallace immediately in mind. *Vital Center*, pp. xxii, 36–50, 159–60.

54. Once again the world was divided into neat opposites and once again men were asked to choose—only this time it was Communism or freedom. Sidney Hook put the issue squarely: "I cannot understand why American intellectuals should be apologetic about the fact that they are limited in their effective historical choice between endorsing a system of total terror and *critically* supporting our own imperfect democratic culture with all its promises and dangers." "From Alienation to Critical Integrity," in George B. Huszar, ed., *The Intellectual: A Controversial Portrait* (New York, 1960), p. 528.

55. Schlesinger, *Vital Center,* pp. 98, 100, 129–30.

56. The formation in 1947 of Americans for Democratic Action (ADA) symbolized for Schlesinger the beginnings of this political awakening. Along with the new breed of State Department officers, men like Sumner Welles, Dean Acheson, George Kennan, and Charles E. Bohlen, the ADA comprised the working nucleus of the anti-communist front he envisioned. *Vital Center,* pp. 51–67, 131–44, 146–47, 245.

57. Ibid., pp. 150–52, 165–68, 182–83, 253–56.

CHAPTER 10

1. John Dewey, "Force and Coercion," *Characters and Events,* ed. Joseph Ratner (New York, 2 vols., 1929), 2: 787. This piece originally appeared in the *International Journal of Ethics,* April, 1916.

2. Morton White, *Social Thought in America: The Revolt against Formalism* (Boston: Beacon Paperback ed., 1961), p. 163.

3. [Alfred M. Bingham], "The Liberal and Anti-Fascism," *CS* 7 (October, 1938): 3–5; "Footnote to Anti-Fascism," *CS* 7 (November, 1938): 5; Bingham, "We Shall Have Peace," MS, n.d., pp. 1–5, Bingham MSS; "Books," review of Mumford's *Men Must Act,* in *CS* 8 (March, 1939): 27–28; *Man's Estate: Adventures in Economic Discovery* (New York, 1939), pp. 436–37; [Bingham], "An Unpublished Speech of Mussolini," *CS* 9 (June, 1940): 28.

4. A. Fleming MacLiesh, "The Assault on Liberalism," *CS* 9 (June, 1940): 10–13.

5. Lewis Mumford, "The Corruption of Liberalism," *New Republic* 102 (April 29, 1940): 568.

6. MacLiesh, p. 11.

7. *New Republic,* 102 (May 13, 1940): 643–44.

8. MacLiesh, p. 11.

9. Mumford, "Corruption," pp. 568–72.

10. Mumford to Brooks, February 10, 1940, *Brooks-Mumford Letters,* p. 181.

11. Mumford to Brooks, November 3, 1939, *Brooks-Mumford Letters,* p. 167.

12. Mumford to Brooks, February 10, 1940, *Brooks-Mumford Letters,* p. 181; Frank, "Our Guilt in Fascism," *New Republic* 102 (May 6, 1940): 603.

13. MacLiesh, p. 11.

14. "Lewis Mumford's 'Mein Kampf,'" *New Masses,* October 15, 1940, pp. 8–19; see also Malcolm Cowley, "Shipwreck," *New Republic* 103 (September 9, 1940): 357–58.

15. "Mr. Mumford and the Liberals," *New Republic* 102 (April 29, 1940): 562–64.

16. James T. Farrell, "The Faith of Lewis Mumford," *Southern Review* 6 (winter, 1941): 417–38.

17. "Review of the Month," *CS* 9 (July, 1940): 18; "The Threat from the Axis," *New Republic* 103 (October, 1940): 466–67. Manfred Jonas argues incorrectly that Bingham defected from the isolationist cause after the fall of France, when, in fact, Bingham was never an isolationist. See Jonas, pp. 217–18.

18. See Jonas, pp. 206–13, 226.

19. Bingham, "Is the Battle of Britain America's Battle?" MS, October 5, 1940, Bingham MSS; Bingham to [?] Godshall, February 6, 1941, CS collection; [Bingham], "'The Wave of the Future,'" CS 10 (March, 1941): 80–81.

20. [Bingham], "Why Short of War?" CS 10 (May, 1941): 144–45; "The Aim Is Victory," CS 10 (September, 1941): 272–73.

21. Bingham to Stuart Chase, January 6, 1941, CS collection; [Bingham], "A Foreign Policy for American Democracy," CS 9 (July, 1940): 3–8; "What Kind of Victory?" CS 10 (June, 1941): 176–77.

22. Bingham, "Foreign Policy for American Democracy"; [Bingham], "How to Beat Hitler," CS 10 (July, 1941): 208–9; "A Domestic Policy for American Democracy," CS 9 (August, 1940): 3–7; "Why Short of War?"

23. Bingham to Chase, January 6, 1941, CS collection.

24. See, for example, [Bingham], "Capitalism: Murder," CS 4 (October, 1935): 2–3.

25. [Bingham], "Guns and Butter," CS 8 (January, 1939): 3–5.

26. "Review of the Month," CS 9 (August, 1940): 19; "Review of the Month," CS 10 (April, 1941): 115.

27. [Bingham], "Whose Sacrifice?" CS 10 (April, 1941): 112–13; Bruce Bliven, "Get Tough, Mr. President!" New Republic 103 (September 16, 1940): 377–78; "Preparedness: The Lesson of Germany," New Republic 103 (November 11, 1940): 649–51. "The Lag in Defense," Nation 152 (May 10, 1941): 545–46; I. F. Stone, "Mr. Knudsen's State of Mind," Nation 152 (May 10, 1941): 550–51. "Wartime Profits," New Republic 105 (September 8, 1941): 293; [Bingham], "Beyond Defense: The Shape of the Future," CS 10 (October, 1941): 291; Bingham to Representative H. Jerry Voorhis, June 3, 1942, CS collection.

28. Bingham, "Whose Sacrifice?"; "Domestic Policy," p. 5.

29. [Bingham], "The Aim is Peace," CS 10 (September, 1941): 272–73; "Grand Strategy," CS 12 (February, 1943): 54–55; "Program for Victory," CS 11 (January, 1942): 18–19; Bingham, The Practice of Idealism (New York, 1944): 3–6.

30. Bingham, Practice, pp. 7, 10–16, 17–19, 21–42, 127–38, 181–83, 193–95; see also [Bingham], "The Future of Germany," CS 12 (November, 1943): 404–5; "Program for Europe," CS 12 (October, 1943): 366–67.

31. Bingham, review of Walter Lippmann's U.S. Foreign Policy: Shield of the Republic, "Books," CS 12 (July, 1943): 262–63; Practice, pp. 120–23.

32. Bingham, Practice, pp. 123–24, 161–63, 168–72, 175.

33. See especially H. B. Parkes, "Using Victory's Opportunities," New York Herald Tribune, April 9, 1944, p. 6; Stuart Chase, "Stuart Chase Says: Five Revolutions," CS 13 (May, 1944): 175–76; Richard Match, "Peace in Our Time," New Republic 110 (June 26, 1944): 855–57.

34. Randolph Bourne, "Twilight of Idols," The Seven Arts 11 (October, 1917): 688–702.

35. I am indebted to Mr. Bingham for allowing me to examine his private papers and correspondence, which proved invaluable to an understanding of his personal crisis.

36. Untitled essay, September 11, 1942, Bingham Personal Papers.

37. Bingham to Hiram Bingham, April 26, May 17, 1941, Bingham MSS.

38. There is a full record of Common Sense's internal affairs during these years in the CS collection; see also "Arrived," Time, December 21, 1942, p. 52.

39. Bingham to Hiram Bingham, January 31, 1942, Bingham MSS.

40. Bingham to Selden Rodman, December 22, 1941; February 25, November 9, 1942, Bingham MSS; Bingham to Rexford Tugwell, February 25, 1942, CS collection.

41. Bingham to Rodman, September 30, 1942, CS collection.

42. Bingham to Rodman, August 27, September 6, September 13, 1942; Bingham to Hiram Bingham, September 6, 1943, Bingham MSS; Bingham to John Dewey, July 11, 1942, CS collection; Bingham, "Law and Politics: Reflections on an Unfulfilled Career," essay, n.d., Bingham Personal Papers. Also in the Bingham MSS.

43. Untitled essay, September 11, 1942; Hiram Bingham to Bingham, November 4, June 9, 1942; Bingham to Hiram Bingham, January 31, April 28, September 4, October 27, 1942; September 6, 1943, Bingham MSS; Bingham to Winslow Ames, September 28, 1943, *CS* collection.
44. Bingham to Hiram Bingham, September 6, 1943, Bingham MSS.
45. Rodman to Bingham, July 3, 1942, January 19, 1943; Bingham to Rodman, March 2, November 29, 1943; Bingham to Sidney Hertzberg, August 25, 1943, Bingham MSS. The *Common Sense* partnership was formally established on December 16, 1941. The partners were Hilda Clausen Rodman, Selden Rodman, Alfred Bingham, and Katrina McCormick Barnes. Later Eliot Pratt joined the partnership.
46. Rodman to Bingham, December 24, 1941; Bingham to Rodman, March 2, 1943; Katrina Barnes to Sylvia Bingham, March 24, 1941; Barnes to *Common Sense* partners, October 28, 1944; Al Grace, "Niece of McCormick Comes Out for F.D.R.," *St. Louis Post-Dispatch*, November 5, 1944. "Niece vs. Uncle," *Time*, March 13, 1944; see also Bingham to Hiram Bingham, September 6, 1943, Bingham MSS.
47. Hertzberg to partners, November 15, 1944; Sylvia Bingham to Bingham, January 21, January 29, 1945; Rodman to Sylvia Bingham, January 23, 1945; Hertzberg to Rodman, February 5, 1945; Rodman to Bingham, February 6, March 5, 1945; Sylvia Bingham to Barnes, June 11, 1945; Rodman to Eliot Pratt, July 31, 1945; Varian Fry to Bingham, September 12, December 31, 1945; Rodman to Barnes, December 6, 1945; *Common Sense* to subscribers, n.d.; Bingham to Fry, July 29, 1945, Bingham MSS. *Common Sense* sold its subscription list to the *American Mercury*.
48. Bingham, "Law and Politics," pp. 5–10, 12.
49. Ibid., pp. 7–10; interview with Bingham, September 7, 1970, at Salem, Conn.
50. Jonathan B. Bingham and Alfred M. Bingham, *Violence and Democracy* (New York, 1970): 178–79; interview with Alfred M. Bingham, September 7, 1970; Bingham's son Stephen Bingham allegedly passed a gun to the imprisoned Soledad Brother, George Jackson, at San Quentin prison. He dropped out of sight shortly thereafter and has not yet been located by the authorities. See Donald Miller, "A Bingham Strain of Rebellion," *Washington Post*, September 5, 1971, p. D3.
51. Bingham, "Law and Politics," pp. 7–10, 12, 15.

EPILOGUE

1. C. Wright Mills, *The Sociological Imagination* (New York, 1959), pp. 15, 165–69; *The Marxists* (New York, 1962), pp. 15–24; *White Collar* (New York, 1951), pp. xvii, xx.
2. Mills, *Sociological Imagination*, pp. 173–74.
3. For a brief and darkly pessimistic essay on the emerging global crisis, see Robert L. Heilbroner, *An Inquiry into the Human Prospect* (New York, 1974). My analysis is not nearly as pessimistic as Heilbroner's. While I agree with Heilbroner that the approaching crisis calls for a new political-economic orientation, we will need, I believe, a dose of the optimistic "skepticism" Lewis Mumford has recently suggested. See Mumford, "Prologue to Our Time," *New Yorker*, March 10, 1975, pp. 42–63.
4. Peter Clecak, *Radical Paradoxes: Dilemmas of the American Left, 1945–70* (New York, 1973), pp. 287–88.
5. Mumford, *Technics and Civilization* (New York, 1934), pp. 364–433; *The Condition of Man* (New York, 1944), pp. 391–423.
6. Warren Susman, "Americanism as Surrogate Socialism: Comment 1," John H. M. Laslett and Seymour Martin Lipset, eds., *Failure of a Dream* (New York, 1974): 443–55.

INDEX